THE WOMAN'S MONEY BOOK

THE WOMAN'S MONEY BOOK

VIVIENNE JAMES

ANNE O'DONOVAN

First published in 1996 by
Anne O'Donovan Pty Ltd
171 La Trobe Street Melbourne 3000
Text copyright © Vivienne James 1996
Illustrations copyright © Beth McKinlay 1996

Edited by Sarah Dawson
Designed, illustrated and typeset by Beth McKinlay
Printed by Australian Print Group

National Library of Australia
Cataloguing-in-publication entry

James, Vivienne.
The woman's money book: it's your money – why not make the most of it.

Includes index
ISBN 1 876026 03 0.
I. Women - Finance, Personal. I. Title.

332.024042

In writing my first book, I was very fortunate to work with a great team of people. My thanks and appreciation to the publisher, Anne O'Donovan, for her enthusiasm and determination; to Lynelle Johnson for making the book more readable; to Sarah Dawson, whose editing skills and diplomacy were first-class; to Beth McKinlay for her creative illustrations; to Mandy McCartney for her selflessness and tenacity researching and helping me write the book; and to my husband, Ian, and our two boys, Matthew and Richard, for their tolerance and support.

CONTENTS

PREFACE

'IT'S NOT WHAT HAPPENS TO YOU IN YOUR
LIFE BUT HOW YOU DEAL WITH IT THAT
COUNTS. WE MUST ALL STAND TALL AND
BELIEVE IN OUR ABILITY TO SUCCEED IN
WHATEVER WE CHOOSE.'

— SUSAN MITCHELL

No two women are the same. We have very varied backgrounds, differing circumstances, and a wide range of opinions and beliefs. We may find ourselves either working or not, partnered or single – but whatever our situation, we share a need for financial security.

Some women relish the prospect of financial independence from an early age, and are disciplined about saving. This is borne out by recent studies which confirm that many women now own a property before they marry. Others of us need a little more help to get started. But no matter how disciplined we are – or are not – every one of us at some stage encounters events over which we have no control. And if we are not prepared financially for these times, there can be many repercussions – emotional as well as economic.

Through my work, I meet many women who have taken steps towards achieving financial independence and security. As far as money management is concerned, these women are clear in their requirements: they don't want to be patronised, they don't want to be treated any differently from men; but they do want financial information presented in a way which makes practical sense.

If this is the case, then, why write a money book for women? Well, the fact is that seldom do the books that have been written about money deal with the day-to-day realities of women's lives, which invariably affect our finances – maintaining financial independence in a relationship, juggling family and work responsibilities, to name but two. Also, there seemed to me to be a need for a book which dealt simply and clearly with what to many people – not just women – is a complex and often daunting subject. *The Woman's Money Book* therefore contains a good deal of common sense and I hope it will provide an easy reference point for a range of real-life situations. You can use it to assess and sort out your personal finances, to manage your money day to day, and (above all) to get ahead by putting your money where it will work best for you.

Another of my reasons for writing this book was to help women think financially for themselves and avoid the pitfalls of trying to conform to work, friendship or family pressures. Women are generally very enthusiastic about learning new skills, which usually translates into great focus and discipline once we decide on a goal. I very much believe in setting goals – in fact, I don't think you can achieve true financial independence without them. But as most of us know from experience, it's all too easy to abandon routines like saving if the prize is too far down the track.

So don't forget to reward yourself along the way! This book is not some kind of handbook to self-deprivation on the path to achieving wealth. There is no intrinsic virtue in having money in the bank, and as Roosevelt said: 'The child who sees his parents sacrifice everything for material possessions will not believe that spiritual values are important'. There must be some balance in our lives. In other words, always remember that your money is a means rather than an end in itself. To me, the 'end' that money brings is freedom – the freedom to make choices about how we live our lives. Even when we fantasise about winning a million dollars, what we are really dreaming of is the means to achieve things which are currently out of reach: a long-awaited trip overseas, leaving an unsatisfying job, or just knowing that we'll have enough to live on when that regular pay cheque stops coming in.

One of the great things about getting control of your money is how quickly you will start enjoying the benefits. You may find you have less debt or that your savings start to grow, but far more important are the choices your money will buy and the truly powerful feeling of security that comes from being in charge of your future. And it is possible! No matter what state your finances are in today, and no matter what age you start, you can make a difference.

Don't wait for some significant event to occur to organise your financial affairs. The sooner you make time, the freer you will be.

Vivienne James
September 1996

1

GETTING ON TRACK

'LIFE IS WHAT HAPPENS
TO YOU WHILE YOU'RE BUSY
MAKING OTHER PLANS.'

— JOHN LENNON

You picked up this book for a reason. Perhaps you've just got your first job. Perhaps you're thinking about giving up work for a while to start a family. Perhaps you've reached a stage in life where you want to make your financial future more secure. Or maybe it's simply that your credit-card debt has blown out again!

All these situations in some way involve money – where it comes from, where it goes, how our priorities for spending it keep changing, and how (for some of us at least) it's not always easy to control what we do with it.

So, in other words, you are interested in becoming a good (or perhaps a better) money manager. And that's what this chapter is about. No, it's not all sums! What we look at mostly are the things that tend to influence our approach to money – why, say, some of us are good at saving and some of us are better at spending – with a few suggestions for easy ways to change your habits if you need to. There is a simple budgeting exercise at the end of the chapter, which you can do if you want a clearer idea of where your finances stand – and if they're in less than perfect shape, this is definitely the best way to start getting back on track. It's worth doing even if your financial affairs are in good order – you might find some spare money you didn't know you had!

But I'd Rather Not Know!

Many people, even successful accountants and bankers, will do anything rather than sit down to sort out their personal finances. So if until now you've handled the whole thing by paying the necessary bills and then burying your head in the sand, rest assured you're not alone.

Probably the main reason why many of us react badly to book-keeping is that, let's face it, doing a budget or crunching numbers can be daunting. And if the numbers aren't in the black, it can be alarming. But while everyone can probably offer a different excuse, research has shown there are a number of reasons why women, in particular, have a tendency to avoid getting their finances under control. Here are some of them:

▲ Many women lack the time to sit down and do a budget, let alone to think about which investments to buy. They are often juggling so many different priorities – work, family, friends – that they don't have the time to give financial decision-making the attention it deserves.

▲ Some women still dream that a knight in shining armour (with a big bank balance to boot) will come along one day, or that a suitcase full of money will fall out of the sky, so they keep putting off organising their long-term finances. The fantasy that someone else will look after us can lurk in subtle forms, even in those of us who are in control of our lives in every other way.

▲ Many women just don't earn enough to put money away for their future needs. Quite often this is because they work reduced hours, or stop work altogether at some stage to accommodate their children's or their partner's needs, or perhaps to study. Alternatively, they may lack education and training, or encounter the 'glass ceiling': even at the end of the twentieth century, women are still over-represented in lower-paid jobs.

▲ Lack of financial knowledge (and uncertainty about where to acquire it) has discouraged many women from being involved early enough in money matters and decision-making. By the time they have to get involved, perhaps because their partner falls ill or dies, they don't know where to start. And the language of money can be very off-putting. It's fine if you work in a field where expressions like 'price / earnings ratio' or 'capital appreciation' are common, but if you don't, these specialised terms can be a turn-off.

▲ Women tend not to be as comfortable as men are about taking risks. Our research has found that a woman is more likely to put money in the bank, whereas a man is more likely to invest in the share market, and this conservatism means that women often receive lower returns on their money.

▲ Women who are in relationships may undervalue the money they earn and view it as 'pocket money' to be spent rather than saved, especially if their partner earns more.

'IT'S NOT REAL MONEY...'

Amanda is a freelance graphic artist who works from contract to contract. Sometimes there are breaks between contracts, but over a year she still makes a reasonable amount of money. Her husband is a businessman who consistently works long hours and earns substantially more money than she does. For this reason, Amanda leaves investing to her husband and uses her salary to buy food, clothes and household items. She regards her wage as a sort of 'kitty' from which they can draw money for day-to-day expenses. She uses any left-over money to buy gifts or flowers.

Amanda believes her husband earns the 'real' money. Because she does not place any significance on her income, she never considers saving any of it.

WHY YOU NEED TO TAKE CONTROL: SOME FACTS

'IN PLAIN FACT, A BUSINESS EDUCATION IS A NECESSARY ADJUNCT TO A MODERN GIRL'S FUTURE.'

— *HELEN'S WEEKLY*, 1934

If you need persuading, there are certainly several good reasons for taking control of your finances – and perhaps more so today than ever before.

If you're single (whether by choice or circumstances) it's obvious that you will have to provide for your own financial security. And even if you're happily partnered, you should always have some financial independence and share any financial decisions that affect you as a couple. Furthermore, statistics suggest that you will be alone at some stage in your life. First, there's the fact that one in three Australian marriages ends in divorce. Second, Australian women on average outlive men by six years, and our daughters can expect to live even longer – in the United States, girls born today have a one-in-four chance of living to 100.

So, now is definitely a good time to start putting in place some strategies for managing your money.

GETTING STARTED

FIRST, YOU NEED GOALS

Knowing that you should get your financial act together is one thing – being motivated enough to do it is quite another matter. For many of us, the missing link here is having a real *reason* to manage our money – in other words, having a goal or two (or more). After all, it's hard to be inspired when you're not working towards something concrete and achievable.

Anyone who has set themselves a goal, and then accomplished it, knows the great satisfaction this brings. Whether you want to learn a new language, to speak publicly with greater confidence, or to finish a relatively uninspiring task such as repainting the bathroom, once you do it you usually wonder why you haven't got around to it sooner! Even gaining control over your day-to-day finances is a great initial goal – and a big step towards financial independence. And being financially independent will, in turn, eventually give you more freedom to make choices about the way you want to live your life, which brings not only peace of mind but a pleasurable sense of fulfilment.

Being financially independent gives you more choices about how you live your life

If you've tried to set yourself goals but have given up before you got there, your goals probably weren't *real* enough. To make them seem real, try writing them down or visualising them in some way: perhaps putting up a picture of the island resort or the dream car will help. And, of course, they need to be attainable – the more distant the reward, the more determination you're likely to need. We look at all this in more detail in Chapter 2.

SECOND, 'YOU GOTTA HAVE ATTITUDE'

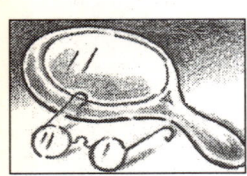

'WE DON'T SEE THINGS AS THEY ARE,

WE SEE THEM AS WE ARE.'

— ANAIS NIN

Your relationship with money will be as individual as you are. Yes, considerations such as how much you earn will affect what you can achieve and how quickly you do so. But believe it or not, this is the least volatile variable. Very well paid people can harbour an attitude to money which keeps them constantly poor; others with very modest incomes somehow have substantial savings or an investment portfolio.

If you have friends who are 'good' money managers, you may have noticed that there is something they all have in common – their attitude to money and how they spend it. Attitude really will make the difference between whether you succeed or fail – and this goes for most things in life, not just money.

The Way Things Are

Attitude may be shaped by family background, by your own experiences, or by social conditioning, and sometimes you may not even be fully aware that any or all of these are affecting your decisions.

Our family history, in particular, tends to play a big part in how we spend and invest our money. We may inherit behaviour patterns, or be tempted to use our parents as role models if they were financially successful. The real issue, though, is that attitudes about money can be passed on in very subtle ways. 'We can't afford that – do you think we're made of money?' or 'It's only money!': does any of this sound familiar? So take a little time to consider how your family's attitude to money may have shaped yours. Are your ideas appropriate for your financial strategy, or did you inherit them along with your blue eyes?

WHAT'S YOUR MONEY PERSONALITY?

For each statement, choose the response that most accurately reflects your feeling or behaviour.

A.   Exactly like me   B.   Somewhat like me
C.   Generally not like me   D.   Not at all like me

YOUR ATTITUDE TOWARDS RISK
1. I like working with a safety net. For example, I will consider investment only when I'm guaranteed not to lose any money.
2. Most people would describe me as adventurous.
3. I think investing is like gambling.

YOUR FEELINGS ABOUT CHANGE
4. I've sometimes stayed in a relationship or job longer than I should have because the idea of making a change was scary.
5. I am open to considering new opportunities, whether they have to do with my career or investments.
6. I feel that change adds zest to my life.

YOUR FEELINGS ABOUT CONTROL
7. I feel that I have control over the direction my life is taking.
8. I rarely send back my meal, return something I've purchased or make a complaint, even if I'm very dissatisfied with the product or service.
9. I'm so busy with work and taking care of my family that I rarely have time to tend to my own needs, financial or otherwise.

YOUR FEELINGS ABOUT THE FUTURE
10. When I think of the future I feel optimistic.
11. I tend to be spontaneous and live for the present: planning ahead is not my style.
12. I'm pretty good about saving money for things I'll need soon, like a new car or a holiday. But I find it a lot more difficult to save for distant goals like retirement.

YOUR ATTITUDE TOWARDS MONEY

13. I know I should save something, but in my heart of hearts, I don't believe financial planning really does that much good unless you have a lot of money.
14. I tend to tune out when friends or colleagues talk about money.
15. I believe that women are just as capable of investing and managing their money as men are.

YOUR MONEY UNDERSTANDING

16. Investment lingo and other financial terms intimidate me.
17. I make most of the financial decisions in my household, either alone or with my partner and I feel pretty good about how we've done.
18. I know very little about different types of investments and the basis of financial planning.

YOUR DECISION-MAKING STYLE

19. I often put off financial decisions because I'm afraid of making a mistake.
20. After making a big decision – whether about my job, money or a relationship – I often worry that I've made the wrong move.
21. When making most major decisions I tend to listen to my heart.

To find out how you rate, tally your score below.

1. A-1, B-2, C-3, D-4		2. A-4, B-3, C-2, D-1	
3. A-1, B-2, C-3, D-4		4. A-1, B-2, C-3, D-4	
5. A-4, B-3, C-2, D-1		6. A-4, B-3, C-2, D-1	
7. A-4, B-3, C-2, D-1		8. A-1, B-2, C-3, D-4	
9. A-1, B-2, C-3, D-4		10. A-4, B-3, C-2, D-1	
11. A-1, B-2, C-3, D-4		12. A-1, B-2, C-3, D-4	
13. A-1, B-2, C-3, D-4		14. A-1, B-2, C-3, D-4	
15. A-4, B-3, C-2, D-1		16. A-1, B-2, C-3, D-4	
17. A-4, B-3, C-2, D-1		18. A-1, B-2, C-3, D-4	
19. A-1, B-2, C-3, D-4		20. A-1, B-2, C-3, D-4	
21. A-1, B-2, C-3, D-4			

DANGER ZONE: *21–36 points*
If your score is in the Danger Zone you may often feel that you're not in control of your life – a feeling that usually extends to financial matters. You probably don't know much about investing or the basics of financial planning, are intimidated by financial terminology and, in the end, may defer decisions about money matters to others. Your choices about where to put your money often reflect a strong preference for the familiar over the unknown, an aversion to risk and difficulty in coping with change. For example, even as your income rises, you're likely to put your savings into money-market accounts and other familiar vehicles that don't lose any money. Trouble is, they won't make very much money either – a fact that is likely to haunt you as you grow older and find yourself still struggling to achieve financial security.

What to Do

Don't despair – but don't delay in trying to get your financial act together. One of the biggest obstacles to you taking charge of your financial life is also the easiest to overcome: lack of knowledge. Learning more about how to manage your money will help you gain a sense of control over the direction your life is taking and increase your confidence in making money decisions. Consider registering for a personal finance course sponsored by a community organisation or a local college. Invite a friend to join you to make it more fun.

You can help yourself further by working on some of the non-financial issues that keep you from taking an active role in managing your money. The sections of the quiz in which you scored lowest are the areas you need to focus on. For example, if you scored low in the control section, you might work on becoming more assertive by pushing yourself to send back a meal that is not to your liking or by demanding a refund for a faulty product. Similarly, if you generally loathe trying new experiences (and investing in stocks is a new experience for most Danger Zone women), practise on a small scale. Try a new type of food or invite a colleague you don't know very well to lunch. It's not how big but how new the experience is that counts.

CAUTION ZONE: *37–52 points*
The ups and downs of daily living preoccupy your thinking if you're in the Caution Zone. You believe you can't do much to shape the future, so you focus on the here-and-now rather than on long-term needs. When prioritising financial matters, for example, you may be motivated to save for a new car but less so to put money aside for retirement and other distant goals. You listen to your heart on

most decisions, so when it comes to money and investing, you often make choices based more on feelings than on facts. You are likely to perceive financial planning as pointless unless you have a lot of money to work with, and to reject any investment that is not guaranteed to protect your principal as too risky. Like Danger Zone women, you prefer the familiar, which keeps you from exploring investments that offer higher returns over time than fixed-term deposits and savings accounts.

What to Do

Your biggest challenge is letting go of preconceived notions about money and investing. Increasing your knowledge of the fundamentals of financial planning through the steps outlined in the Danger Zone should help you change some of your attitudes towards money and get you to base your financial decisions on fact rather than feeling. To overcome your resistance to planning for the future, give some concerted thought to your wants and needs over the long term. Since the first steps to achieving a goal is to visualise it, start by making a list of your financial priorities for the next year, five years, 10 years and beyond. For example, you might aim for a new car in one year, a big house in five years, a college fund for your kids in 10 years and a retirement nest egg for yourself in 20 years or more. With these specific goals as incentives, set up separate savings accounts, specifically earmarked for each one, and add a little bit to each on a regular basis. To make the process easier, consider signing up for an automatic savings account at a bank or building society. Most important, be sure to put the money you allocate for long-term goals into growth investments that have historically outpaced inflation – i.e. stocks and the managed funds that invest them.

COMFORT ZONE: *53–68 points*

If you're in the Comfort Zone, you usually feel in control of your life. You're likely to be optimistic about the future and to realise the importance of taking responsibility for your finances. In addition, you feel capable of understanding money and investing, and have learned at least the basics about types of investment and financial planning principles. The problem is that you are sometimes too comfortable. You may wish you were more active in managing your investments, but take solace in the progress you've made. Still, since you don't experience a sense of urgency and aren't alarmed by fears of failure, inadequacy or insolvency, it's easy to put off making financial decisions or investigating new investment options. In fact, you usually find conversations about money and investment boring.

What to Do

This is a wake-up call. Regardless of your current financial, career, marital and health status, circumstances can and do change. To make sure complacency doesn't keep you from achieving financial security, make planning a top priority. Set aside at least an hour or two each month to review money matters – for example, researching a new managed fund or checking to see whether you need to make any changes in your portfolio – and mark the time in your calendar, as you would any important appointment. If you are considering a new investment or face another kind of financial decision, set a deadline by which you make your choice. By doing so, you won't let yourself procrastinate indefinitely.

ACTION ZONE: *69–84 points*

There's little to prevent you from becoming an accomplished investor. You are open to a wide range of investments and understand that you must put some money in riskier, growth investments like stocks to earn higher returns. You aren't easily intimidated by financial lingo, and you'll ask questions until you are sure that you understand. What's more, because you're generally assertive about your rights, you will challenge a financial professional who gives you poor service or questionable advice. Though you value your ability to enjoy the present, you want to be in control of your financial future, and you regard planning as essential to meeting that goal.

What to Do

Congratulations. You are either an active and accomplished investor or are set to become one. If you haven't fully taken the plunge, try to analyse why by examining your scores in the individual sections of the quiz. Are your totals similar in all seven sections, or are one or two substantially lower than the others? If so, these are the areas you need to work on to make smarter choices about your money. For example, if your scores indicate that you tend to procrastinate, set a deadline each time you are faced with a financial decision. If your totals are low in the financial knowledge section, bone up on personal finance by reading books or magazines or by attending a financial-planning seminar. Whatever your weak spot, create a plan of action to overcome it. Then just do it.

First appeared in *Working Woman* in February 1995. Reprinted with permission of *Working Woman* magazine. Written by Chris Hayes. Copyright ©1995 by *Working Woman* Magazine.

Can't, Can't, Can't

'IF YOU HAVE MADE MISTAKES ... THERE IS ALWAYS ANOTHER CHANCE FOR YOU ... FOR THIS THING WE CALL "FAILURE" IS NOT THE FALLING DOWN, BUT THE STAYING DOWN.'

— MARY PICKFORD

OLD HABITS DIE HARD

Felicia is a highly paid researcher in the finance industry. In 1990, she applied for a mortgage to enable her to buy an investment property. Despite the fact that she approached the very bank she worked for, the unenlightened manager who handled her application actually asked if she was certain she wasn't likely at some stage to get married or have a baby and therefore stop working. And what if she lost her job? As Felicia pointed out, she was hardly likely to risk her deposit on a whim, and in any case what's to stop a man from being retrenched? Felicia eventually got her loan, but was disillusioned by this confidence-sapping experience.

Another attitude which discourages many of us from making the most of our money is the fear of making a mistake. In 1994 Janet Bodnar wrote an article in the US magazine *Kiplinger's Personal Finance*, which quoted research suggesting that women are more self-critical and less confident of their financial ability than men are. This is not surprising when you take into account all the extra obstacles women have had to encounter as far as money management is concerned. The old stereotypes have lingered in some quarters until quite recently.

Yet sometimes it isn't other people who sap our confidence, it's our own self-doubt. Fear of making a mistake can be a great paralyser. Perhaps you've tried investing, but lost money. Well, don't let the fear of losing money stop you – no one is born a money genius. Even those brilliant entrepreneurs who never seem to fail have all lost at some stage, but they picked themselves up and continued on the path to wealth by treating their mistakes as a learning experience. After all, you may be disappointed if you fail, but you're nowhere if you don't try.

Hey, Big Spender!

 'NEVER KEEP UP WITH THE JONESES. DRAG

'EM DOWN TO YOUR LEVEL. IT'S CHEAPER.'

— QUENTIN CRISP

It is very tempting, in this consumer age, to spend beyond our means. We have all at some time or another felt pressure to be one of the group and to keep up with our friends – to buy that expensive suit or flash car when our real wealth is close to zero.

Unfortunately, access to money has never been easier. As the press keeps telling us, any postwar baby has had a very good run financially. The previous generation suffered the 1930s depression and learnt to be cautious and frugal, to 'cut the suit to fit the cloth' by saving for what they wanted. We, on the other hand, live in a society awash with credit, have easy access to our money through ATMs and EFTPOS, and are offered the incentive of picking up points towards other purchases if we outlay even more. Smart Cards and computer banking will soon become common.

The upshot of all this is that we are a society notorious for spending, not saving – which inevitably affects our attitude towards our personal finances. Breaking the pattern of spending is not easy, especially when it is emotionally grounded. How often have you said 'I was feeling miserable, so I went out and bought something to cheer myself up'? This may not be a problem if you are rarely 'down', but if it happens regularly you could be spending big dollars.

The question to ask yourself is whether your current habits are leading you where you want to go. Even giving up an expensive habit such as smoking can make a big improvement to your budget. If you smoke one packet a day and give up, you will save $30 a week: over a year this adds up to $1500, which is a very useful amount of money to put towards a deposit for a house! And if you invested $1500 for ten years at an interest rate of 8 per cent, you'd be even better off and end up with a tidy sum of $3238.

Whatever your attitude to money, the point is that if you *think* your financial position could be improved, it undoubtedly can be. Having a practical plan is a great first step in the right direction, and a budget is a good way of getting started.

BUDGETING – NOW'S THE BEST TIME TO DO IT

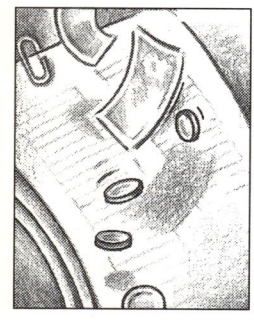

'A BUDGET IS TO HELP YOU KEEP YOUR EYE ON WHERE THE MONEY IS SUPPOSED TO GO AND WHERE, IN FACT, IT WENT.'

— SHIRLEY CONRAN, *SUPERWOMAN*

Chances are that you find the idea of doing a budget as appealing as doing your tax return – and about as much fun. If, on the other hand, you're one of those people who find budgeting easy, who pay off credit cards before the interest becomes due, who don't feel deprived of life's little rewards: congratulations, you may not need to complete the exercise that follows unless you want to review your current situation. For those of you in the first group – just remember how good you felt when your tax return was in the mail, and read on.

You can probably think of a hundred other things you would rather do than comb your files and drawers for old receipts, bills and bank statements. But doing a budget will probably only take you a couple of hours, and it is definitely time well spent. And if you think you haven't got the time today, consider that there may come a point when you have the time but not the money (when you retire, say) and you'll regret not having made the most of your income when you had the chance.

BUT I CAN NEVER STICK TO A BUDGET!

If you have tried budgeting before but have always given up, it's most likely that your figures were either unrealistic or too inflexible. You may have been overly strict about the amount you allowed yourself for expenses, which made you feel a failure because you kept having to dip into the part you'd set aside for savings. Or perhaps you had some change in your circumstances (a new job, even unemployment) which made your budget unworkable, so off it went to the 'too hard' basket.

If you've tried budgeting before and have always given up, it's likely your figures were unrealistic or too inflexible

And even when we think we know where we stand financially, budgets always have some surprises in store. Don't let this put you off: regardless of what your figures reveal, it's the first step towards gaining control of your finances and it will give you a great sense of accomplishment.

The aim of doing a budget is definitely not to make you miserable for the rest of the year because it feels like a millstone around your neck, preventing you from doing the things you enjoy because you 'can't afford them'. In fact a budget can have quite the opposite effect. Next time you're sitting in a restaurant about to order a three-course meal, or you're going out to buy some clothes, you won't have niggling doubts about whether you really can afford it: you'll know you can – and you'll be able to relax and enjoy it! And you might even have reached the point where you know you've got some savings to invest.

Q *Do I need a computer to do a budget?*

A No, you certainly don't need a computer to get started: a piece of paper and a pen will do just as well. At the same time, if you have one there are quite a few software packages geared to personal finances: Microsoft Money and Quicken (for Windows and Macintosh) are both priced well under $100; the spreadsheet program Microsoft Excel is more sophisticated (and quite a bit more expensive). Have a good look at the program before you buy, to make sure that the extra features are worth the money.

The beauty of all these programs is the inbuilt calculator which makes it very easy to update your budget once it's been set up. And when computer banking services are available, your home software will enable you to do most of your banking and bill-paying at home.

JUST A FEW SUMS AND YOU'RE THERE!

So, down to work. The step-by-step guide below should mean that doing your budget this time round will be a stress-free exercise. Some tips: be realistic, give yourself some flexibility and, above all, build in some 'rewards' now and then. Good luck!

Your personal Budget Planner on page 20 is divided into three sections: Income, Fixed Expenses and Controllable Expenses. It is set up so that you can list your incomings and outgoings month by month, but if you are paid fortnightly or weekly you may prefer to record everything on that basis (this will make it easy for you to see when the greatest number of bills come in, so that you can put aside some extra cash to pay them).

STEP 1 *List your income from all sources.* Some of your income (such as salary) may be fixed for the year, making it the most reliable reserve from which to pay your expenses. Other earnings, such as overtime, bonuses and tax refunds, may vary: to estimate these figures, dig out past statements but also consider whether things may change in the future. It's best to under-estimate rather than over-estimate any variable earnings, so that anything above the predicted amount is a bonus. If your income is spasmodic or you are self-employed, it's business practice to enter your income against the month you invoiced it.

When you have listed income from all sources, total the amount on the right-hand side of the page.

STEP 2 *List each of your fixed expenses*, either under the month in which they are incurred or the one in which you pay them – the important thing here is to choose a method and stick to it. Fixed expenses are typically those expenses over which you have no control without a major change in your lifestyle: council rates or rent, for example, would only vary if you moved house.

Your fixed expenses include any money paid into investments such as superannuation or a savings plan, or money you're setting aside as an emergency fund or for a holiday. (Superannuation contributions are shown on your pay slip if you're an employee; your bank or investment statements will show the other amounts.) These are treated as expenses because they reduce your available income, but they will also be included as both a source of income and as an asset in your Personal Net Worth worksheet (page 26).

You may find that some of the expenses included under the heading 'Fixed' on the Budget Planner are, in your circumstances, controllable. Child-care costs, for example, may be fixed for working mothers but are controllable where you only use child care or a babysitter from time to time. If there isn't an appropriate category for any of your fixed expenses, list them as 'Other'.

When you have listed all your fixed expenses, total the amount on the right-hand side of the page.

STEP 3 *List your controllable expenses*. These are the ones over which you have some discretion (hopefully, without causing any major changes to your lifestyle): you are the one, for example, who decides how often you dine out or go to the movies. Even food costs are controllable to the extent that you can decide whether to buy gourmet or no-name brands. It is how much you spend in this category that will determine whether there is anything left over that you can start saving.

The easiest way to work out how much you spend in this area is to gather together any receipts, cheque butts, and credit-card and bank statements. Look for any items, like clothes, which you may buy over a few months, and then average the amount to estimate your monthly expenditure: if, for example, your clothing expenses totalled $600 over three months, your estimated monthly figure would be $200.

Credit-card payments deserve a special mention, as they can so easily blow out your budget. The reason they are listed as controllable rather than fixed expenses is because many credit-card purchases are a result of impulse buying and are therefore within your control. You may already have allocated the things you pay by credit card to the appropriate category, but if you are being charged interest or have an outstanding balance you should estimate the amount you expect to repay each month and record this in the Controllable Expenses category. The amount of interest you pay may shock you and firm your resolve! You can adjust this amount once you have done your initial budget plan.

When you have listed all your controllable expenses, total the amount on the right-hand side of the page.

STEP 4 *Now, the moment of reckoning!* Deduct your total expenses from your total income. Don't panic or be discouraged if the amount left over is less than you thought, or even negative. There are lots of things you can do to tip the balance in your favour, as we show in Chapter 2.

PHEW!

So now you know where your hard-earned dollars are going. And with your figures on paper, you should find it easy to jot down your assets and liabilities on your Personal Net Worth worksheet on page 26. This will give you a snapshot of your total financial position.

Congratulations – you have begun to take control! Now it's time to look a bit more closely at what you're spending your money on and why, and to try to establish your real priorities. This is what the next chapter deals with: setting yourself goals, finding ways to free up some money, and (if necessary) making some changes to ensure that your day-to-day cash is going where it will do you the most good.

LIFETIME HABITS FOR MONEY SUCCESS

- Set yourself financial goals that are achievable.
- Always keep track of your income and your expenses.
- Treat your income seriously, and use some of it to secure your future.
- In your job, put your hand up for more lucrative positions.
- Control your money, don't let it control you.
- Spend less, so that you can save and invest more.
- Continue to educate yourself about the financial options available to you.
- Treat any mistakes as a learning experience.

BUDGET PLANNER

	JAN	FEB	MAR	APR	MAY
INCOME					
Salary (before tax)					
Bonus					
Overtime					
Investment income					
Trust distribution					
Rent					
Dividends					
Other					
Interest on bank accounts, etc.					
Allowances (e.g. pension, child)					
Tax refunds					
Other					
TOTAL MONTHLY INCOME	$	$	$	$	$

JUN	JUL	AUG	SEP	OCT	NOV	DEC	TOTALS
$	$	$	$	$	$	$	

TOTAL ANNUAL INCOME $

BUDGET PLANNER

	JAN	FEB	MAR	APR	MAY
FIXED EXPENSES					
Superannuation					
Investments (e.g. savings plans)					
Rent/mortgage					
Council rates					
Water rates					
Electricity					
Gas/oil					
Telephone					
Maintenance & repairs					
Loans (e.g. car)					
Car registration					
Licence/motor associations					
Petrol and oil					
Car maintenance					
Public transport					
House/contents insurance					
Car insurance					
Life insurance					
Income protection					
Medical insurance					
Child care					
School/university/ self-education fees					
School uniforms					
School excursions					
Tax on salary					
Provisional tax					
Tax on investment earnings					
Other					
TOTAL MONTHLY FIXED EXPENSES	$	$	$	$	$

Jun	Jul	Aug	Sep	Oct	Nov	Dec	Totals
$	$	$	$	$	$	$	

TOTAL ANNUAL FIXED EXPENSES $

BUDGET PLANNER

	JAN	FEB	MAR	APR	MAY
CONTROLLABLE EXPENSES					
Food (groceries, meat, vegies)					
Clothing & shoes					
Hair care & cosmetics					
Credit-card payments					
Pharmacy					
Dentist					
Doctor					
Optometrist					
Gym & fitness					
Electrical appliances/furniture					
Restaurants/bars/alcohol					
Concerts/theatre					
Holidays					
Home improvement (garden, decorating)					
Hobbies/club fees					
Drycleaning					
Taxes					
Newspapers/books/subscriptions					
Gifts & decorations					
Other					
TOTAL MONTHLY CONTROLLABLE EXPENSES	$	$	$	$	$
TOTAL MONTHLY BALANCE*	$	$	$	$	$

(*Total monthly income less
total monthly expenses)

JUN	JUL	AUG	SEP	OCT	NOV	DEC
$	$	$	$	$	$	$

TOTAL ANNUAL CONTROLLABLE EXPENSES $

$	$	$	$	$	$	$

TOTAL ANNUAL BALANCE $

YOUR PERSONAL NET WORTH

ASSETS: [WHAT YOU OWN AS AT   /   /19   ]

		current value ($)	% of total assets
Cash	Cash on hand	$	
	Bank accounts	$	
	Bank accounts (cheque, etc.)	$	
	High-interest savings accounts	$	
	Building societies/credit unions	$	
	Loans	$	
	Other	$	
Personal property	Motor vehicles	$	
	Clothing/jewellery	$	
	Art/antiques	$	
	Other	$	
Property	Family home	$	
	Holiday home	$	
	Contents	$	
Investments	Shares	$	
	Fixed interest	$	
	Property	$	
	Managed funds (e.g. unit trusts)	$	
	Other	$	
Superannuation	Schemes	$	
	Pension	$	
TOTAL ASSETS		$	100%

LIABILITIES: WHAT YOU OWE [AS AT   /   / 9   ]

		current value ($)	% of total assets
Credit card balance		$	
Bank overdrafts		$	
Loans	Mortgage	$	
	Car	$	
	Personal	$	
	Other	$	
Other		$	
Total liabilities		$	100%
PERSONAL NET WORTH			
(Total assets less total liabilities)		$	

2

GETTING IT TOGETHER

'IF YOU DON'T KNOW

WHERE YOU ARE GOING,

ANY ROAD WILL TAKE

YOU THERE.'

— ADAPTED FROM ALICE'S
ADVENTURES IN WONDERLAND

So how do your finances look? Are they in good shape, or is there room for improvement? Doing your budget in Chapter 1 will have revealed where you spend your hard-earned dollars, and in particular where you overspend. This chapter suggests some ways of keeping your finances on track.

First, we focus on spending habits. Is most of your income going where you want it to go, or is it all just disappearing with very little to show for it? If this is the case, you are probably living from emergency to emergency, juggling your finances to meet bills and everyday living costs. If you are keen to get off the never-ending treadmill of spending everything you earn (and sometimes more), the answer lies in setting goals and working towards something you really want. Otherwise, why would you bother?

Next, we offer guidelines to help you free up some money to put away – the key to having a financial plan that works – and a few practical tips on how to do this by spending less without feeling totally deprived. Then there's the day-to-day reality of making the most of what money you do have. We explore the maze of financial institutions, with some suggestions to help you pick the best accounts (and loans) for your particular needs and to help you get back on top of things if you find your debts are out of control. And last but not least, we look at protecting yourself through insurance, including some down-to-earth advice about picking the most appropriate form of cover.

FACING THE 'C' WORD: COMMITMENT

There is no way around it, saving money can be pretty tiresome, especially when you are continually told to be patient, to think long-term and to forego pleasurable spending. At weight-loss centres, counsellors sometimes ask a new client to rate on a scale of 1–10 how committed they are to losing weight. They know that no matter how good the diet, no matter how good the intentions, clients will fail if they are not completely committed.

The same principle applies if you want to get ahead financially. If you really want to improve your finances, you have to be committed. So if you are not where you want to be, stop and work out why. There may be no quick fix, but the mere act of drawing up a plan to improve things will be a big – and arguably the most important – step forward.

WHAT ARE YOU SAVING FOR?

Now for the fun part! It's time to look at what you'd really like to be spending your money on, put these goals in some sort of order of priority, and then work out the most effective (and the quickest) way of saving for them.

THINK POSITIVE!

- Don't think that you cannot save or get out of debt. You may only need to make a small adjustment in your life to improve your situation. If you can't afford much, remember that there are many pleasurable things in life which are absolutely free. Visiting friends, sitting beside a blazing fire in winter, or enjoying a day at the beach cost you virtually nothing.
- Enjoy the feeling of being in control. Sit down and work out your debt-reduction or savings plan, and take pride in the fact that you are in charge of things.
- Set major goals – and work towards them.
- Set some easy goals too – a weekend away, a special ('would-love-to-own') piece of clothing – and put some money (even $5 would do) in a jar each week to achieve them, one after the other. Getting some quick results, however small, will give you a sense of achievement and keep you on track for the big goals.
- Make some bargains with yourself – there is nothing wrong with a little bribery and corruption! Perhaps you could take your own lunch to work two days a week (at $5 a lunch, that's $520 saved for the year) or borrow your favourite glossy magazine from the library instead of buying it (another hundred or so dollars saved over the year) – and reward yourself with a week away at Christmas.

Setting Goals

If you have trouble saving – or even balancing the books – it's likely that you don't have any goals to which you're really committed. It really is as simple as that. Why would anyone in their right mind forego the pleasure of a new outfit or a dinner out, or the convenience of a taxi ride, if it wasn't for another, more substantial, pleasure down the track?

But this is not why most people fail: many of us lose the plot because our long-term goals are too vague – we suffer from 'big-picture paralysis'. By setting yourself realistic goals and realistic time-frames for achieving them, you will benefit along the way from a sense of accomplishment which will in turn give you greater confidence for the next step.

Don't Forget Your Emergency Fund

This is the old rainy-day principle reinvented for the nineties. When you sit down to work out your priorities, consider whether one should be an emergency fund to meet unexpected costs. If, for example, your car broke down or your fridge needed replacing or, even worse, you lost your job, you could use this fund to tide you over.

Of course, how much you allocate for emergencies will depend on how much you feel you need for comfort's sake, but a couple of months' pay is a reasonable kitty. You should keep this money where it is immediately accessible: a savings account will do, though a cash-management account may offer higher interest (but make sure the money can be withdrawn easily). If you have a flexible home loan that allows you to draw money back at no fees, this may be a good place to 'invest' some of your emergency fund.

Getting Your Goals on Paper

To overcome big-picture paralysis, all you need is a piece of paper. First write down the headings for the three main time-frames:

▲ SHORT TERM (1–2 years)
▲ MEDIUM TERM (2–5 years)
▲ LONG TERM (5 years+)

Under each heading, list all the things you want to achieve during that time (these don't have to be financial goals). Try to be as specific as you can for the short-term goals, but you will find that the goals become vaguer or 'bigger' as the time-frame becomes longer.

Put your list aside for a couple of days, or even a week, then look at it again. What do you need to add? What can you do without?

How Much Will You Need For Each Goal?

The next step is to put a dollar figure on your goals, including any borrowings you will need to achieve them. If you don't know the cost of any one particular goal, leave the amount blank until you find out.

If you've been honest and uninhibited, your goals (particularly the short-term ones) will be numerous and you've probably woken up to the fact that not all of them are achievable given the money you've got available. The answer is not to reach for the moon: even if you manage to accomplish two of the goals in each time-frame, you'll be more in control of your finances than you are today.

The final step, then, is to put the goals in each time-frame in order of priority, and number them accordingly. Give yourself lots of time to do this: once again, leave the list and come back to it a few times, and don't be surprised if your priorities change.

Some Typical Goals

SHORT TERM (1–2 years)	MEDIUM TERM (2-5 years)	LONG TERM (5 years +)
Save for emergency fund	Pay extra $10 000 off mortgage	Retirement plan in place
Holiday in Bali	Start a school-fees saving fund	Buy investment property
Paint house	Investment porfolio	Own business
New car	Study for degree	

Use the table on page 32 to work out how much you'll need to save each month or year to achieve your priority goals. You could break the figures down further into weekly amounts to make it all seem more manageable.

How Much Should You Save Each Month to Meet Your Goals?

$ Goals (today's value)	5 000	10 000	25 000	50 000
At the end of				
1 year	420	845	2110	4215
2 years	210	420	1050	2095
3 years	140	280	695	1390
4 years	105	205	520	1035
5 years	80	165	410	825
6 years	70	135	340	685
7 years	60	115	290	580
8 years	50	100	255	505
9 years	45	90	225	450
10 years	40	80	200	400

This example assumes an annual return of 5.16 per cent (after fees and taxes), and an inflation rate of 4 per cent.

WHERE TO NEXT?

So now you've got your wish list, the next step is to work out some ways of freeing up money so that you can attain it.

LEARN TO PAY YOURSELF FIRST

The bulk of your income will always go towards paying the wages of others – the butcher, the landlord, the bank, the child-carer. But what about you?

The most effective way to make sure that you treat saving seriously is to consider any money you can save as being your pay to yourself. And setting aside something from your income for savings before paying your other expenses will ensure that you always get paid.

▲ Ask your employer if you can have your salary paid into two bank accounts – to separate your everyday funds from the money you do not want to touch. (For information about the range of accounts which may be suitable, see the section 'Banking On It' later in this chapter.)

▲ If direct credits from payroll are not an option, organise with your bank to direct-debit a set sum regularly from your everyday account into a separate savings account.

AIM TO SAVE TEN PER CENT OF YOUR INCOME

You should try to save at least 10 per cent of your net income. If you can't manage this much, start with a smaller proportion but try to increase it as circumstances allow – when you receive a pay rise, for example.

Of course, everyone's circumstances are different. Your stage of life will have a direct bearing on the percentage you manage to save, and should also influence where you place that money. If, say, you're in your twenties, thirties or forties and have a mortgage, the interest you earn on any savings is unlikely to be anywhere near the level of interest you're paying on the loan (and you have to pay tax on any interest earned on the savings), so it may make more sense to use the money to reduce the mortgage. If, on the other hand, you're in your fifties or sixties and contemplating retirement, you may be best off topping up your superannuation contributions.

Budgeting For It

In the end, though, no matter what amount you are able to earmark for savings, the key to success is putting the money aside *regularly*. And your attitude to budgeting will directly influence how you go about this.

As we've already said, there are lots of computer programs available to help you set out and update your budget. But don't think you have to shell out for fancy software in order to get started – the Budget Planner at the end of Chapter 1 is equally effective.

The 'Bottom-up' Approach

With 'bottom-up' budgeting, you first look at your income and then deduct your expenses from it, so that you know you can save whatever is left over. This suits those of us who are organised, enjoy keeping records, and like to keep control of our budget.

If this sounds like you, you should have no trouble working out how much you can save. Your main challenge is to set yourself a workable budget and, if you have unexpected expenses, do your sums until the figures balance again.

The 'Skimming' Approach

With the best will in the world, some of us just can't keep track of a budget, through either lack of time or a lack of interest (or both). Does this sound like you? You've probably started a budget a million times, but only ever kept it up for a week or two. And when you're faced with a choice between another caffe latte and saving the money, the caffe latte wins every time. Anything available will be spent, and then some!

If this is the case, the solution is probably the 'you-don't-miss-what-you-don't-have' approach. In other words, the only way you will save is if you skim it off the top first. You should still do a budget at least once so that you know how much you really have available for saving, but when you've worked out the amount you should convert it into a percentage of your income and this percentage should be removed from your salary immediately every pay day and deposited in a separate account.

The Dangers of a 'Bread and Water' Budget

Don't over-react and decide to save all you can now. It's unlikely that you'll be able to keep it up, because at some point you will feel deprived and abandon the saving habit to catch up on some good living. It's the old diet truism – changing your eating patterns rather than crash-dieting, because if you are too rigorous you'll soon be into the chocolate-cake mixture to compensate for weeks of self-denial.

If you really can't live on the money you have allowed yourself, go back to your budget. You can only save what you can afford, so don't put yourself through the hoops. Instead, readjust your goals to provide a better balance between 'what you can afford to save' and 'what you can afford to spend'.

How Can You Save If Your Income Is Spasmodic?

It can be harder to save if you are self-employed and have a varying income, or if you work irregularly (on a casual basis, for example). The trick here is to give your budget an annual (rather than weekly or monthly) base. Although your income may go up and down from week to week or month to month, if you've worked in this way for more than a year and you check your tax returns you will probably find the annual figure is more consistent, so base your weekly budget on this.

For anyone whose income is unpredictable, the skimming approach to saving is probably the best way to go. Every time you bank some earnings you should cream off your set percentage of savings: the amounts may vary, but you will still end up with your percentage target by the end of the year.

'BUT I NEVER HAVE ANY MONEY LEFT OVER ...'

For those of you wondering what's the point of having goals when you never have any spare cash or if you are in debt, the answer is simple: freeing up cash or getting your debts under control could be your first goal (and a little further on we look at ways to help you do it). If this is your first goal, understandably you may not be very excited by it, but if you want to get to a point where you can save for something more interesting – such as a holiday, or a deposit on a house – it is an essential step. And it's not as difficult as you might think. Basically there are two ways of achieving it: by increasing your income through a pay rise or a second job, or changing your spending habits.

'EXPENDITURE RISES TO MEET INCOME.'

— C. NORTHCOTE PARKINSON

Unfortunately, most people find that the more money they have in their pockets, the more they seem to find to spend it on; in other words, they always live up to their means! So regardless of your income, it is probably best to concentrate on your spending habits.

First, Look at the Essentials...

You will always, of course, have to pay for food, transport and a roof over your head – which together tend to account for around 30–50 per cent of most people's spending. The way you spend your money and your ability to save will, though, largely depend on your individual circumstances – your stage of life, your income and your family structure. To some extent this is a matter of personal choice, but if you don't seem to be able to save because one part of your of life is draining your resources, perhaps it's time for a rethink. Should you move if your housing expenses are too high? Is your car costing too much?

...Then at the Things You Enjoy Spending On

As for spending on 'non-essentials' – variable expenses like eating out, clothes and entertainment – the trick is to work out what you most enjoy spending money on and cut back on the rest.

Last, Find a Few Painless Ways to Cut Back

It's so easy to fritter away a few dollars every day without noticing it – on an extra coffee at lunchtime, or a last-minute birthday present – but it's also surprisingly easy to cut back if you want to, and it will make a difference.

Imagine, for example, that you could free up even an extra $50 a month and add it to your existing savings of $1000. After five years your account balance would have grown to $4974.31 (assuming that you get 8 per cent interest on your money and that you have paid 34 per cent tax on the income), of which $724.52 is interest. Without that $50 a month, your balance would only have gone up to $1286.04.

So, as you can see, it's definitely worth trying! For a start, look at the simple money-saving ideas that follow and see if you can make use of any of them.

Saving on Day-to-day Shopping

▲ Plan your meals in advance to avoid running to the corner shop for last-minute items. The prices there are usually quite a bit higher than at the market or supermarket.

▲ Eat before you shop, because research shows that if you are hungry you're likely to buy more food than you really need.

▲ Convenience food and pre-packed meals come at a cost. Try to buy fresh food whenever possible.

▲ Often there is little difference between 'gourmet' and no-name brands, so swallow your pride and keep the change.

▲ Buy refills rather than new containers or applicators every time.

▲ Make a list before you shop, so you're less tempted to 'impulse-buy'.

▲ If time is short we often sell ourselves short. When buying big-ticket items like electrical goods or furniture, there is no substitute for research: you can save literally hundreds of dollars by taking the time to shop around. And even when you've found the best price in town, don't be shy, ask your local supplier to better it!

Cutting Clothing Costs

'CUT YOUR COAT TO FIT THE CLOTH.'

— PROVERB

▲ Set yourself an annual limit for clothes purchases, and divide this between the two major seasons – summer and winter. Go looking for a few weeks, then plan a day for the big spend and buy everything at once. The beauty of this approach (apart from being great fun) is that you're more likely to achieve a perfectly co-ordinated wardrobe and you won't be tempted to spend later on a skirt here and a coat there. It doesn't matter whether you come home with several cheaper outfits or one expensive one – that's your choice.

▲ Visit some of the recycle shops specialising in designer clothes, which are springing up everywhere. They offer high-quality gear at very affordable prices, and you can also sell them any of your own clothes you no longer need.

▲ Buy samples and seconds from factory outlets. These clothes usually have a small fault, but often it's fixable or not noticeable. A word of warning, though: factory outlets are becoming so popular that some manufacturers produce special cheap lines of new clothes to stock them, and these are merely cheap clothes rather than a good bargain.

▲ If you have friends who wear a similar size to you, consider each buying one expensive outfit which you share on a rotating basis. This will save you at least a couple of special purchases.

Good-value Gifts

▲ It's easy to overspend on gifts, particularly if you buy them at the last minute, so snap up presents at bargain prices throughout the year if you've got somewhere to hide them for a few months.

▲ Home-made gifts that reflect the interests of the person receiving them are always appreciated, so if you have a talent – use it! A batch of home-made mustard or a pot of plants raised from seed can go a long way, and cost a fraction of the bought equivalent.

▲ If you belong to a large family, put everyone's name in a hat and have each person pick one out. They then buy a present for that person only, up to an agreed price. If there are children, why not agree with friends and siblings to buy for the children only?

Making Entertainment Affordable

▲ For most of us, dinners out are meant to be a treat. If you find yourself eating out too often, consider occasionally 'eating out' at home: get out the tablecloth and candlesticks and make a romantic meal, or pack some surprises in a basket and have a picnic. Even a simple meal at a middle-range restaurant can cost $60 for two, so cutting back on just one meal out a month could save you $720 a year.

▲ Take-away meals are generally cheaper than eating out, but these too can eat into your budget. The average Australian family spends about $12 a week on take-aways – and many of us spend lots more than that. If you cut out even a couple of take-aways a month, you'll save several hundred dollars a year. But use your common sense: while you can use a ready-made pizza base and still feed the family fast for a few dollars, the price of a take-away spiced chicken may well beat the home-cooked price.

▲ Take advantage of entertainment discounts – many cinemas offer books of tickets, which reduce the cost significantly. Motor associations, health-insurance companies and some company staff clubs are able to bulk-buy for a range of social events and pass on these savings to members or employees.

▲ Don't forget your local library: it's a source of audiotapes, CDs and videos as well as reading matter.

▲ Needless to say, cutting back on alcohol or cigarettes will not only make you healthier but improve the well-being of your bank balance too.

▲ The best things in life are free! It doesn't cost you anything to go for a walk – be it along the beach, in the park, or just around the neighbourhood. You'll get fitter, and you have the chance to catch up with friends or family along the way.

▲ Take advantage of the free concerts or activities provided by local councils, especially in school holidays.

SOME SIMPLE SAVING STRATEGIES

'A PENNY SAVED IS A PENNY EARNED.'

— ANON.

Hopefully by now you have got your goals down on paper, worked out how much money you'll need to achieve them, and seen some areas where you could free up some cash. Next you'd like to know the quickest way to make your savings grow. Well, there are a few ways to do this.

THE MIRACLE OF COMPOUND INTEREST

There's no doubt that when you start to save you will soon find that there's a hidden reward, because money makes money. This comes about through the power of compound interest – which the fabulously rich John D. Rockefeller is reputed to have called 'the eighth wonder of the world'.

Put simply, compounding is where you earn interest on your interest. The longer you save, the more compounding works in your favour – another good reason for starting early! No matter how small the amount you start with, the sooner you start saving the sooner you will reach your financial goals. And even if you never increase the amount you put away each week, compound interest will eventually contribute more to your savings than your weekly payments do.

The 'Compounding' Adventures of Jenny and Sue

Jenny and Sue work together and both save $2000 a year. The only difference is that Sue started saving at the age of 21, whereas Jenny began at 43 (which is when she met Sue). Let's see how they would stand when they each hit the age of 65 and have saved $2000 a year for twenty-two years, if we index their contributions at 4 per cent annually and average their rate of return at 8 per cent per annum (or 5.16 per cent after paying tax).

	Age they started saving	Contribution	Value at age 65	Value in today's dollars
Sue	(21)	$44 000	$359 229	$63 959
Jenny	(43)	$44 000	$281 444	$50 110

As you can see, because Sue started early, even though she contributed exactly the same amount as Jenny she will actually have earned about $77 785 more (though, of course, taking inflation into account, every dollar will be worth significantly less). In other words, the combined effect of starting early and having your money grow through compounding will increase your balance dramatically – all the more reason to start saving early and to make it a regular habit.

The higher the earning rate, the more amazing the 'magic' of compounding becomes. If Sue and Jenny earned 10 per cent rather than 8 per cent, their savings at age 65 would amount to $545 018 and $326 542 respectively.

And What's More ...

The other important thing to know about compounding is that the more frequently your interest earns interest, the better off you'll be. So when you are choosing an account or an investment, as well as looking for the highest interest rate ask the provider how often interest is calculated and paid. Usually interest is calculated daily, monthly or yearly, and paid monthly, quarterly, half-yearly or yearly, so it stands to reason that the best deal for you is an account that calculates interest daily and pays it monthly.

Your Savings Account: The Best Deal for You, a free booklet which is put out by the Australian Bankers Association, helps you work out the effective interest rate on your account, so that you can see its overall effect on your savings. For a copy of the booklet, phone the Australian Bankers Association on 1800 033 652.

INTERESTING SUMS

Penny was considering opening a savings account. She investigated several and finally it came down to a choice between two accounts with similar features and both offering 5.5 per cent interest per annum. Although both accounts calculated the interest daily, one paid it monthly and the other paid it half-yearly. Penny got a copy of the booklet *Your Savings Account: The Best Deal for You* and was able to work out that the 'effective' interest rate (that is, the interest rate adjusted for the effect of compounding) was 5.64 per cent on the account which paid the interest monthly and only 5.57 per cent on the account which paid interest half-yearly. The difference may seem exceedingly small, but Penny knew that it would have a significant impact over time and as her savings grew. Not surprisingly, she went for the monthly-interest account.

BANKING ON IT

There has been nothing short of a total revolution in the banking industry over the past fifteen years. Since deregulation in the 1980s, formerly 'non-bank' institutions such as building societies, credit unions and insurance companies have come into the marketplace to compete for your business.

This increased competition is good news for you, because it means that there are now far more options available. You don't have to accept the first account or loan you're offered: you can shop around and negotiate for the best deal. Because you are more likely to swap institutions if you're not happy with the terms your bank is offering, there has been a huge power shift in favour of the customer.

Like all good retailers, financial institutions want to buy your loyalty. That is why there are now so many extra benefits attached to simple bank accounts, including free insurance, travel discounts or a shopping hotline. Some of these services are provided by independent companies who thus get access to the bank's huge customer base.

Also like good retailers, banks are now working hard to 'target' you with the right 'product'. Private banking for high-net-worth individuals was an early example of this, but it will become far more sophisticated and some banks are already talking about 'lifestyle' accounts. More and more, you will be able to choose the exact account you want and to choose how you want to access it, be this in person, by telephone, by computer or via a mobile consultant.

These extra services can only increase as banks and building societies face greater competition. If you choose and use these accounts carefully they can save you a lot of money, especially if you have big items to purchase or are considering travelling, but remember there are usually higher account-keeping fees associated with such accounts. It certainly always pays to ask about the extras on offer as you shop around for accounts – but be realistic about whether you really will use them and then weigh up the benefits against the costs involved.

What's the Competition?

Many of us still don't think past the 'big four' banks (the National Australia Bank, Westpac, the Commonwealth Bank and ANZ) when shopping for bank accounts or finance. And even if we do look elsewhere, it is generally to one of the smaller, state-based banks. Whilst these institutions offer good products and services, they now face stiff competition which any financially savvy person should consider. The same goes for building societies and credit unions, which have enjoyed a surge in new customers fleeing from what they perceive to be excessive bank fees, although this honeymoon in reduced fees is unlikely to last.

How Safe Is Your Money?

At the close of the 1980s the collapse of building societies such as Pyramid gave many Australians a shock, as we tend to consider our money safe when we place it with a bank or other financial institution. The reality is that no financial institution can absolutely guarantee you your money back, but there are now stricter regulations governing these organisations and their activities. In 1992 an agreement to establish standards for all building societies and credit unions (friendly societies are also covered from 1996) came into effect in every state and territory. The scheme is administered by the Australian Financial Institutions Commission in Brisbane and Financial Institutions Commissions (FICs) in every other capital city.

LET'S GO SHOPPING

With all these options, how do you find the account that is best for you? How can you make sure that your savings will keep growing but that you also have an account that is flexible enough for you to manage your day-to-day expenses? How do you stop fees and charges eroding your money? Well, it isn't easy, but there are ways to use accounts effectively once you understand how they work and how the fees are charged. So let's have a look at these issues.

Which Account?

While they may go under many different names, there are really only a few types of bank account:

▲ basic accounts

▲ transaction accounts

▲ savings accounts

▲ fixed-term deposit accounts

▲ cash-management accounts

▲ children's accounts

But it's not quite as simple as this. With about fifty banks and more than 300 credit unions and building societies operating around Australia by the late 1990s, there are hundreds of variations on these basic themes. Below, we look at the main things to consider when you are shopping around for any account.

▲ BASIC ACCOUNTS were introduced largely in response to community concern about bank fees, especially their effect on low-income earners. You don't pay any bank fees on these accounts provided you stay within the bank's withdrawal guidelines (although they are still subject to government charges), but then they pay little, if any, interest, so they are definitely not the best vehicle for your savings. Also, few of them offer a cheque facility, which you may find restricting.

▲ TRANSACTION ACCOUNTS, as the name implies, are designed for day-to-day use and include a chequebook facility. Most banks offer a reasonable interest rate on these accounts, and waive account-keeping fees provided you keep a minimum amount in the account. But once you have a good sum of money there, it is usually better to maintain the required minimum balance (to avoid account-keeping charges) and transfer the rest to a straight savings account with a better rate of interest, or perhaps to a cash-management account or term deposit.

▲ SAVINGS ACCOUNTS typically offer us some incentive for saving – or at least some discouragement to withdraw. The encouragement to put your money in such an account may include a higher interest rate than you'll get with a transaction account, or a bonus rate if you make regular deposits. The encouragement to keep your money there may include a fee if your balance falls below the required minimum (which averages

YOUR ACCOUNT SHOPPING LIST

- What interest rate will your money earn in this account?
- How often is the interest calculated and how often is it paid?
- Will the interest rate vary depending on the amount you have in the account?
- What fees will you be charged on the account? Is there a minimum number of free transactions?
- What constitutes a transaction? Are, for example, EFTPOS, ATM or telephone withdrawals counted as transactions?
- Can you get access to the account in ways that suit you (e.g. chequebook, phone, credit card, and electronic link-ups including Internet)?
- Are there any minimum withdrawal/deposit limits or minimum balances required?
- Are there any associated special benefits, like cheaper insurance or home loans?

$500 – $1000), or a minimum being set for withdrawals. You can open these accounts with as little as $1, but the interest rate is often tiered, so the higher the balance the more interest you earn. These accounts are characterised by a lack of 'bells and whistles' such as cheque facilities. With some banks, if you have the minimum balance on the day when they assess your account (usually towards the end of the month – ask your bank), but fall below the minimum elsewhere during the month, you may not incur fees.

▲ With a FIXED-TERM DEPOSIT, your money is commonly locked away for somewhere between six months and five years. You can usually retrieve the money before the term expires, but you may suffer a fee or a reduced interest rate. Some banks allow you to access part of your money after a specified time without incurring a penalty, so shop around if you think you will need this flexibility.

▲ A CASH-MANAGEMENT ACCOUNT usually offers high interest rates, but you may need a minimum deposit of $2000 or as much as $5000. The interest rate is usually calculated daily based on the prevailing rates in the short-term money market. If you want to add to or withdraw money from such accounts, there is usually a minimum amount (typically $1000). Some of these accounts offer cheque-book facilities. (You invest in a cash-management trust through a managed fund: these are dealt with in Chapter 3.)

▲ CHILDREN'S ACCOUNTS differ from standard accounts in that account-keeping fees may be waived if the account-holder is under 18 or if the account is held in trust for a child. Children's savings accounts were originally designed to teach children to save, but banks now also offer a children's transaction account with such extras as ATM access, in which case account-keeping fees may be charged. Account-keeping fees on general accounts are also often waived for full-time students.

LOOKING FOR A BETTER INTEREST RATE?

Each type of account pays a different level of interest – basic accounts tend to pay the least, and cash-management accounts and fixed-term deposits tend to pay the most. Even within the same product category, different institutions may pay different rates of interest – and these are adjusted regularly. Again, it pays to shop around.

When the consumer magazine *Choice* last compared the interest rates for standard transaction accounts, it came to the conclusion that fees and charges mean a person with a low account balance (say $100) and medium–high use of the account will effectively lose money over the year no matter what the institution offers in the way of interest rates. If this applies to you, all you can do is minimise the loss by shopping around for the best account. Even if you keep the minimum balance in your transaction account, the interest you earn usually only offsets fees and charges, which is why 'savings' is a misnomer for many of these accounts.

You may also see offers of a tiered level of interest on different balances – up to seven steps in some institutions. Don't be dazzled by the interest rate for the top tier and leap straight in: also check how the interest is calculated if your balance slips down a step (some accounts don't pay you a cent

Two Interesting Points

How Often is the Interest Paid?

As we pointed out when talking about compound interest (see page 39), when you are choosing an account always look at when the interest is calculated and paid. An annual interest rate of 5 per cent paid monthly earns you effective interest of 5.1 per cent: this may not make much difference over a year, compared with daily and quarterly calculations but could do so over several years.

And What About Inflation?

Inflation also affects the interest rate you're paid. If inflation is running at 5 per cent and your interest rate is only 4 per cent, you'll be making a loss — even before fees and taxes are taken into account. The difference between the interest rate and inflation is known as the 'real' interest rate.

of interest if your account balance falls below a certain amount).

If you have a home mortgage, you could consider a 'mortgage offset' (or 'mortgage reduction') account. This offers the same facilities as a transaction or savings account, but you are not taxed on any interest earned on the account as this is immediately credited against the interest you owe on your mortgage. Even better, if your home-loan account offers a redraw facility (which means that you can borrow back, up to an agreed limit, any amount of the principal that you've already repaid), you may be able to arrange to have your salary and income paid directly into this account: by reducing the loan principal as well as the interest, you will effectively earn a much higher interest rate than you could from a standard account. Of course, this is only useful if the bank allows you to draw down on the additional repayments to meet your regular expenses: you shouldn't use it as a transaction account, but perhaps once a month withdraw enough to cover your day-to-day expenses and your credit-card bill. We look at these options in more detail in the section 'Buying a Home' in Chapter 4.

A Reminder: always lodge your tax-file number with your bank. For as long as the bank doesn't have it, you will be charged the top marginal tax rate (47 per cent plus Medicare levy) on any interest you earn. (Once you put in your tax return, though, you can claim a credit for any excess tax you've paid.)

Accounts That Give You More For Your Money

The erosion of interest earnings by factors such as fees, inflation and taxes means that in the long term it is generally far better to put some of your savings into property, shares, or some other investment which offers capital growth (that is, it has the potential to continue to increase in value). These alternatives are discussed in the next chapter. If you have savings of $1000 or more – too much to keep in a low-interest bank account but not quite enough to invest in property or shares, or if it's your emergency fund and you want easy access to it – consider putting it in a cash-management account or trust (see page 46). These usually provide better rates of interest than standard accounts.

A Word (or Two) on Fees and Taxes

There are so many ways in which fees are levied that it is worth sitting down with a few bank statements to see exactly what the fees add up to – and then keep this in mind when looking for an everyday account.

How to Minimise Fees
Account Fees
▲ Shop around for an institution which has waived account-keeping fees and, if possible, the requirement for a minimum balance on basic and transaction accounts.
▲ If your account requires you to keep a minimum balance, make sure you adhere to this. Can you consolidate a couple of accounts to help you do so?
▲ Check whether you are eligible for an exemption from fees. This may be the case if you have a home loan or other investments with the institution, if you are under 21 or are a full-time student, or if a pension is paid into your account.
▲ If your account offers benefits such as telephone banking or bill-paying, ask if there is a fee for these services. If there is and you are not making use of these facilities, consider transferring to another account with lower fees.

▲ If you are no longer using an account, close it as soon as possible so that you don't continue paying account fees.

Transaction Fees

▲ Find out how many free transactions you can make per month – and stick to it. Or switch to an account which better suits your spending style.

▲ Use your own bank's ATM whenever possible. Using those of other institutions can attract a fee as high as $1 per withdrawal once you have used up your monthly ration of free transactions.

▲ Find out whether your institution counts EFTPOS transactions or phone banking as part of the monthly maximum. If so, limit your use of these facilities. If you use EFTPOS at retail outlets, check with the retailer whether tacking on a withdrawal attracts a fee.

▲ Wherever possible, pay bills by direct debit as many accounts do not charge a fee for these transactions. What's more, it will make sure that your bills are paid on time.

▲ If you are likely to be accidentally overdrawn on a regular basis, choose an account which charges a low (or no) fee for this.

From BAD to Worse: the Taxes on Your Account

We are all pretty familiar with bank fees, but lately have you added up the tax you pay to the government every time you make a deposit or withdrawal? In

---

HOW TO MINIMISE 'BAD' TAXES

• One way to avoid BAD is by choosing an account which does not have a cheque facility. But don't fall into the trap of thinking that you can avoid BAD if you have an account with a cheque facility and simply don't use it – you can't.

• BAD is charged as a specified percentage of different withdrawal amounts: currently it costs you around 40 cents if you withdraw between $1 and $100, 70 cents if you withdraw $100–$499, and so on. So you can lessen its impact both by making as few small withdrawals as possible and by trying to keep larger withdrawals just under the next fee level.

all states bar Queensland you pay FID (Financial Institutions Duty) on every deposit you make; and in every state and territory except the ACT you pay BAD (Bank Accounts Debit or, as it's becoming known, Debits Tax) every time you make a withdrawal from a cheque-bearing account.

BAD was well named – it has a far worse impact on your savings than does FID, and hits small withdrawals particularly hard: it is said to cost you, on average, $5 a month. But both taxes are a disincentive to change accounts, as any money which you withdraw and then deposit elsewhere attracts both BAD and FID in the move. There is little you can do to avoid FID, though you can claim any FID paid on salary deposits or interest earnings as a tax deduction.

WHEN YOU WANT TO BORROW

'A BANK IS A PLACE WHERE THEY LEND YOU AN UMBRELLA IN FAIR WEATHER AND ASK FOR IT BACK WHEN IT BEGINS TO RAIN.'

— ROBERT FROST

While Robert Frost's comment was undoubtedly aimed at lending institutions, it should also be seen as a reminder of what can happen if you over-extend yourself. There is nothing wrong with borrowing money, but never forget that it does have to be paid back – with interest. And, of course, it is relatively easy to borrow money: the main challenge is to be in control of any debts you have and to be ever-aware of their impact on your financial well-being.

If you need to buy something it's preferable to save up for it, as you won't then have the additional cost of interest on a loan. In addition, retailers will often give you a discount if you pay for large purchases with cash, so you could end up saving money in more ways than one. But, of course, this isn't always possible: if you are buying a house or a car, for example, or spot a bargain which may not still be around by the time you have saved the money for it, then borrowing may be the best (indeed the only) option. If, on the other hand, you are borrowing merely to cover bad spending habits, it could become a difficult cycle to break and you may find yourself with unmanageable debt.

YOUR CREDIT RATING

'THE RICH ARE DIFFERENT FROM

YOU AND ME BECAUSE THEY HAVE

MORE CREDIT.'

— JOHN LEONARD

Responsible lenders, whether they are offering an overdraft, a credit card or a consumer loan, want to make sure you're a good credit risk. Good payers tend to stay good payers, so your loan history is an important part of the equation. If you've never borrowed money you won't have a credit rating, but although this makes it more difficult when you do want to borrow, it won't exclude you from doing so.

Credit bureaus are there to check out and record the credit history of potential borrowers. When seeking information from a credit bureau the lender must use a special code, which is intended to prevent snooping by unauthorised persons. The lender will be given any information about you that the bureau has on file, which includes all your other applications for credit and any 'delinquencies' on your part. (In this context, delinquencies mean serious misdemeanours like skipping town and leaving debts or bankruptcy, rather than such things as paying last month's Bankcard late.)

Because credit applications usually go through a credit bureau, their file says a lot about you: if you constantly borrow for small consumer items, for example, or if you told the bank you'd saved for a home deposit when you'd really borrowed it from another provider, all will be revealed here. The only catch can be if you were genuinely shopping around for a good deal and put in more than one application (which is particularly common when looking for housing finance), as the credit bureau does not indicate whether the loan was denied, abandoned or proceeded with, only that an application was made.

SHORT-TERM BORROWINGS

Here you borrow a relatively small amount of money – anywhere from a few hundred dollars to a few thousand, say – which you'll pay back within a year or two. The main sources for such borrowings are credit cards (yes, this money is a loan!), bank overdrafts and, though less commonly, lay-by arrangements and pawnshops.

Fantastic Plastic
Other than bank overdrafts, the most familiar forms of immediate credit are credit and charge cards. The word 'credit' has such warm-and-friendly connotations that it's often easy to forget that credit equals debt. Credit cards can cause more budget havoc than just about anything else, so it's important to use them well – or don't use them at all.

As credit cards are relatively easy to acquire, your biggest headache is likely to be deciding which of the numerous cards available will give you the best deal. The 'big three' are Visa, MasterCard and Bankcard, but just about every financial institution offers its own version. In addition the big three also offer 'affinity cards' (or loyalty cards), and large retailers such as Myer–Grace Brothers, David Jones, Sportsgirl and Freedom Furniture have their own 'store cards'.

Credit cards either offer an interest-free period or charge interest immediately the purchase is made but at a lower rate; some also charge an annual fee. Just as you should put your bank account through its paces, you should crunch some numbers on your credit card. Your spending style will dictate whether an interest-free period is useful or not.

Finally, look after your credit card. You may be responsible for all debts incurred up to the time you report a card missing, so a thief can quickly wipe out all the good that your careful spending habits have achieved. Know your credit-card number and the number to ring if your card is stolen or goes missing, and act quickly to report it. Do not disclose your PIN number or lend your card to anyone, and be wary of giving your card number over the phone unless it is to a reputable company.

Being Credit-card Clever

Most people have a love–hate relationship with their credit cards. They love the convenience and the 'free' money, and hate them when the bill comes in. Obviously the best way to manage your card is to choose one which matches your spending style, but here are few ideas on ways to lessen the pain when the statement arrives.

IDEA 1   *Set yourself a limit*

Often the key to handling credit cards cleverly is to set yourself borrowing limits and not be tempted by flattering letters of the 'You have been such an excellent customer we have upped your credit limit to $5000' variety. These letters can be disastrous for bad managers of credit cards.

Consider applying for two cards: one with a low limit, for convenience purchases; and one with a higher limit, for larger, longer-term purchases. On the low-limit card, look for a decent interest-free period (45–55 days, say) and for the higher-limit card go for no interest-free period but a lower interest rate.

Repaying any credit-card debt should be a high priority

If your credit card has a debit facility, use it. In this way you'll be spending your own money instead of the bank's when making a purchase. You can deposit funds into the card, earn interest and still enjoy the convenience of plastic.

When selecting a credit card, don't

Most people

have a love-hate

relationship

with their

credit cards

necessarily go for the 'gold' or 'platinum' varieties which offer a higher credit limit. Benefits such as the wine club, preferential theatre bookings and travel insurance typically come at a price, usually a higher membership fee. If you're after a higher credit limit apply for this on your standard card.

IDEA 2 *Pay it off in full*

Try to avoid paying only the monthly minimum off your credit cards, as you will then pay a high level of interest on the outstanding balance and may lose the interest-free period entirely.

Use the interest-free period to your advantage by paying off your card at the last possible moment, but then again don't have money sitting in the bank earning a few per cent interest while you are paying high interest rates on your outstanding credit-card balance.

Unless you are desperate, avoid drawing cash on your credit card. This is a very expensive way to get money, as interest is usually charged from the date the cash is drawn and you forfeit the interest-free period.

IDEA 3 *Leave it at home!*

If you love to shop till you drop or can't resist a bargain, try to leave your credit cards at home when you feel the urge to spend. That way you can have a cooling-off period to reconsider whether you really need that 'bargain'.

Beware of the Christmas holidays, as this is a time when credit-card debt can spiral out of control, a situation which is not helped by the fact that some cards offer a 'Christmas holiday' from your minimum repayment. Don't even be tempted.

IDEA 4 *Have your own card*

It is wise for you and your partner to have separate credit cards. This will ensure three things: that you will not be in the position of having the card frozen should your partner die and you are not the primary card-holder; that you are less likely to find yourself left to repay someone else's debt; and that you will have your own credit history, which will be important if you need to borrow money in the future. (These and other money issues in partnerships are considered in more detail in the section 'Marriage and De-facto Partnerships' in Chapter 5.

A Warning About 'Interest-free Periods'

When you receive your monthly statement, you have the option of repaying the minimum amount (usually this is a small percentage of the amount outstanding) or repaying part or all of the remaining balance. Now, you'd think an interest-free period would be an interest-free period – but it isn't if you didn't pay last month's balance in full. With some cards, you lose your interest-free period if you miss a payment or fail to pay the full balance, and all purchases from that time accumulate interest from the day of purchase until the balance is paid in full. This means that the interest is not only backdated but applied immediately to any further purchases – and in some cases this can triple the interest owed. So check the terms and conditions for your card.

'THAT'S NOT TRUE!'

- If you suspect that there is incorrect information on your credit file, you have the right to inspect it, and if you can prove any errors the bureau must alter your file. All information is kept for five years, so if you default on a loan it will not haunt you forever.
- The Credit Reference Association of Australia has published a leaflet, CRAA and Your Right to Privacy, which outlines the steps you need to take to access your file. For a free copy, phone 1300 364 141.
- Your right to privacy is protected by the Privacy Act, and if it comes to light that information about your credit history has found its way into inappropriate hands you can contact the Privacy Commissioner in your state for further help.

KEEPING THINGS TOGETHER

Kate and Matthew have always had a clear goal – to pay off their house by the time they are 45. Kate looks after the household accounts, and takes pride in her careful management of the books (and some old-fashioned thrift). She pays their water and rates accounts by direct debit, and she and Matthew consolidate all their buying and whatever bills they can (such as the phone bill) on one credit card.

Kate always pays the card off in full when the account comes in. She therefore uses only a few cheques a month (thus saving on bank charges) and can see almost all the household expenses at a glance on the credit-card statement, which really simplifies her book-keeping. She and Matthew chose a credit card which which offers Fly Buys points, and wherever possible they shop for petrol, clothes and food with companies that are part of the scheme. Kate's mother lives 1200 kilometres away, and last month Kate used her accumulated Fly Buys points to attend her mother's eightieth birthday party.

If you use credit cards and their interest-free periods wisely, they are a very cheap means of borrowing for a short time. If you make a purchase just before the date your statement is drawn up (this tends to be around the same time each month), you can also benefit from an additional month interest-free. But if you don't pay back the full amount, the interest rate will be higher than most other forms of borrowing, so repaying any credit-card debt should be a high priority.

Some stores also offer an interest-free period (typically six months) as an inducement to buy their goods. These deals are usually underwritten by a finance company and you will be required to sign a contract if you take up the offer. So, what's the catch? Well, as with credit cards, if you're disciplined and pay off the whole amount by the end of the interest-free period there's no catch – it's free money. But if you don't pay in full, the store passes your debt on to the finance company and you'll pay a very high rate of interest.

'A CREDIT CARD IS A MONEY *TOOL*, NOT

A SUPPLEMENT TO MONEY.'

— PAULA NELSON

Store Cards

These cards were the forerunners of credit cards and most big retailers still offer them. But it is hard to see why you would use a store card for short-term credit today: the interest rate is steep compared to the terms offered by a credit card, and there can be harsh penalties for not paying the account balance in full. If you have one of these cards, check to see if there are any special attractions – such as long interest-free periods, extended warranties, or bonus discounts – associated with owning it. If there are, make the most of these and pay the card in full each statement. If you can't do this, cancel the card.

Charge Cards

The best-known charge cards are American Express and Diners Club. The main difference between these and credit cards is that you must pay the total amount outstanding on your charge card each month, rather than spreading repayments through the use of 'credit'. The charge card also typically has an annual fee.

Charge cards can be used overseas, but then so can a number of credit cards including Visa and MasterCard. The charge cards' market share has taken a battering from credit cards in several ways in recent times. It's far more convenient for consumers to carry plastic which has credit attached, and charge cards tend to take a higher merchant fee from retailers, which has discouraged retailers from accepting them. This is now being counter-acted by the charge-card companies entering the credit arena (American Express, for example, now offers a credit card). When choosing these cards, apply the same criteria that you would for any credit card.

COVERING YOURSELF – CREDIT INSURANCE

You can take out insurance to cover yourself in case you can't make credit or loan repayments owing to unemployment, illness or some other mishap. General credit insurance (for example, for a loan to buy a hi-fi system) is available from insurance companies. Many banks also offer credit-card insurance. The terms and premiums will differ from bank to bank, but this type of insurance is relatively inexpensive (typically it's a flat fee per month or year, or you are charged a certain number of cents per $100 of the monthly closing balance). Income or disability insurance (see page 74) is usually a cheaper and better alternative, however.

Lenders cannot force you to take out credit insurance, nor can they force you to insure with their chosen insurer. (They can, though, insist that the goods you are buying with their loan are insured against theft or damage.)

As with any kind of insurance, it pays to shop around, because cover offered by the lender may not be the best deal in town: for some tips, see the section 'Insurance – Protecting What You've Got' on page 69.

Reward Schemes: Something for Nothing?

'Affinity' cards are appearing everywhere. They are usually issued by banks and are similar to ordinary credit cards except that every time you make a purchase you accumulate points towards some benefit with the associated company. Company-branded cards, such as Telstra and GM, provide a range of rebates: the GM card, for example, reduces the cost of your next GM car purchase relative to what you have spent via the card.

Then there are the points schemes, such as Frequent Flyers and Fly Buys. Always look carefully at these reward programs, as you can end up spending far more than you intended just to accumulate the points. Not only may you be buying things you don't need, but you may be less likely to shop around for the best price because you favour the providers participating in the scheme.

So always think about what you are likely to gain from using such schemes. Consider the interest rate, the annual fee and the interest-free period – in the end, these can have a greater impact on your financial situation than a discount. The rule of thumb is not to change your spending habits to accommodate the reward system. Buy what you need from whomever you want at the price you want, and if you accumulate enough points to earn a reward – good luck to you.

Bank Overdrafts

Bank overdrafts for small amounts are usually fairly easy to organise, and are attached to an existing account.

Most people use an overdraft if they have bills to pay and the account temporarily doesn't have enough in it to cover them. If you borrow in this way you will pay interest from the time the account is overdrawn. If the overdraft limit is relatively low, the loan is usually unsecured (i.e. not tied to one of your assets for the sake of security). If the overdraft is large enough to be 'secured' by a mortgage over an asset, it attracts stamp duty and establishment fees, which means it's not really a good bet for one-off short-term borrowings. If, on the other hand, you run your own business, a secured overdraft may be essential to help you manage your cash flow.

Although many people don't realise it, the interest rates for overdrafts are usually negotiable. Variable interest rates are used, which means that the rate may move up and down. The bank then adds on a margin, which reflects both the extent of risk they believe you pose and the amount borrowed. These margins may vary significantly and can make borrowing very expensive, so shop around. Use your history with the bank, your credit reliability and your assets (if you are negotiating a secured overdraft) to negotiate both the interest rate and the bank fees.

If you run a business and need to make significant purchases, you may choose to have more money added to your overdraft (which is referred to as having a 'fully drawn' account). These accounts attract the same interest rate as your overdraft and are also subject to the usual fees and duties. The main difference is that you have to make regular repayments to bring the debt down.

Lay-bys, or Whatever Happened to Good Old Patience?

In days past, if you didn't have the money for a purchase you didn't have to miss out, you just put it on lay-by. This facility is still offered by many stores: usually you pay a deposit on the goods and make regular payments off the purchase price; the goods remain with the retailer until you have fully paid for them. You are not usually charged interest, but there may be cancellation charges if you change your mind. As with any agreement, you should always check the written statement of the lay-by terms, including:

▲ the purchase price
▲ the deposit paid, and the balance owing
▲ dates and amounts of each instalment and the final payment
▲ cancellation charges (if any)

The supplier can cancel a lay-by and keep the cancellation fee only if you have broken the terms of the lay-by agreement (by being late with a payment, for example), but first they must write to you and give you a reasonable chance to fix the problem.

MEDIUM-TERM BORROWINGS

'IN THE MIDST OF LIFE WE ARE

IN DEBT.'

— ETHEL WATTS MUMFORD

In the world of finance the medium term is usually defined as three to five years, so you should keep borrowings of this kind for large purchases – a new car, an extension to your home, a pool.

These loans are reasonably straightforward: they don't involve interest-free periods and annual fees, so you don't have to juggle those figures (as you do with credit cards) and you don't have to agonise as much over fixed versus variable interest rates (as you do with a longer-term loan). At the same time, you shouldn't rush into such an agreement: you still have to consider the interest rates, the terms and any charges.

Most financial institutions lend money – banks, credit unions, building societies, finance companies and, more recently, insurance companies. It's therefore a competitive market and the institutions want your business, so never be afraid to negotiate. Go into these negotiations fully armed: think of the business you could bring the bank by way of accounts, loans and insurance policies, and ask what they can offer if you transfer your custom across. You will, of course, need to be sure you have a good credit rating: contact the Credit Reference Association on 1300 364 141.

Personal Loans

Personal loans, which are available through most financial institutions, allow you to borrow an agreed amount over a fixed period of time (though the period may be negotiable). They are most commonly used to buy a car or other big item (the section 'When You Need to Buy a Car' in Chapter 4 covers the ins and outs of such loans in more detail). There is rarely an application charge for a personal loan (or a nominal one only, around $2), but the rate of interest is usually a few per cent higher than for a standard housing loan.

If you take out a personal loan, it is worth considering consolidating into it any other debts you may have (on your credit card, say) that carry very high interest rates. First, the interest rate on a personal loan is invariably lower; second, you will have the discipline of repayments to keep you on track. A big 'but', though: don't be tempted to rob Peter to pay Paul by consolidating your debts and then running the credit card back up again.

Will Your Loan Be Approved?

Whether or not your loan application is successful will usually depend on a mix of factors. In the past, personal loans were granted on the say-so (or otherwise) of your bank manager. Nowadays, banks tend to be more scientific about risk management and use around sixteen different factors (such as length of employment, credit rating, where you live and how long you've lived there) to determine whether you look like a good credit risk – if not, the loan is a no-no. The good news is that, apparently, this system pointed out the fact that young women, in particular, are a good credit risk.

WHAT'S IN A RATE?

There are several ways in which loans are set up.

A *flat interest rate* is calculated on the original amount you borrow: that is, the repayments stay the same, no matter what has been paid off the loan. This is not a good option unless you want to borrow the money for a few months only.

A *fixed interest rate* may be calculated on the reducing loan balance, but the rate is fixed for an agreed number of years: this means that you know exactly what your repayments are for the fixed period, after which you revert to a variable rate and the repayments then increase or decrease.

A *variable interest rate* is calculated on the reducing loan balance and may go up or down depending on the general direction of interest rates. If the variable rate drops below the fixed rate you'll be advantaged, but if it goes up your repayments will too.

Consumer Finance

A secured loan from a finance company, often organised via the retailer, is a common form of financing largish consumer goods such as hi-fis and cars. This type of finance is discussed in more detail in Chapter 4 in the section 'When You Need to Buy a Car'.

'Rent and Buy' Plans

Some retail companies offer an arrangement whereby you rent the goods (most commonly television and audio equipment) for a fixed period before buying. While you are renting the item, you don't have to pay for any repairs and you can generally update the equipment at any time (but you may pay a higher rental fee for the new version). In most cases this is an expensive way to buy, so do your sums.

Putting It on the House

If you already have a mortgage, it may be worth considering increasing this loan to cover further borrowings. You have to pay stamp duty if you increase the initially approved amount, but the interest rate may be more attractive and, depending on your mortgage arrangement, you may have more flexibility to increase your repayments if you can afford to do so. A further benefit is that if you have a 'redraw facility' on your mortgage, you can borrow back (up to an agreed limit) at a later date any amount of the principal that you've already repaid. You can usually do this with as little as 24–48 hours notice, and most banks don't charge a fee for the facility.

There are two main dangers inherent in these options. First, your repayments may not be scheduled; and second, your mortgage is likely to be a long-term loan (commonly twenty-five years). It is false economy to use the lower rate of interest available through your mortgage and then stretch the repayments over a much longer period – you will pay a great deal more interest in the long run.

Long-term Borrowings

If you are borrowing a very large amount of money – to buy a property or a business, for example – you are likely to need a long-term (five years or more) loan. Here, what concerns most of us is the amount of interest we pay on the loan, and the fact that, because big dollars are involved, the lender will require some security over the loan in case we default. The dos, don'ts, ifs and buts of such loans are covered in the section 'Buying A Home' in Chapter 4.

Know Your Rights as a Borrower

Yes, borrowers do have rights. As lenders have been known to persuade people to take out loans which they cannot really afford, or to charge unjustifiably exorbitant interest, there are now laws to protect consumers. The Department of Consumer Affairs in your state can answer simple queries over the phone, and if the problem is complex they will refer you to someone who can help.

First of all, obtain a copy of the loan agreement, make sure you fully understand it before you sign, and do check that the full cost of the credit has been divulged. Following are some examples of your rights as a borrower.

▲ If you are refused a loan, based on a report from a credit agency, the lender must inform you of this in writing. The notice must include the name and address of the agency. You can then write to them for a copy of your credit report.

▲ If you dispute the amount owed on a credit card, ask the institution to send you a copy of the relevant receipt. Once you have this information, you should pursue the matter immediately.

▲ If you cannot keep up your repayments, you have four weeks to ask the credit provider to vary the terms of your contract (lowering the repayments, for example, or extending the repayment term). No legal action can be taken before this time. If the creditor will not renegotiate your contract, you can ask the Department of Consumer Affairs to intervene on your behalf. If the lender still refuses to negotiate, the matter is referred to the relevant appeals tribunal.

PAYING COMMISSION FOR YOUR CREDIT

If you don't go directly to the bank or finance company for your loan, but deal through a third party such as a broker, there is likely to be a commission component in the credit contract. This is particularly common when buying a new car: after you've looked over the new model with the dealer, you are introduced to the 'finance rep', who will work out a deal for you. There are two things to consider in such situations:

GOING GUARANTOR

It sometimes happens that you're asked to act as a guarantor for someone else's debt. As such requests are often from a partner or other family members, there is a strong emotional impulse to agree. But never forget that by 'going guarantor' you are saying, in effect, that if they cannot pay back the loan you will. So always think seriously before signing on the dotted line.

1 The finance rep is likely to offer you a deal from one finance company only, and there is no guarantee that this will be the best deal going or that this institution will be the best one to borrow from.

2 The seller may be paid a commission, and this charge will be passed on to you.

There may also be a commission paid when you use a leasing, insurance or finance broker. In this case it may still prove a worthwhile deal if the broker has access to wholesale rates of interest which, even with a commission, are cheaper than you could negotiate on your own behalf.

But, as a rule of thumb, always find out the 'effective' interest rate you'll be charged (this is the interest rate plus the commission, which is calculated as a percentage of the total amount owed, divided by the period of the loan). And never feel pressured to take the deal: in most cases it will be cheaper to negotiate directly with the credit provider yourself.

To Her Credit

Melanie was on a good salary, but she never seemed to have any money left over at the end of the month. She decided to change a few of her spending habits and was surprised to see how quickly it made a difference to the amount of cash she had available. She then decided to tackle the problem of her mounting debt: she owed $2500 on one credit card, at 18.5 per cent interest, $4000 on the other credit card, at 16.5 per cent, and had a personal loan of $10 000 on which she was paying 13.5 per cent.

Melanie paid an additional $400 a month off the card with the highest interest rate, while continuing to meet the minimum payments on the other two debts. This meant she was benefiting from reduced interest rates on her overall debt, as well as reducing the term of the debt. Once she was free of the first credit-card debt, she was able to focus on paying off the second one. And when this was achieved, because the repayments on her personal loan were fixed and she couldn't pay it off any sooner, she decided to put the extra $400+ a month towards a deposit for a house.

HELP, I'M IN TROUBLE!

If the occasion arises when you find you cannot manage your debts, you need to act quickly. This is one time when you can't be an ostrich – the debt will not go away if you don't open your bills. The longer you are in debt, the longer you will take to get out of it again. Here are eight suggestions for dealing with debt when it seems to be out of control.

STEP 1 *Stay calm*

Try to keep things in perspective: plenty of people and businesses get into trouble, but manage to work their way out again. The important thing is to formulate a plan.

STEP 2 *Determine whether the problem is short-term or is serious*

If the blow-out is temporary or the result of changeable factors such as unemployment or illness, you will be better able to handle it through a plan of action. If you are behind in your credit-card repayments, you generally have four weeks grace before the provider can take any action. If the problem is likely to continue (you are facing long-term unemployment, for example) or you are facing bankruptcy, get professional help immediately. Contact a lawyer or accountant for advice. A financial counsellor (see box on page 67) may also be able to advise you.

STEP 3 *Contact your creditors as soon as you get into difficulties*

Creditors want the loan repaid. Most will work with you to find a solution, which usually involves extending the repayment period and thus lessening the amount you pay off each time.

STEP 4 *Back to the budget*

Have another look at your budget (see Chapter 1). Redo it if necessary, making sure that you are realistic and trying to free up some money to put towards paying off your debt. Consider other ways to make money, such as taking on a second job.

STEP 5 *Protect your credit rating*

You may need a loan at a later date, so try to keep up to date with your bills. Even an unpaid electricity bill could show up on your credit rating if they chose to notify the Credit Reference Association.

STEP 6 *Stretch your money*

Take note of due dates and pay all your bills on the latest possible day. Don't necessarily pay all of one bill and nothing on another: at worst, just pay the minimum amounts due.

STEP 7 *List your debts in order of importance*

Write down all your debts, including the interest rate applicable for each. Aim to pay off first the debt with the highest interest rate, but still keep paying the minimum balances on all other debts. Once you have paid back the most costly debt, start on the next most expensive, and so on down the list.

STEP 8 *Consider consolidating all your debts*

As we said earlier, this doesn't mean robbing Peter to pay Paul. Consolidating your debts is only an option if several of the debts carry high interest rates (as with credit cards). If this is the case, consider organising a personal loan for the total debt (try to choose the shortest practicable payback term), with scheduled repayments

If you have a mortgage, also investigate collapsing the debts into it. But beware: if debt got you into trouble in the first place, why risk your home for it? If you can make higher repayments, you will be ahead; if you can't, you will be paying more interest on the extra amount you've borrowed. In other words, you will need to be very disciplined to manage this solution.

FINANCIAL COUNSELLING

If you have financial problems – you can't meet your loan or credit-card repayments, for example – it may be worth going to a financial counsellor. The sort of assistance they can provide includes helping you negotiate with the lending institution to change the size or timing of your repayments. Financial counselling is free (for contact numbers, see the Useful Contacts list at the end of the book).

Q *I'm having trouble meeting the loan repayments for my computer system. Can the bank repossess it?*

A If a lender takes a mortgage over goods for which you're borrowing to buy, they then have a legal interest in those goods and can take possession of them in some circumstances if you cannot keep up the repayments. The lender must, however, fulfil certain criteria before they repossess the goods: they must give at least one month's notice in writing that you are behind in your repayments, obtain your permission (or a court order) before they enter your home, and get an order from the state Appeals Tribunal, if you have paid more than 75 per cent of the price of the mortgaged goods. While it's not as dire as repossession, banks may have the power to do an 'account sweep' if you fall behind in your repayments. This means that they can literally sweep money from any account you hold with them, to pay the debt. They can't, though, sweep money from accounts you have with other financial institutions.

Bankruptcy – the Last Resort

If you are unable to repay your debts, always try to come to an arrangement with your creditors first. Alternatively, investigate Part X of the Bankruptcy Act, which suggests various possible arrangements between debtors and creditors, such as an agreement to accept money or property instead of full repayment of the debt. For further information, telephone or visit your State Library for details of the Act in your state, or contact your local community legal centre.

The last resort if you have unmanageable debts is to file for bankruptcy. Obviously, you should only contemplate this if the situation appears to be irretrievable – after you have exhausted all other avenues and have sought professional advice. If you are in this situation, contact the Insolvency and Trustee Service, Australia (ITSA), the Federal Court Bankruptcy Registry, a financial counsellor (see page 67) or an accountant.

Bankruptcy has long-lasting ramifications, and to deter people from choosing this as the 'easy' option, it carries a range of penalties: these include having to get permission to leave the country and, if you seek credit for more than $3000, having to inform lenders of your bankrupt status. The fact that you have been bankrupt remains on your credit record for seven years; it also takes a heavy emotional toll.

How is it Done?

You can declare yourself bankrupt on any amount, although creditors cannot declare you bankrupt if all your debts together do not total more than $1500.

Bankruptcy typically lasts for three years (after which it is discharged). But it is ultimately up to the Federal Court and the trustee to decide, and may in certain circumstances (for example, where the trustee believes that you have not disclosed all your assets) last indefinitely. If you have few assets and only a small income, it may only last six months. Bankruptcy can be annulled if you pay off all your debts or if the creditors agree to accept an 'offer of composition' (in other words, as much as you can afford to pay off the total debt).

Insurance – Protecting What You've Got

'Experience is a good teacher, but she sends in terrific bills.'

— Minna Antrim

Once you accumulate possessions and investments, it makes sense to safeguard them with insurance. So, while the only form of insurance you are legally required to have is Compulsory Third Party for your car, you should also give serious thought to allocating a portion of your income for protecting what you've got. Nobody enjoys paying insurance premiums, and it's tempting to believe that they are a waste of money. On the other hand, recovering financially from an expensive loss – be it loss of income through sickness, or having your house go up in smoke – could take you years. The following section deals with 'personal' insurance: health, life, disability and income-protection cover, and insurance when you're travelling. We look at insuring possessions such as your home and your car in Chapter 4.

People tend to hold one of two basic attitudes towards insurance. There's the 'It'll never happen to me' approach, which leads some people to have inadequate cover or no cover at all; and there's the 'It always happens to me' approach, which leads others to have too much (or in some other way inappropriate) insurance. When insurance companies set premiums, they do so on the basis of complicated calculations about the amount of risk you pose – and this is not a bad approach to take in reverse. 'What can I afford to lose?' and 'How long would it take me to recover financially?' are good starter questions if you are considering insurance.

The decision as to which forms of insurance are 'must-haves' and which are 'only-ifs' will depend on your situation. But whatever type of insurance you are looking for, there are some common guidelines to follow.

▲ Shop around and obtain quotes from a number of organisations. You will find that prices vary dramatically and the cheapest policy (or the most expensive, for that matter) may not be the best for you.

▲ 'Contract before cost'. Choose a policy that best meets your needs and only then consider the deals available. To do this you will need a clear picture of your needs, so it is worth putting a reasonable amount of time into this.

▲ Make sure you are absolutely clear about what the policy does and doesn't cover. Read the fine print, and never hesitate to ask questions if something is ambiguous.

▲ When you fill out the application form, answer every question honestly and accurately. This is largely to protect yourself, because if you make an error the insurance company can use this as a reason not to pay a claim.

▲ Check with the insurance company to find out whether you are entitled to any reduced premiums because of your age, sex, occupation and state of health.

▲ Find out what you can about the insurance company's approach to dealing with claims. What percentage of claims do they pay? How quickly do they settle?

HEALTH INSURANCE

'WHEN YOU DON'T HAVE ANY MONEY, THE PROBLEM IS FOOD. WHEN YOU HAVE MONEY, IT'S SEX. WHEN YOU HAVE BOTH, IT'S HEALTH.'

— J. P. DONLEAVY

Medicare, it would seem, is here to stay — more or less. But most of us at some stage worry about whether it is adequate for our needs and whether we should have private health cover.

Obviously your insurance needs will vary according to your general state of health, your family history and your stage of life. So, how do you decide whether to have private health cover or to rely on Medicare?

The main benefits of private health cover are as follows:

▲ It gives you access to private hospitals and to the doctor or surgeon of your choice.

▲ The waiting period for elective surgery is reduced significantly. A survey by *Choice* magazine in May 1994 found that 30 per cent of people who opted for private health insurance did so mainly to avoid waiting lists.

▲ Private health cover can help meet expenses not covered by Medicare, such as dental treatments, physiotherapy, optometry and ambulance costs.

Yet an increasing number of people are opting out of the private health system, and by 1996 little more than a third of all Australians had private cover. The reasons for this are simple. The young, the aged and others on lower incomes often struggle to meet the costs of premiums and the 'gap' between what they are charged and what they can recoup from their health fund, when such treatment may have been free under the public health system. (In an effort to stem the declining membership of private funds and the spiralling cost of maintaining the public-hospital system, the government has introduced a cash rebate for those with private insurance, which will come into effect in 1997, as well as reviewing the Medicare system.)

Then, of course, there's the assumption that Medicare will cover you in the event of an emergency. And it is a fact that if you do need emergency treatment, you're more likely to be taken to a public hospital, because this is where most emergency and specialist departments are – and in such situations you will receive the same standard of care whether you are a private or public patient. If you go to a public hospital as a public patient, you don't have to pay for your accommodation or your treatments, but you cannot choose your doctor. You can, even if you have private insurance, choose to go to a public hospital as a public patient: in this way you will not pay for anything, but then again you will not be able to choose your doctor. If, on the other hand, you go to a public hospital as a private patient, you will be

---

GOING INTO HOSPITAL

What You Need to Know if You Have Private Cover
- Will your policy cover all the costs, including accommodation, treatment, anaesthetist if required, and other services such as theatre fees?
- If your policy covers less than 100 per cent of the costs, or the cover has a dollar limit, ask for the estimated costs in writing.
- What arrangements are there for paying? Are you required to pay in advance?
- Does your health fund have a contract with your doctor and with the hospital? This type of contract is convenient when it comes to settling the accounts, and some may cover you for up to 100 per cent of your costs.
- Have you fulfilled the qualifying period for cover?

charged (although the costs may be covered in full by your health fund).

Probably the two times when you are likely to reassess your position as regards health insurance are when you start a family and when you hit middle age or beyond. The specific needs of each these groups are covered in the sections 'Having a Child' in Chapter 5 and 'Health Issues' in Chapter 6.

LIFE INSURANCE

If you have substantial debts (such as loans for your house or car) or dependants who rely on the income you provide, you should consider taking out insurance to cover you for illness, disability and death. If you are young and have no dependants, there is no need to waste significant amounts on life cover, but it's definitely worth considering some insur-

TAKING COVER

Miriam is the main breadwinner in the family. Her husband John works part-time and they have two school-aged children. They have just moved into a bigger house and taken on a substantial mortgage, which they aim to have reduced significantly in ten years' time. They also hope to send their children to private schools in a couple of years.

When discussing their need for life insurance, they realised it would be primarily during the next ten to fifteen years that they would be in difficulties should something happen to either of them. Also, they couldn't afford the higher premiums attached to 'whole-of-life' cover at a time when they were trying to reduce their mortgage. They decided to take out term insurance for fifteen years, with a value of $200 000 for Miriam (as she is contributing most of the mort-gage repayments and education costs), and $100 000 for John.

ance to cover you for loss of income in case you become ill or have an accident. Equally, even if you are staying at home to raise children and not earning an income, you should consider having life insurance. If you die, the chances are that your partner would have to keep working to support the family, in which case he would undoubtedly need help with child care and with keeping the household functioning. And, as many of us know, this help doesn't come cheap.

How Do You Choose The 'Best' Policy For You?

How much life insurance you need will reflect the value of both your assets and your debts. The fewer debts and the more unencumbered assets you have, the less you need life insurance.

Choosing the most appropriate life-insurance policy can be difficult, as the policies vary so much and incorporate so many different features. To simplify what can be a fairly complex area, there are two basic types of life insurance: those which pay an amount on death up to a certain age (known as 'term insurance'), and those which combine this cover with a savings element (known as 'whole-of-life' and 'endowment' policies). The key determinant is the price you are willing to pay and your circumstances at the time you take out the cover.

Term insurance covers you for a certain period of time. You may take out term insurance for a set number of years or to age 65, after which time your cover will cease and you will not receive any benefits. With some policies the cover extends beyond age 65, although an annual medical statement may be required. The insurance premiums for a set amount of cover generally increase with age: if, for example, you want life cover of $100 000 you can expect to pay about $65 a year at age 25, rising to $540 a year once you reach 55. This type of insurance is useful if you are going through a period where your financial commitments are steep and you have dependants who would be left in dire straits should you die.

Whole-of-life and **endowment policies** offer a savings component as well as life cover, and thus the premiums are more expensive in the early years than those for term insurance. In effect the 'savings' give your policy a cash value, which can be withdrawn or borrowed against. If you are considering this form of insurance, think about whether this benefit is worth the extra you'll pay for it. Cancelling the policy before the contracted date usually means that your 'savings' will have grown very little, if at all.

PROTECTING YOURSELF AGAINST LOSS OF INCOME

Many people go to great lengths to ensure that they have adequate life insurance, but fail to cover themselves against the loss of income they would face if illness or disability prevented them from working. This is quite frightening when you consider that your earnings may be your biggest asset.

Statistics show that one in two Australians will at some stage suffer a disability or illness which prevents them from working for three months or more. Research (and logic) also suggests that if you're between 25 and 65 you are more likely to suffer from a severe disability than you are to die.

It appears that women in particular need to come to terms with this reality, as far fewer women than men have some form of income insurance. This may have been understandable in days gone by, when women were not, by and large, the major breadwinners.

A Sporting Chance

Helen is the coach for a gymnastics team. Her job is very active, but she no longer takes part in competitions so she was surprised to find that the company she approached for income-protection insurance regarded her job as high-risk and would only offer her cancellable insurance. After weighing up the costs and benefits of this type of policy, she decided it was too much money to pay if there was a chance the policy would be cancelled at a future date, possibly due to changed circumstances over which she would have no control. So she decided instead to put a portion of her income each month into a savings plan - this would be her 'insurance', which she could cash in if she was unable to work.

But today, with more women working, with more families relying on two incomes and with the rapid increase in the number of women starting their own businesses, it is time to think about whether you can afford not to protect yourself.

Today, as well as income and disability insurance, you can also take out trauma insurance, which provides a lump sum if you suffer from a major illness or condition like cancer, heart attack, stroke or dementia. Importantly, unlike income protection, this cover is available whether you are working or not. The premiums are typically lower for women than for men, because statistics show that men are more likely than women to suffer from these conditions.

Income-Protection Policies: What To Look For

Income-protection insurance can provide you with an ongoing income of up to 75 per cent of your salary if you become ill or have an accident. This should cover your day-to-day bills while you're not working.

When shopping around for income-protection insurance, look first of all for a policy that is 'guaranteed renewable', which means that the insurer must renew the policy each year (as long as you keep paying the premium) even if your state of health or your occupation changes. This is crucial, because if you buy a cancellable policy and then change jobs to what the insurers consider a higher-risk occupation, or your health deteriorates, they could refuse to renew your policy.

Read very carefully the terms of any policy you're considering, and make sure the wording is as specific and unambiguous as possible. Where the policy sets out the conditions under which you qualify for a benefit, for example, go for one which will pay you if you are unable to perform 'the main duties of your usual occupation' rather than one which has a broad or ambiguous description like 'all of your duties'.

Also look for a policy which contains a fair definition of the 'disabilities' that qualify for benefits, as these can vary from policy to policy. Above all, avoid policies with definitions that may allow the insurer to reassess your claim after a period of time, such as 'after two years of being unable to perform duties in your usual job, you may be assessed on the basis of your ability to perform tasks in another occupation requiring similar levels of education, training and experience'.

Similarly, choose a policy which has the broadest possible definition of 'income'. Ideally the policy will include any sources of income (such as regular overtime, or a car allowance) and other benefits that might constitute your salary package. Make sure you are fully aware of any 'offset' items (income from other sources that will reduce the benefit you receive) listed in the policy. If you run your own business, the benefit can be calculated to cover the expenses involved in running the business, as well as your salary (the business overheads will, of course, need to be substantiated).

To ensure that the value of your policy goes up over time, buy one that will reflect any increases in your income. In addition, check that payments continue to increase in line with inflation while you are off work and receiving the benefit.

Many of the features that we recommend you look for in a policy will mean a higher premium, and receiving a benefit for as long as possible is no exception. Some insurers offer policies which will pay benefits for as short a period as one year, while others continue to pay claims until you reach the age of 65. You will pay a higher premium for the latter, but the peace of mind it brings may well outweigh the extra expense.

The waiting period before you are entitled to a benefit is a further consideration. If you have money set aside to cover emergencies, this may free you up to choose a policy with a longer waiting period, which will reduce the premium.

Do You Need Disability Insurance?

While you may be covered by workers compensation if you have an accident at, or when travelling to or from, your job, disability insurance usually covers you twenty-four hours of the day.

Total and permanent disability insurance provides a lump sum if you suffer a permanent incapacity (through the loss of two limbs, for example), or absence from work for more than six months through injury or illness, and which leaves you incapable of ever returning to work. Unfortunately, many claims for this benefit have been refused by insurers because the claimant has not met the strict criteria set out in the policy.

At issue here is the fine print of the policy. Not only does the insurer have to be of the opinion that you are so incapacitated you can never return to work, but policies differ as to the definition of the occupation you can return to. Avoid policies which are vague in this regard (citing, for example, 'any occupation you could be suited to'): if, for example, you cannot resume your work as a doctor but could work as a hospital administrator, would you get paid the benefit?

The value of total and permanent disability insurance is in providing a lump-sum payment at a time when your medical expenses could be substantial and home modifications may be necessary. Purchasing this and life cover through your superannuation fund can have some tax advantages, so discuss the possibility with an accountant. In the end, though, it is no substitute for the ongoing payments provided by general income-protection insurance.

Q *Are my insurance premiums tax-deductible?*

A No, premiums for life and/or disability insurance cannot usually be claimed as a deduction. The only exception is where you purchase this cover through your superannuation fund: in such cases, the premium can be deducted from any before-tax super contributions you or your employer make, which can almost halve the cost to you. Income-protection insurance can, however, be claimed as a tax deduction even if you pay for it outside your superannuation fund, as it is treated as an expense incurred in earning income. In fact, where your benefit entitlement lasts for longer than two years you would really be better off paying for the policy outside your super fund, because these benefits will count towards the maximum amount of super you can receive at the concessional tax rate.

TRAVEL INSURANCE

When it comes to travel, take Murphy's Law to heart: 'Whatever can go wrong, will go wrong.' That is why it's important to take out travel insurance before you go. You can choose to be covered for a range of mishaps including cancellation of your holiday, loss of luggage or money, personal liability in case you damage someone or something in another country, and the cost of overseas medical and hospital expenses. These insurances are generally offered as a package, with varying levels of cover, depending on the premium you wish to pay.

Although it will be costly if your luggage goes missing or you have to cancel your holiday due to unforeseen circumstances, this is nothing compared to the financial burden you can face if you fail to take out medical insurance. Medicare does not pay for medical or hospital expenses incurred overseas, unless Australia has a reciprocal agreement with that country. Currently we have such agreements with Finland, the UK, Italy, Malta, the Netherlands, New Zealand and Sweden, but they don't cover non-emergency treatment, private hospitals and travel home. In such countries, you need to carry your Medicare card as well as your passport.

In countries where no such agreements exist, particularly the US, medical

TIPS WHEN CHOOSING TRAVEL INSURANCE

- Choose a policy which suits your needs, not the first policy offered by your travel agent.
- Check if the policy covers you for pre-existing medical conditions, for ambulance costs and for an emergency flight home.
- If you have a credit card, check to see if it offers you free insurance up to a certain level, or emergency global assistance.
- If you are going to travel more than once in a year, an annual policy may be cheaper.
- If you are going on an activities holiday, check that the activities you intend to pursue are covered, especially adventurous sports such as scuba-diving.
- If you have private health insurance, check if it gives you any overseas coverage.

bills can be astronomical. Even if you're fit and healthy, medical insurance is one area where you shouldn't skimp.

WHERE DO I GO TO BUY INSURANCE?

There are all kinds of insurance policies out there, and they are available through general insurance companies, life-insurance specialists and, increasingly, banks and other financial institutions (especially for home and car insurance, though the policies they sell are usually insurance-company products). The best place to start investigating the field, other than asking friends or relatives for recommendations, is to look under 'Insurance' in the Yellow Pages. Most companies have agents who will come to your home or office and explain the policy, the disadvantages of this service being that agents may try to pressure you into buying and may only present one company's policies. You can also contact an insurance broker, who will broker a deal for you, which is particularly useful if you have an unusual insurance request.

LOOKING AHEAD

This chapter should have helped you to start 'getting it together' financially – or, for those of you already along this path, to firm up your financial strategy – by allocating your income in ways that will work best for you.

With a savings plan, an emergency fund, and insurance, you have the building blocks of your future – the foundations of the path to financial and personal freedom. So it's time to take a step further: while you may be good at saving, if you want your money to work harder on your behalf, you should think seriously about putting some of it into shares, property or other investments which will increase in value and/or give you even more income. This is what investing is all about, and we look at it in the next chapter.

3

GETTING AHEAD: PUTTING YOUR MONEY TO WORK

In financial terms, what does 'getting ahead' mean to you? For many of us it simply means being free of money worries. For some people it might mean having enough money to be free to make choices. And for others, money is a ticket to the high life.

The point is not, though, how we choose to spend our money – it's that just about everyone would like to have more than they've got. Yet the reality is that anyone on an average salary will earn well over a million dollars during his or her lifetime. It's what they do with their income that distinguishes successful money managers from those of us who live from day to day. Successful money managers get ahead by investing any spare money they have – which is the focus of this chapter.

Anyone on an average salary will earn well over a million dollars in his or her lifetime

Think It Looks Too Hard?

Many people who are good at saving find the next step, becoming an investor for even greater gain, a difficult one. Yet investing is not complicated: if you take a little time to understand the basic principles outlined in the following pages, you'll find it much easier to make investment decisions – and a lot of people enjoy doing so. And if you think you need heaps of money – think again: you can start investing with as little as a thousand dollars.

So what sorts of investments are there, and when might they perform best? Which ones might suit you, and how do you go about acquiring them? And how do you choose the right financial adviser if you need one?

UNDERSTANDING INVESTING

'YOU DON'T HAVE TO BE WEALTHY TO BE AN INVESTOR. YOU HAVE TO BE AN INVESTOR TO BE WEALTHY.'

— ROB FERGUSON

Investing simply means buying something with the aim of earning an income from it now or making a profit on it in the future.

Being a successful investor shouldn't, though, be confused with instant wealth – get-rich-quick schemes always carry with them a high chance of losing money. The best approach to investing is to see it as a long-term, or get-rich-slow, process. It also helps if you are investing for a purpose, whether it be to give you a regular income now, to pay for a holiday or your child's education a little further down the track, or to support you when you retire. If you start at 25 or if you have a good deal of spare income to invest, obviously you'll have a headstart. If you start later, you may have to work a bit harder but you can still do it.

WHAT DO YOU NEED TO KNOW?

Women as a group have traditionally been cautious when it comes to investing: we usually prefer to put our money in the bank or 'invest' it in a home. No doubt in many cases this stems from a fear of making a mistake and losing money.

And certainly the range of investments on offer can be daunting. Unit trusts, mortgage trusts, bonds, shares, corporate debentures, futures – the list is apparently endless, and the terms used to describe them can be

---

YOUR MARGINAL TAX RATE

Basically, the more you earn the higher the rate of tax you pay. If you are an investor, it's useful to know your marginal tax rate, which determines what you owe the Tax Office (plus Medicare, where applicable). You can use it to work out whether income from any of your investments will take you into a higher tax bracket.

TAXABLE INCOME ($)	TAX PAYABLE ($)
0–5400	Nil
5401–20 699	20% on any amount over $5400
20 700–37 999	$3060 + 34 per cent on any amount over $20 700
38 000–49 999	$8942 + 43% on any amount over $38 000
50 000+	$14 102 + 47% on any amount over $50 000

confusing too. But it really isn't as complicated as it looks. For a start, although there are lots of variations on each theme, investments can all be placed within one of four broad categories: cash, fixed interest, property and shares. We look at each of these in detail later in the chapter.

When you come to invest, do choose a path with which you feel comfortable – in terms of both your purse and your personality. You may enjoy playing a very active role, by making direct investments such as

---

GETTING THE BALANCE RIGHT

Just as most of us strive for balance in our lives (well, at least a semblance of it), financial experts all advocate a balanced mix of investments – known in the trade as 'a diversified portfolio'. A balanced portfolio contains a mix from all four investment sectors:

- CASH
  In investment terms, 'cash' means money which is at call (that is, you can retrieve it within 24 hours). You can invest in this way through bank accounts and cash-management trusts.
- FIXED INTEREST
  Here you invest your money for a longer period at a pre-arranged, fixed rate of interest. Such investments include fixed-term deposits and bonds.
- PROPERTY
  While most of us think of real-estate investments as a block of land, a house or an apartment, today there is increasing interest in commercial, retail and industrial property, which may offer better returns.
- SHARES (STOCKS OR EQUITIES)
  Through shares, you become part-owner of a company. You can purchase existing shares via the stock exchange and new shares through a 'float' (when they are first made available to the public, usually to fund expansion by the company).

COLLECTABLES: INVESTMENTS OR NOT?

Works of art, antiques, gems, stamps, coins, toys and even luxury cars are often dubbed 'investments'. In fact, while they may indeed be valuable, and bring you status or enormous pleasure (or both), you can never be a hundred per cent sure that their value will increase, let alone that there will be a buyer for them should you want or need to sell. They are, in other words, a high-risk area in investment terms, as your money will be tied  up with no guarantee of income or profit. As the editor of *Kiplinger's Personal Finance Magazine* has commented, 'Don't include collectables in your long-range plans for financial security. That would be confusing a hobby with an investment strategy.'

buying a property yourself or purchasing shares through a stockbroker. Or you may like to invest indirectly by joining with other investors in a managed fund (see page 128).

'Income' and 'Growth'

Some investments give you a regular income, and others are chosen for their potential to grow in value. Of course, your need for income and for growth will change according to the stage of life you're at. When you are working full-time you probably don't need income from your investments, but should you take time off to have a baby or to travel, or if you work part-time, this situation may change. Certainly when you retire you will need income to replace your salary.

Each of the four investment areas provides some level of income. The interest you receive from fixed-interest investments makes them a good source of regular, though often set, income. Property and shares, on the other hand, have the potential to provide increasing income (through rising rents and increases in company earnings/dividends, respectively).

Many of us need a combination of income and growth. You should always try to structure your investments so that you are receiving income from a number of sources, and also achieve some growth so that your money does not run out too quickly.

The Risk–Return Equation

Your attitude to risk, and the returns you need or want, will together underpin your investment decisions.

How do you know how risky a particular investment is? Well, there is a simple rule about risk, which holds true for all investments: the higher the possible return, the greater the risk and potential loss. So whenever you are considering buying an investment, judge the risk by this rule. If it is offering to double your money in six months, or is paying a higher rate of interest than most other investments in its class, there may be more risk of losing your money.

Risk and uncertainty lie at the heart of every investment decision

But – and it's a big but – this doesn't mean that you should avoid all risk. An investment carrying minimal risk, such as a bank account, rarely provides sufficient returns to counter the effects of inflation, tax and fees. In this case, you risk the value of your money going slowly backwards.

You will also find that the level of risk varies between the different investment areas and according to the amount of time you are prepared to hold on to the investment. Shares and property, for example, tend to be more risky than cash investments in the short term, yet generally outperform all other asset classes over a ten-year period.

Risk can be reduced by purchasing at the 'right' time. If you buy shares or property towards the end of a recession, chances are that they will increase in value over the long term. Equally, if you lock into a bond when interest rates are high, it's likely that the interest rate will drop at some point and make your rate of return look very attractive.

SIX SOUND INVESTMENT PRINCIPLES

'TENDING AN INVESTMENT PORTFOLIO IS A LOT LIKE GARDENING. MOST SMALL GARDENS DON'T REQUIRE MUCH ATTENTION AND LARGE ONES REQUIRE MORE. BUT THEY BOTH REQUIRE SOME.'

— *BARRON'S GUIDE TO MAKING INVESTMENT DECISIONS*

There is no sure-fire formula for being a successful investor: risk and uncertainty lie at the heart of every investment decision. This fact can be disappointing to potential investors, who constantly want to know what the 'best' investment is.

Although there will always be stories around about the person who made a small fortune on one speculative share, or picked up a real-estate bargain, these successes usually depend on a fortuitous mix of luck and talent. This is not everybody's lot, so if you are new to investing or want a long-term strategy, it's worth following a few time-honoured rules.

1 THE RIGHT BALANCE

Although there have been well documented examples of people growing rich on a diet of real estate alone, no one is smart enough to pick the best-performing investment sector all the time. By spreading your money across a number of different investments, you not only reduce the overall risks but

EVERYBODY HAS A GOOD TIME WHEN THINGS ARE BOOMING

When the stock market was booming in the early 1980s, Sue bought some big, safe 'blue-chip' shares, including BHP and CSR, and made quite a bit of money. She used her earnings to invest in more shares, this time in speculative areas like new technology.

Then, in October 1987, the market collapsed. Sue lost her nerve and tried to offload all her shares: she couldn't find a buyer for her speculative shares for some months, but she was able to cash in her blue-chip stocks, albeit for a much lower price than she would have got prior to the crash. *Her mistake:* she bought the technology shares when the market was overvalued, and then compounded this error by selling her blue-chip shares at the bottom of the market, instead of waiting until things picked up.

increase your total return. The share-market crash of October 1987 was a real lesson in the benefits of having a mix of investments. If at that time you only held shares, you would have lost a lot of money when share prices fell dramatically. If, on the other hand, you also had some money in cash, property and fixed-interest investments, this may have offset your stockmarket losses. In much the same way, when the property market fell in 1989 and 1990, having a spread of investments could have saved you from having to sell and allowed you to wait till prices picked up again.

As well as diversifying between the major investment areas, you should also consider diversifying within them – in the case of shares, by perhaps having both industrial and resources stocks. It's also worth considering international shares, which are covered in more detail on page 123.

Of course, the most appropriate mix of investments for you will depend on your needs and your goals, and may change over time as these factors change. Not having all your eggs in one basket has several things going for it. You will be educating yourself about a wide range of investments, and as you become more comfortable with the different sectors you are likely to see ever-more investment opportunities.

2 THE IMPORTANCE OF TIMING

There are, of course, right times to invest, and if you follow a particular type of investment – be it shares or property – you'll soon learn to recognise when the market is booming or rising (known as a bull market) or when it's falling or depressed (a bear market).

When a major store has a sale and cuts prices (a bear market), shoppers rush in looking for bargains. And when a store lifts its prices (a bull market), shoppers are soon conspicuous by their absence. While the logic of this behaviour is clear, many people don't seem to apply the same common sense when it comes to investing, particularly in the case of the share market. When share prices fall, fear tends to strike: new investors are hard to find and existing ones panic and scurry to get out, although the market is at its cheapest after a fall. When the share market is 'running' and prices rise, on the other hand, investors tend to rush to buy, not wanting to miss out – yet they are buying when the market is at its most expensive. The property market works slightly differently. When property prices are down, people resist putting their houses on the market and this often leads to a shortage of stock. When prices rise, buyers fear that they will get locked out of the market and tend to pay over the odds. So, you can make a good start by resolving to look at your investments as part of an overall strategy. Don't chop and change when returns vary in the short-term – instead be patient, with an eye to the long-term rewards.

Of course, investment bargains don't always present themselves when you have money to spend. And even if you have some spare cash when an opportunity comes up – be it real estate, shares, fixed interest, or whatever – how do you know it's the right time to enter the market? While there are ways to reduce your chances of buying at the worst time (when prices have already soared, for example), for most investors it is probably safest to follow the adage, 'It's not the timing of the investment, but the time invested that counts'. This is dramatically illustrated by a look at the Australian share market over time: if, every year since 1970, you had invested $100 in the All Ordinaries Accumulation Index at the worst end-of-the-month price, by December 1995 you would still have made an average annual return of around 14 per cent before tax.

3 GET THE HABIT

It's not the timing of the investment, but the time invested that counts

At the risk of sounding repetitious, the key to successful investing is to be disciplined. The principles of 'paying yourself first' and putting money aside regularly – which, as we discussed in Chapter 2, are the best ways to increase your savings – also apply to building investments.

If you invest a set sum on a regular basis, regardless of market conditions, you will buy more for your money when prices are down and less when prices are high. This tends to reduce the average cost of your investment, which is why it is often referred to as 'dollar cost averaging'. While such an approach is not as advantageous as buying when prices are at their lowest, you'll find it a far better strategy than waiting for the 'perfect' time to buy.

4 KEEP AN EYE ON THE ECONOMY

Another characteristic of a successful investor is the habit of keeping a 'weather eye' on which way the larger economic winds are blowing. The outlook for inflation is particularly important, as some investments are better suited to times of high inflation and others to low inflation.

Property is regarded as one of the best investments in periods of high inflation, as there are likely to be both strong capital gains and increased income as prices and rents go up. Property is generally less appealing in times of low inflation, when real-estate values tend to level off. Shares, on the other hand, can be more appealing in times of low inflation: lower interest rates and lower operating costs are both good for company profits and thus the value of your shares.

No matter whether you are dealing with high or low inflation, you should do your homework before investing and always reassess your strategy in times of economic change. It is also worth pointing out that as we lived with high inflation for two decades – a whole generation – there will be many older people committed to investments which suited that environment. If, say, you choose to invest in shares rather than property, you could well be discouraged from doing so by investors who have enjoyed profits from property but had a bad time with their shares. Just remember that times change and what worked then (or now, for that matter) may not be appropriate ten years later.

As well as inflation, you should also consider current interest rates when choosing investments. Obviously, you would think twice about borrowing to buy a share portfolio or investment property if interest rates are very high, but would quite happily think about locking into a term deposit.

5 Don't Base Future Expectations on Past Performance

Although an investment's performance over the long term gives an indication of its relative merits, it's unwise to make your decision solely on this basis. As a graphic example, the Australian share market returned over 45 per cent (including both dividends and capital growth) in 1993, yet the following year it returned minus 12 per cent. In fact, based on the calendar returns over the last fifteen years, no sector has been the top performer for more than two years running.

Keep reminding yourself that simply because a particular investment has done well in the past there is no guarantee that it will continue to do so in the future. There are a number of factors that affect the performance of an investment, such as changes in management or in government policies, which reinforces the importance of considering a range of investments. So when you are considering an investment, by all means make your decision in the light of present conditions and anticipated performance, but keep monitoring the situation in case things change.

6 Consider the Investment First, Then Its Tax Merits

Many of us want to use our investments to reduce our tax bill. If this is your top priority, you may be tempted to choose an investment primarily for its tax benefits rather than for its potential returns. But in fact nowadays there are only a few ways to reduce your tax without sacrificing something else: superannuation, for example, receives many tax concessions, but our access to the money is pretty restricted until we retire. All in all, it's generally better to choose an investment first for its potential returns and then for its tax-effectiveness – though ideally, of course, it will offer both.

Capital-gains Tax – No Free Lunches?

We discuss the tax merits of the different investment sectors as they occur later in this chapter. But as capital-gains tax impacts on all our investment decisions, it's perhaps worth a special look.

If your investment increases in value, the Tax Office usually takes some of the profit ('capital gain') you make when you sell it. They achieve this through capital-gains tax (CGT), which was introduced in September 1985. If you make a loss when you sell, this can't be offset against other income, only against other capital gains, although it can be carried forward and used against capital gains in future years. Thankfully, some things are exempt from capital-gains tax, such as your principal family home, your car(s), compensation payments for injury, and lottery wins.

Capital-gains tax does advantage some investments over others. With shares and property, for example, not only can you deduct some expenses but the investments are sheltered from tax up to the value of inflation: in other words, provided you hold your shares or property for more than one year, capital-gains tax only applies to that part of your profit which is greater than the rate of inflation over that period. For example, if the value of your investment went up 8 per cent on average each year and inflation during that time was 5 per cent, only the 3 per cent gain over and above inflation is taxable; the remaining 5 per cent growth is tax-free. Also, a special formula is used to ensure that this gain doesn't, by itself, push you into a higher tax bracket. With cash and fixed-interest investments, on the other hand, the total return is usually taxed.

As any assets aquired before September 1985 are exempt from capital-gains tax, it's advisable to think carefully about cashing them in as any future increase in their value is yours tax-free.

You're Part of the Equation, Too

'I THINK I COULD BE A GOOD WOMAN IF I

HAD FIVE THOUSAND A YEAR.'

— BECKY SHARP IN *VANITY FAIR*

So how do you decide which is the right investment for you? Your choices will, to some extent at least, be influenced by personal factors such as your age and stage of life, and your attitude to risk.

What's Your Time-frame?

All of us have a number of personal and financial goals, which may be short-term or span many years. Throughout your life your needs and wants, and hence your goals, will change. This will, in turn, affect your choice of investments: generally speaking, the more time you have, the more comfortable you can be with investments that offer greater growth and therefore carry a higher level of risk. If you have a short time frame and can't afford to risk your initial capital, your investment options will be more limited.

So if you're young – in your twenties, thirties or even forties – and have a long-term investment plan, you can afford to ride out the ups and downs

---

FIVE QUICK QUESTIONS YOU NEED TO ASK

- How quickly might I need to access this money?
- Will I be able to sell this investment easily?
- Do I need income or growth, or a combination of both?
- What tax do I pay and how might this investment affect it?
- Will this investment affect any social-security payments to which I'm entitled?

The aim of investing is financial security rather than sleepless nights

to which many investments (like shares) are prone. If you don't need money from an investment for a long time (ten years, say), you can afford to take some risks.

At the other end of the spectrum, if you're older, you may not have this luxury: you may be retiring in two years and want access to your money then. If so, you may wish to reassess your portfolio (by, say, having fewer shares) to give you more steady income and to reduce the risk of your investments going down in value in the short term.

WHAT'S YOUR ATTITUDE TO RISK?

'IF YOU DON'T RISK ANYTHING,

YOU RISK EVEN MORE.'

— ERICA JONG

Everybody would prefer to own investments that have a good chance of going up in value and only a small chance of going down, but the reality is that every investment carries some risk. While, as we've said above, your age and stage of life will determine how much risk you can bear, your personality will also play a part.

The fact is that some people just aren't comfortable with shares, because of the risk of losing money; others are constantly attracted by speculative investments. In this regard, there's no easy formula. While certainly the aim of investing is financial security rather than sleepless nights, being worried about the amount of risk associated with a particular investment doesn't mean that you should avoid it altogether. At the same time, highly speculative investments where you could lose all your money are not the basis for a sound investment strategy. The question really is: are the investments you're most attracted to going to get you where you want to be financially?

WHAT'S YOUR RISK PROFILE?

Choose the level of risk that is appropriate for you by thinking along these lines:

- **What is my stage in life?** If you're young, you can afford to take greater risks with a view to higher returns in the long term. If you're older, security becomes more important, although you shouldn't totally forego capital growth for the sake of perceieved security.
- **Is my goal short-term, medium-term or long-term?** Again, you can afford riskier investments if your goal is longer-term. If you need that money to buy a car in two years, don't take risks with it.
- **What kind of 'money personality' do I have?** (If you're not sure, try the quiz in Chapter 1.) Some people are risk-takers and some aren't, so don't try to be what you are not – rather, understand your attitude to money and risk, and what you expect to earn from your investments.
- **How willing am I to accept short-term ups and downs in the value of my investments?** If watching shares go up and down makes you tense, perhaps you could limit your share investments until you feel more comfortable.
- **Am I prepared to accept higher risk for greater return?** No risk equals little return, so try to find a level you are comfortable with.

GETTING FINANCIAL ADVICE

To be a successful investor, then, you have to take into account your personal and financial situation, as well as doing some crystal-ball gazing. Knowing your goals is one thing, but finding the best investments to help you reach them can be difficult without some guidance. This is why, at some point, most people find themselves seeking the help of experts. So how do you get good advice?

Although many of us have occasion from an early age to visit an accountant or a lawyer, many people wait until they approach retirement and need advice about their superannuation to seek out a financial adviser. Yet enlisting the services of a professional adviser is just as valid as consulting a doctor, dentist, or any other specialist – after all, who has the time to keep up to date with changes in the superannuation system, to read every new prospectus, or to understand the tax aspects of every investment?

If you want financial advice, you can visit a bank, a stockbroker, an accountant, a financial planner or an insurance agent. When it comes to investment, though, you should start by consulting a financial adviser. Not only can a good adviser tailor an investment plan to suit your particular circumstances, but he or she is likely to know more than you about the opportunities available and can also keep you on the right track.

As with any profession, the quality of advice available from investment experts does vary. So just as you do your homework before selecting a doctor, dentist or tax agent, you should ask around before deciding on a financial adviser.

'AN EXPERT IS SOMEONE WHO KNOWS

SOME OF THE WORST MISTAKES THAT CAN

BE MADE IN HIS FIELD AND WHO

MANAGES TO AVOID THEM.'

— WERNER HEISENBERG

Where to Look (and What to Look for)

The first and best place to start is word of mouth, so ask friends and colleagues for recommendations. The Financial Planning Association can also provide a list of financial advisers in your area, along with a booklet called *Don't Kiss Your Money Goodbye* (issued with the Australian Securities Commission) which contains some sound advice on choosing an adviser.

Before discussing your own financial situation, you should be confident about the adviser's expertise. Don't be shy about asking questions – a good adviser will be frank and professional. And do choose a person you are comfortable with, as this is likely to be a long-term relationship.

Here are the kinds of questions you should ask:

▲ **Are you licensed to provide investment advice?** They should have a licence issued by the Australian Securities Commission, or authority to act for a licensee.

▲ **How much will your services cost?** What do they charge for an initial consultation? Are they paid by fee or by commission, and what is the total cost including any ongoing commissions? Can you pay for differing levels of service?

▲ **Are you affiliated with any financial institution?** In other words, are they able to provide independent advice?

▲ **What experience do you have in the industry?** Some advisers have a particular area of expertise, such as tax advice or managed funds.

▲ **What educational and professional qualifications do you have?**

▲ **What research do you have access to?**

▲ **What sort of ongoing service can I expect?** How often will you see them once your investment plan is in place?

▲ **Do you have professional indemnity insurance?**

▲ **If I have a problem outside your area of expertise, can you refer me to other professionals?**

YOUR INVESTMENT PLAN

The next step is to provide as much information as possible about your financial situation. This will make it easier for them to put together a personalised investment plan which gives a snapshot of your position now and attempts to predict your future needs.

If you did the budgeting exercise in Chapter 1, this is where it will come in handy. Take details of your assets and liabilities along on your first consultation, together with a wish list of your goals (financial and otherwise) from Chapter 2.

How Much Will It Cost?

While the first consultation with a financial adviser is usually free, a fee (typically $150–$500) may be charged for the preparation of an investment plan. This fee should be agreed before the plan is drawn up.

Financial advisers have traditionally been paid by way of commission or a fee, or a combination of the two. Bear in mind that the quality of the advice should be your main concern – and good advice does cost money. You should, though, establish up-front how much you will have to pay, and whether a commission is involved.

Commissions have in the past been the source of much misunderstanding – one of the reasons why the industry has suffered image problems. A number of planners are now moving towards fee-based services: they give a full rebate of any commission associated with the product they are selling, to indicate that their recommendations are not biased. This approach also brings them in line with other professionals such as solicitors and accountants. The fee may be a percentage of the amount invested, or an hourly rate, and there may also be ongoing service fees. If you have a relatively small amount to invest, paying an entry fee which includes a commission to your adviser can be far cheaper than paying on an hourly basis.

Many financial advisers are still compensated solely by commissions. The Australian Securities Commission and the Insurance and Superannuation Commission have strict rules to ensure that any commissions are disclosed in full.

It's Your Money!

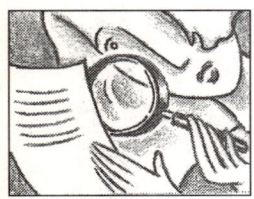

'WHERE LARGE SUMS OF MONEY ARE

CONCERNED IT'S ADVISABLE TO TRUST NO ONE.'

— AGATHA CHRISTIE

No matter how good the adviser or the advice, don't remain passive. Remain involved by checking the statements you receive, requesting reviews of your portfolio, and asking lots of questions. Never agree to

YOUR INVESTMENT PLAN

Your investment plan should include the following elements:

- A summary of your current financial position, including your income and expenses, assets and liabilities.
- Your current tax position. Bring along your last two tax assessments so that your adviser can assess the level of tax you pay and whether any tax-effective investments may be suitable.
- A list of your financial goals for the short, medium and long terms.
- Details of any relevant personal circumstances (such as divorce, or illness in the family). These may need to be taken into account before any recommendations are made.
- A summary of your attitude to investment risk. How important is it to you that your money is secure?
- A list of recommendations which reflects your financial goals and indicates the appropriateness or otherwise of your current investments.
- Details of the documentation needed to put the plan into effect. It is important that you read any prospectuses or other documentation carefully before signing.
- An analysis of your superannuation and insurance requirements.
- A reference to estate planning. Do you have a will, and if so does it need to be reviewed? Should you consider setting up a family trust, now or in the future? These matters may be outside your adviser's domain, so you may be referred to a solicitor or accountant.
- The assumptions used for projecting investment returns. The anticipated returns will also indicate the level of risk in the portfolio.
- An estimate of your cash flow, taking into account your future income and expenses.
- A clear outline of all costs. Licensed investment advisers must set out all commissions and fees.

invest in something you don't understand. Always make any cheques payable to the trustee of the fund in which you are investing.

If understanding all this entails some extra research on your part, remember that you will be educating yourself about investment markets at the same time. The more knowledge you gain, the more confidence you will have when it comes to making future investment decisions.

Finding Your Way Through the Investment Maze

Now it's time to look in more detail at each of the investment areas – cash, fixed-interest investments, property and shares – in terms of what they have to offer and how you go about acquiring them. And as more and more Australians have money in managed funds (including super funds), we also look at how these work.

Investing in Cash

Cash is the least risky investment and offers the most predictable rates of return. Cash investments are suitable for both short-term and long-term goals, although over the longer term cash tends to be a poor performer relative to other investments.

People usually invest in cash for reasons of security and ease of access rather than for the anticipated returns. Having said this, some cash in an investment portfolio acts as a buffer against fluctuations in your other investments. But as cash investments are vulnerable to inflation and you pay tax at your marginal rate on any earnings, you should look to other investments if you are after long-term capital growth.

HOW TO INVEST

'Investing' cash doesn't just mean parking it in an everyday bank account. Once you have saved around $5000, you may be able to get a higher return by putting it in a cash-management account or trust, which usually means your money will be invested on the short-term money market.

To open a **cash-management account**, you simply apply to a bank. These accounts are hit with the same fees and charges that afflict all bank accounts (see Chapter 2 for a discussion of these). If you don't make any transactions, you won't be liable for any government charges (except when you make the deposit and eventually withdraw your balance), but as most facilities allow deposits and withdrawals, the bank fees can make a difference to your overall return.

To invest in a **cash-management trust**, you get a prospectus from the financial institution offering it, or from your financial adviser. You don't usually pay any entry or exit fees with this type of investment, but there is an annual management fee of 1–1.5 per cent of your balance (which is deducted from your interest). You can assess how safe your money will be by asking what the company's Standard and Poor security rating is (AAAm is the highest). As for interest rates, these will fluctuate and are usually

---

CASH INVESTMENTS: KEY POINTS

- A good investment if you don't want to risk your capital.
- Low risk, but generally lower returns than the other investment categories.
- Easy access – you can usually retrieve your money within 24 hours.
- More suitable for your short-term goals.
- Little, if any, potential for capital gains, so your returns can be eroded by tax and inflation.
- No tax benefits – all income is fully taxed at your marginal tax rate.

published daily in financial and metropolitan newspapers, or you can ring the institution whose product you are considering. Some institutions have a user-pays system when it comes to government fees and charge them on your individual transactions, whereas others charge these fees across the total fund. If you are not planning to use such an account for regular transactions, why pay for someone else who does? Instead, assuming the interest rate stacks up, go for the user-pays system.

FIXED-INTEREST INVESTMENTS

'IT IS REMARKABLE...WHAT A CHANGE OF TEMPER A FIXED INCOME WILL BRING ABOUT.'

— VIRGINIA WOOLF

For every person who's got some spare money, there's someone who'd like to borrow it. If you have a fixed-interest investment, you are agreeing to lend money to the institution issuing it. In return they agree to pay you a fixed rate of interest at regular intervals (known as a coupon payment) and to repay your money on a fixed date (referred to as the maturity date). So you are likely to choose fixed-interest investments if you want a regular income and you want to know exactly how much it will be. They can be useful because you can choose how long you invest for and thus tailor them to your own time-frame. As a rule, the more money you invest and the longer you invest it for, the higher the rate of interest you get.

Term deposits are one of the most common fixed-interest investments: here you lock into a fixed interest rate for an agreed period which is often between six months and a few years. As the direction of interest rates is

FIXED INTEREST: THE RISK HIERARCHY

When you lend money, always consider the borrower's ability to repay you.

- **Government and semi-government bonds** sit at the top of the security tree in this regard and provide the highest guarantee of repayment (and because there is less risk, they usually offer the lowest interest rates).
- **Debentures** are most commonly offered by finance companies, which are often bank subsidiaries (such as Esanda and AGC). How secure they are is a direct reflection of the financial health of the company: you can check whether any debenture you are interested in has been rated by the rating agency Standard and Poor (an AAA rating is the best)
- **Unsecured notes** are also a fixed-term loan to a company, but unlike debentures your 'loan' is not secured against the company's assets. This interest rate is usually higher, to compensate for the greater risk.
- **Convertible notes** differ from other fixed-interest securities in that you can choose to (or, in some cases, must) convert your investment into shares or hold on to it until the maturity date and continue receiving interest payments. Their risk level is about the same as unsecured notes.

uncertain over the long term, most people usually only lock into a fixed rate for up to three years, and quite often stagger the maturity dates. Some institutions offer term deposits which allow you to make limited withdrawals over the term, but this will usually be reflected in a lower interest rate.

You can also invest in **fixed-interest securities** such as company debentures or government bonds. The investment period is usually longer than for a term deposit (in the case of government bonds, up to ten years). The main difference between a term deposit and a fixed-interest security is that you can sell a security (at the market price, which means you can make a

WHEN THE TIMING'S NOT RIGHT

Helen had saved $1000 and decided to invest in a three-year company debenture offering 8 per cent interest. Six months later, though, she had the opportunity to work overseas for two years. With the costs involved in moving, she now needed the money: having purchased a debenture, she knew it was tradeable.

In the six months since she had bought the debenture, interest rates had risen to 10 per cent. So in order to sell she had to accept a lower amount than she had invested initially, to compensate for the lower rate her debenture was paying. If, on the other hand, interest rates had *fallen* 2 per cent, she would have made a profit when she sold.

profit or a loss) before the end of the agreed term. If you buy a fixed-interest security and hold onto it until maturity, your initial capital will be repaid in full at the end of the term, in the same way as a term deposit.

HOW TO INVEST

To invest in a fixed-term deposit, you simply apply at your bank. Debentures and convertible notes can be bought direct from the issuing company (look for their advertisements in newspapers, or ask your financial adviser) or through a stockbroker. You can also invest in fixed-interest securities through a managed fund, of which there are basically two types – those which guarantee to repay your initial outlay ('capital guaranteed'), and those where the value of your initial outlay will go up or down reflecting the movements in interest rates ('market-linked'). To invest through a managed fund, contact the fund manager or your financial adviser to obtain a prospectus.

GETTING THE BEST OUT OF YOUR INVESTMENT

Fixed-interest securities generally do best when interest rates and inflation are falling. By locking into the higher interest rate, you will benefit from the additional income, and you can make a capital gain if you sell before the maturity date. The importance of timing when trading fixed-interest securities was made clear in 1994 when the interest rate on a ten-year Commonwealth bond rose from 6.5 per cent to 10.5 per cent. As a result, the value of that bond over its ten-year term fell dramatically – in fact by over 25 per cent. This was widely reported in the media as a 'collapse' of the bond market, and gave a shock to investors, who considered they had a relatively safe investment. As a result, many people panicked and sold, thus missing out in 1995 when investors virtually recovered their losses. The chief lesson to be learnt from this story is that, while fixed-interest investments have traditionally been considered 'safe', they can make a loss under certain market conditions.

The other factor you should consider is when and how the interest is paid. You can choose either to have it paid to you regularly as income, or

FIXED-INTEREST INVESTMENTS: KEY POINTS

- They are a good source of regular income.
- As a general rule, the more money you invest and the longer you invest it, the higher the rate of interest you'll receive.
- Most fixed-interest investments are suitable for both short-term and long-term goals.
- They generally perform best when inflation and interest rates are falling.
- Unlike cash, you can expect some capital gain from fixed-interest securities if you manage to sell at the right time. However, they are not as good as shares and property for long-term growth.
- Compared to cash, it is more difficult to get access to your money with fixed-interest investments.
- There are no tax benefits, except with insurance and friendly-society bonds.
- Fixed-interest investments help reduce risk in your overall port-folio, because they can provide a predictable return.
- You can invest with as little as $1000.

to have it reinvested and therefore start the interest compounding. A word of warning here, though: some institutions quote interest rates which are added only at the end of the term, in which case you won't get the benefit of compounding interest.

Fixed-interest investments are not a good choice if you are looking for tax relief. Any earnings are taxable in full, and typically you also pay tax on any capital gains you make through trading. If you are on a high tax rate, friendly-society or insurance bonds can be a tax-effective alternative: though dubbed 'bonds', these investments are really managed funds, and are dealt with on page 130.

INVESTING IN PROPERTY

Australia's love affair with property has been fuelled by a couple of decades of high inflation, which saw significant price rises in residential properties. This, combined with tax advantages when you borrow to buy, made such properties a good investment choice. In times of low inflation, it is your choice of property that dictates how good an investment it will be.

When you think about buying your own home there are lots of variables to be considered, not least how much you love the place. Happily, this is one less consideration when buying property as an investment – remember, you don't have to live there. The only things to think about are how rentable it is (and for how much) and whether it's likely to appreciate in value. While some of these questions will be answered by applying the same kinds of tests you'd use when buying a home (see page 161), others require a different way of thinking.

Historically, residential property has offered good returns over the longer term. Annual rental returns on an investment property, after maintenance costs and various fees are taken into account, may only average about 4–5 per cent of the value of the property, so it has been the prospect of making a profit when they sell which has excited most potential investors. But this may change: the current low-inflation environment means that property prices will no longer necessarily gallop ahead, yet the real cost of your borrowings may stay relatively high. It's not all gloom, though, as a period of lower inflation will provide more stable housing prices because building costs should be contained.

So is property still a good investment? The answer is 'Yes', provided that you have the time and talent to find a good buy, and that you understand the special cycles through which real estate moves. Even if you do buy when prices are low, these cycles can mean that it's a number of years before you benefit from prices going up. So if you are thinking of investing in property, you need to think long-term.

DOING THE SUMS

With an investment property you have to think beyond the initial price – which includes the same extras (fees and more fees) that apply if you buy a home. (For a rundown of these, see the section 'Buying a Home' in Chapter 4.) Your sums should also take into account your ongoing expenses and the rent you are likely to receive. If you cannot meet the expenses and, worse still, are forced to sell in a market downturn, you will wave goodbye to capital growth – and this is what property investment has traditionally been about.

But the Figures Don't Add Up!

When you do the sums, it's quite likely you'll find that the expenses do indeed exceed your anticipated rental income. Now do your sums again, but this time take into account the possibility of the property being vacant for four or even ten weeks of the year. Then consider the shortfall between the rental income and your expenses, the tax benefits and the expected increased value of the property. This should determine whether or not you should buy the property – the key element being whether you have enough income from other sources to make up the income shortfall week to week.

If you don't have the money to buy an investment property, or the time to look for and maintain one, you could invest in a property trust (this is a form of managed fund: for more details see page 128).

Now for the Good News – the Tax Deductions

There are several tax deductions available on investment properties. It's definitely worth discussing the tax aspects with an accountant to make sure you claim all you're entitled to.

If you borrow money to buy the property, the interest on your loan will probably be your largest expense. This can be claimed as a tax deduction in the year it was paid, provided you do not prepay the interest for more than thirteen months in advance. (You can only deduct interest, not any repayments of the initial sum you borrowed.)

If the property is new (built after 1985) you can deduct from your assessable income an allowance for the costs of building it. The present rate is 2.5 – 4 per cent of the construction cost, depending on when it was built. In addition, if you rent out a property furnished, you can claim depreciation on any large household goods until you write off the purchase price. Claiming deductions for repairs can be tricky. According to the rules, 'repairing' means restoring something rather than improving it. The cost of improvements can, however, be taken into account when calculating any capital-gains tax payable.

Expenses such as the agent's fees, rates, cleaning costs, insurance, and government and bank charges on your account when your rents are paid by cheque, are all tax-deductible.

Q *I earn $50 000 a year and have paid a substantial amount off my own home. A friend has suggested that I invest in a property and negative-gear. Can you please explain how this works?*

A The expenses you incur when earning an income can generally be claimed as a tax deduction. In addition, when the interest you're paying on a loan to buy an investment property, and any other regular expenses associated with the property, exceed the income you're earning from it, you can claim the shortfall as a deduction against your salary or other forms of income: this is referred to as negative gearing.

Many people see negative gearing as a way to reduce their tax, but it's only of value if you make a capital gain: if the property does not increase in value, you can lose money. And remember that the higher your personal tax rate, the more valuable the tax deductions.

CHOOSING AN INVESTMENT PROPERTY

While position and eye appeal are always important, the criteria for choosing an investment property aren't quite the same as for a home.

- **Do your homework.** The economic environment – the level of inflation and economic growth, and the employment rate – all have a direct impact on demand for (and ultimately the value of) the property.
- **Investigate the prices of comparable properties,** to make sure you are not paying too much.
- **Don't buy the best you can afford.** Mansions can be as hard to rent out as fibro shacks beside a railway line. Experts say that the best bet is a middle-priced property.
- **Small is beautiful.** Today, small households are the norm.
- **No frills please.** That gorgeous garden, pool and white carpet cost money and time to maintain, so leave them to the home-buyers. In other words, beware of over-capitalising: most real-estate agents recommend that if you renovate you do so selectively – replacing a small and dingy kitchen with an inexpensive but functional one can improve the rentability of a property, as can a simple coat of paint.
- **Don't buy in the area where your home is.** Doing so means you're putting all your eggs in one basket, and if prices fall you are hit twice.
- **Read the rules for strata or company titles.** If you buy a unit, consider how much freedom you have to rent out or make structural changes to the property.

Do You Need a Managing Agent?

Employing an agent to look after the property can be money well spent, although the agent's fees will reduce your rental income by 5–7.5 per cent and you have to pay a leasing fee, generally of one week's rent. The fee is often negotiable, though.

Ask friends and associates for their recommendations. Compare fees, but don't be swayed entirely by cost: the cheapest agent may not be the best. Before signing any agency agreement, understand what it means and what you are getting for your money. A good agent will thoroughly screen prospective tenants, make sure you are receiving the market value rent, inspect the property regularly, and take responsibility for evicting tenants if necessary. Agents will also be commercial (and more detached than you) in their treatment of tenants. It's hard for you not to be swayed to reduce rent because of a hard-luck story.

INVESTMENT PROPERTY: KEY POINTS

- In times of high inflation, property has provided the best returns.
- There is less likelihood of substantial increases in property prices in periods of low inflation when demand is low.
- Property is more suited to long-term goals: if you choose selectively, it can still provide good returns over the long haul.
- Property can be a source of income, through rents, but as steady rents depend on stable tenancies the returns are not as secure as the income from fixed-interest investments.
- It can be harder to access your money quickly if it is invested in property (except in the case of a listed property trust).
- Unlike cash and fixed interest, property does have some tax benefits.
- If you own a home, investing in commercial, retail or industrial properties gives you diversity.

INVESTING IN SHARES

The number of share investors nearly doubled between 1991 and 1994. And with good reason: over the long term, shares usually provide higher returns than any other investment sector, so they are essential to a balanced portfolio. Although shares can provide income in the form of company dividends, they are primarily a good investment choice if you are looking for some capital growth; they usually perform best in periods of low to medium inflation. Shares in larger companies are usually quite easy to sell, which means that you can access your money, and they also have some tax benefits.

Yet many people see shares as the most risky of all investment areas (at least as a short-term venture), and not without cause: few people have forgotten the crash of October 1987, and nor should they. But there are ways in which you can reduce the risk: we look at these on page 115.

As with any investment, there are many things to consider before you buy shares. Your main questions will probably be along the following lines: Where and how do I buy shares? How will I know which ones to buy? How safe will my money be? While the answers are by no means straightforward, understanding shares is really no more difficult than understanding any other investment, and there are a number of professionals who can help you along the way.

How the Share Market Works

The share market is simply that – an exchange where you can buy and sell 'shares' or 'stock' of publicly listed companies and listed trusts. It is a medium for companies who need extra capital (usually to allow them to expand) and for people who are willing to provide this money.

The Australian share market is made up of more than 1700 companies. Together, about 70 per cent of these comprise the 'industrial' sector and include building companies, banks, transport companies, media companies and insurance companies. The remaining 30 per cent make up the 'resources' sector, which includes minerals and mining companies such as Western Mining Corporation and Santos Ltd.

The actual process of raising capital by offering shares for sale (called a 'float'), is known as the primary market; the trading of shares on the stock exchange is known as the secondary market. To become a public or listed company, a business must satisfy stringent criteria set by the Australian Stock Exchange (ASX) and the government corporate watchdog – the Australian Securities Commission (ASC).

The daily movements of the markets are recorded and translated into the All Ordinaries Index (familiarly known as the All Ords), which reflects the performance of a group of over 300 Australian shares, weighted by size, which together account for around 95 per cent of the total value of the Australian market.

Learning the Ropes

Before investing in shares, try to get some understanding of how the market works. You might start by attending one of the free lunch-time seminars run by the Australian Stock Exchange , which currently operate in every capital city except Canberra and Darwin. The ASX also runs courses and other educational programs for new investors, and their bookshop and research library are open to the public. They also provide an introductory information pack (phone the Stock Exchange in your state to ask for this).

Reading the financial news, including the share-market page, is another good way of keeping informed about company trends and the investment environment generally. It has to be said that anyone opening up a newspaper at the shares page for the first time could be forgiven for closing it again straight away. The rows of columns and the cryptic headings can be totally daunting, and the jargon even more so – but once you know how to read this page, you'll be able to get at a glance much of the information you need.

ARE SHARES RIGHT FOR YOU?

Share prices can fluctuate considerably in the short term, but they do tend to reflect the long-term profitability of the business in which the shares are

WHEN THE CHIPS ARE DOWN

You've undoubtedly heard people say 'Go for blue-chip shares, they're the safest bet'. So what is a blue-chip share and why do they have such a good reputation?

In a casino the highest-value gambling chips are blue, and in the world of investment the term has traditionally meant shares of the highest market value – as opposed to speculative stocks, which normally have a low market value. Being blue-chip reflects the company's size ('the bigger the company, the bluer it gets') and the fact that it has a long and handsome track record (speculative stocks tend to be relatively new companies with no track record), which means their share price is likely to be less volatile and their dividends steady.

To qualify as blue-chip, the company should be listed in the 50 Leaders index compiled by the Australian Stock Exchange, and preferably be ranked in the top 20. Classic blue-chip companies include BHP, a few top industrial stocks like Amcor and CRA, and the big banks.

Today, however, the notion of blue-chip stocks is considered by the experts to be too subjective and the description is no longer an iron-clad guarantee of a company's performance. Even large companies can be beset by financial difficulties or other problems, and their share prices inevitably suffer as a result. It is also a fact that all industries go through cycles which can affect any company, whatever its size. So don't just put your 'blue-chip' shares in the bottom drawer and never give them another thought: keep an eye on the market and research these shares as carefully as you would any other share.

held. While some people have certainly lost money on the stockmarket, it also presents many opportunities to gain higher investment returns over the long haul.

If you are young and looking for investments suitable for long-term goals, like saving for your child's education or for your retirement, shares are a good choice because time is likely to be on your side and you can afford to take some risks. If, however, you are saving for an upcoming expense like a university course in a year or two, shares could be too risky.

Another advantage of investing in shares is their favourable tax treatment. First, you only pay tax at your personal tax rate on any capital gain over and above the inflation rate. Secondly, any income you earn from Australian shares may be tax-free, depending both on how tax has been paid on the dividend you receive and on your personal tax rate – this benefit is called 'dividend imputation' and we discuss it in more detail later.

The effect of this favourable tax treatment is shown in the chart on page 119: you can see how the after-tax returns on shares are much better than those for property, cash and fixed-interest investments.

MY STOCKBROKER SAYS...

While financial advisers can give advice and work with a stockbroker to buy shares for you, only stockbrokers are allowed to do the actual buying and selling. They must be members of the Australian Stock Exchange and are strictly regulated.

Word of mouth is the best way to find a good stockbroker, so ask your friends and colleagues for recommendations. The Stock Exchange in your nearest capital city can also provide a list of recommended brokers. You can select either a full-service stockbroker or a discount broker. If you are a first-time investor, it's sensible to use a full-service broker, because he or she can give you advice. (In fact, even if you are a seasoned investor, you may benefit from the research that full-service brokers provide.) If you are more experienced, just want to buy one company's stock or don't need advice, a discount broker may be enough for you: all they do is place your order, usually for a lower fee than full-service brokers charge.

Understandably, if you place your money with a stockbroker you'll want

---

INTERVIEW WITH A BROKER

- What services do you provide, and how much will each cost?
- What is the size of your research team? How many (and what type) of shares do you research?
- What confirmation of my transactions will you give me?
- Do you require a minimum order or have a minimum charge?
- Will you phone me if you think I should sell any of my shares?

---

to know what protection you have. In the unlikely event that your stock-broker runs off with your money, there is a National Guarantee Fund which you may be entitled to access by applying to the Australian Stock Exchange.

THE RISK FACTOR

Of course, when you buy shares in a company you share the risks as well as the rewards. Many factors affect the profits (and ultimately the value) of a business, including inflation, interest rates, the demand for the company's product, the level of competition, and the prices the company receives for its products. A change in any of these conditions is almost instantly reflected in the share price, and even expectations about future events can tip the scales up or down. This 'volatility' is one of the main reasons why so many people see shares as risky.

Diversifying your portfolio is one of the best ways to reduce the possi-bility of losing money, no matter what the investment. With shares this is especially true, because there will always be a number of factors beyond your control which can negatively affect share prices. (If, for example, you've invested in a bakery which experiences a food-poisoning scare, the share price is likely to plummet.) You can diversify by buying shares in different but complementary industries.

Another way to reduce risk is to select 'good' shares. While there is no foolproof formula for choosing winners, there are a number of indicators

How to Read the Share-market Page

Industrial Market

52 week high	52 week low	day's high	day's low	ASX code	company name and par value	last sale	+ or –	vol 100s	quote buy	quote sell	DIVIDENDS, ASSETS, EARNINGS dividend c per share	times cov	net asset back	div yield %	earn share c	P/E ratio
2.70	2.20	–	–	APE	AP Eagers 50c	2.44	–	–	2.44	2.64	10.00f	–	4.45	4.10	–	–
.24	.091/2	.11	.11	ACQ	A.C.Equi 20c	.11	–	25	.11	.14	–	–	.35	–	5.50	2.0
3.194	2.52	2.67	2.63	AGL	A.G.L. $1	2.63	–4	6611	2.62	2.63	14.00f	1.67	2.37	5.32	23.40	11.2
.18	.03	–	–	AJF	AJP.Grth 40c	.041/2	–	–.041/2	.08	–	–	–	–	–	–	–
.75	.26	.34	.34	AJFIN	AJP.Inc 93c	.34	–1	49	.34	.36	8.42	1.00	.93	24.76	8.42	4.0
1.55	1.19	1.35	1.35	APN	AProvnews 40c	1.35	–2	80	1.34	1.35	2.00f	–	–	1.48	–	–
5.20	4.52	5.09	5.05	ACS	AConPress 50c	5.05	–4	844	5.05	5.08	8.60f	1.34	5.03	1.70	11.50	43.9
.96	.44	.62	.62	ADD	AIDC 50c	.62	–	71	.57	.62	–	–	.83	–	–	–

| 1 | 2 | 3 | 4 | 5 | 6 | 7 | 8 | 9 | 10 | 11 | 12 | 13 | 14 |

1   52 WEEK HIGH/LOW: the highest and lowest price for the share over the year.

2   DAY'S HIGH/LOW: the highest and lowest price for the share on the previous day.

3   AUSTRALIAN STOCK EXCHANGE (ASX) CODE: the code the Australian Stock Exchange assigns to a particular share. It is used on the board where the latest details about shares' trading price are given.

4   PAR VALUE: the price at which the share was issued, which is often quite different from the share's market price.

5   LAST SALE: the price at which the share was last traded.

6   + OR -: the difference between the price of the last sale for the day and the last sale for the previous day.

7   VOL 100s: the total number of shares sold on the previous day.

8   QUOTES: the *buy quote* indicates how much someone is prepared to pay for a particular share. The *sell quote* indicates the price a seller is prepared to accept for a particular share.

9   DIVIDEND PER SHARE: the amount of company profit (in cents) paid per share. There are yearly (final) dividends, and half-yearly (interim) dividends. An 'f' following the number indicates that the dividend is franked (i.e. paid out of taxed company profits).

10 TIMES COVERED: the number of times the company's profit covers the dividend. The figure is calculated by dividing the earnings per share by the dividend per share, and indicates how much of the profit is being paid in dividends.

11 NET ASSET BACKING: the net value of the assets owned by the shareholders.

12 DIVIDEND YIELD: the dividend yield is like a current interest rate for the share. It is expressed as a percentage, and is calculated by dividing the dividend per share by the last sale price.

13 EARNINGS PER SHARE: one of a number of gauges of a company's performance. It is calculated by dividing the company's profit by the number of shares on issue, to give the profit earned per share.

14 PRICE/EARNINGS (P/E RATIO): this is generally considered a good yardstick for measuring the value of a company's shares. It shows the relationship between the market price of a company's shares and the earnings per share.

PICKING SHARES: THINGS TO LOOK FOR

- What assets does the company own? What debts does it have ?
- Does the company have a good track record of solid growth in sales and earnings, at least over the last few years? And what are its future earning prospects? Find out the company's share of its market: can it be increased?
- Is the company expanding? What funds are there for research and development?
- What is the quality of the company's management? Good managers will not try to cover up any negative aspects of the company, but instead will provide reasons for these and suggest how things will be improved.
- Who are the largest shareholders? If they include successful companies which have kept their shares for several years, their holding is obviously a 'seal of approval'.

---

which can help you decide whether a company's prospects are good, and whether the current price of the share represents fair value: the main pointers are 'price–earnings (P/E) ratios' and dividend yields. They can be tricky, however, and shouldn't be taken at face value without further research to establish their true significance. Company annual reports can usually throw some light on the figures.

HOW TO INVEST

There are four ways of investing in shares: buying shares when a company is first floated, buying listed shares through a stockbroker, buying 'pre-packaged' shares, or buying units in a managed fund which invests in the share market.

The Commonwealth Bank, Qantas, GIO, Woolworths and David Jones all offered shares to the public in the last few years and enjoyed enormous support from small investors. When buying into a **float**, consider the share price carefully. If you have a broker or a financial adviser, ask them whether it looks like a fair deal and what they know about the company's expected profitability. Floats are usually widely advertised, and to invest you simply contact the company or a stockbroker, and fill out an application. If the float is very successful and there are more buyers than shares, you may find you cannot buy as many shares as you applied for. If you do miss out, don't leap in and buy shares in that company as soon as they are listed on the exchange, as the pent-up demand can artificially inflate the price. It is usually best to wait for the price to settle down – probably a few days later.

Small investors' increased interest in shares hasn't been lost on the financial marketers, and as a result you can now buy **pre-packaged shares**. The Commonwealth Bank, for example, offers ready-made portfolios including shares in some of the top Australian companies, like BHP and the National Australia Bank. You can select a package of shares in three companies for about $3000. The number of shares you get for your money will depend on the price of the shares at the time you invest.

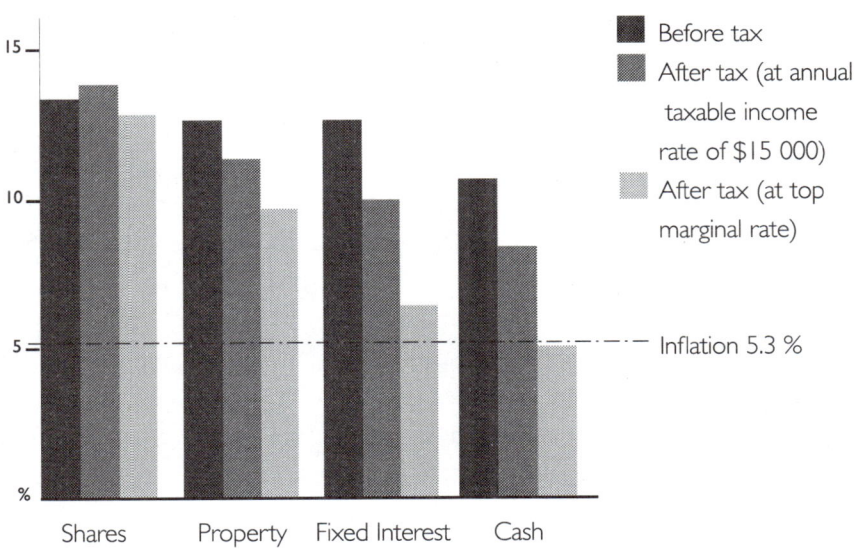

INVESTMENT RETURNS FOR 10 YEARS TO FEBRUARY 1995

Before tax

After tax (at annual taxable income rate of $15 000)

After tax (at top marginal rate)

Inflation 5.3 %

Shares   Property   Fixed Interest   Cash

Source: ASX Investments Report prepared by Towers Perrin

Before buying this sort of parcel, it is important to research the companies offered to make sure that the price is fair. Also, do your sums on the brokerage rate (the cost of buying and selling the package), particularly if you think you might want to sell each company's stock separately. Compare the rate with those charged by a few stockbrokers, as you may find it is relatively high, particularly for smaller parcels: for a $3000 parcel the brokerage rate is around 4 per cent, but for a $5000 package it is a more competitive 2.5 per cent. Finally, bear in mind that brokerage doesn't include advice, so if you need it you will have to pay for it separately.

Another simple way to buy shares is to invest in a **managed fund**. If you consider doing this, it is more important to research the fund manager and its products than it is to research the share companies (a financial adviser can help here). We offer some tips about this in the section 'Managed Funds' later in this chapter.

How Much Will I Need?

While theoretically you only need a very small amount of money to invest in shares, in practice anything less than $4000 is probably uneconomic. This is because of the way in which brokerage rates are applied when you buy or sell. If you use a full-service broker, expect to pay about 2.5 per cent for any transactions less than $10 000; the rate reduces for larger amounts and it's always worth asking if brokerage is negotiable.

While 2.5 per cent may not sound all that expensive, do bear in mind that most stockbrokers charge a minimum fee which can range from $40 to $120. So, if your stockbroker's minimum fee is $100, you would need to purchase $4000 worth of one stock to get the 2.5 per cent rate – any less than this and you would pay a higher rate, which may make the deal unprofitable. Discount brokers usually charge a flat fee, typically around $55 per trade on amounts under $6000.

The other thing to know is that a broker's minimum fee usually applies to each line of stock. If, for example, there is a minimum fee of $100 and you buy three different shares for a total of $3000, you will pay a $300 minimum fee. With both full-service and discount brokers you will also pay stamp duty of 0.15 per cent on each purchase or sale of shares.

TIPS WHEN BUYING AND SELLING SHARES

- Take the time to learn about any shares you are thinking of buying – give your investments the attention they deserve.
- Know what level of risk you are prepared to accept in a share, and don't be persuaded by anyone else.
- Have a guiding strategy when choosing shares and stick to it. You may decide to buy only blue-chip shares (a common strategy for first-time investors) or shares that provide you with regular dividends. If you take this approach, at least until you become more experienced, you are less likely to be swayed by 'hot tips'.
- Be an active rather than a passive investor, and monitor your investments. Remember that your broker may have hundreds of clients: if the market falls quickly, with the best will in the world he or she will not be able to ring and warn all of you.
- Be careful of 'hot tips', whatever the source. Ask yourself why the person is giving you the tip – if it is so hot, why wouldn't they keep it to themselves and make a lot of money?
- Don't panic if the value of one or more of your shares starts to drop. If the reasons for buying the shares still stand (for example, they still have good earning potential) don't sell. In fact, it could be the best time to consider buying some more – while the price is low. The greatest risk when investing in shares is to let your emotions run away with you, so that you buy or sell at the wrong time.
- If you have access to the Internet, you can get some of the market and company information that was previously only available to brokers and research houses – so use it.
- Whatever advice you receive, in the end it is your money. So do your homework, research carefully and first and foremost listen to your own instincts.

DIFFERENT CLASSES OF SHARES AND OPTIONS

- **Ordinary shares** are the most common form, and give you part-ownership of the company and the right to vote and to receive any profits through dividends. Ordinary shareholders bear most of the financial risk if the company is wound up, as they rank behind all other creditors.
- **Preference shares** normally have a fixed dividend level, which guarantees you a certain income. The dividends on these shares are paid before those on ordinary shares, and preference shares rank ahead of ordinary shares in the event a company is wound up. They are normally more expensive than ordinary shares and not as commonly available.
- **Contributing shares** have only partly been paid for and will require additional payments at future dates. From time to time, the company may ask such shareholders to contribute outstanding amounts until the shares are fully paid. Shareholders must pay these amounts if the company has limited liability, but if not they can choose to forfeit the shares rather than make the payment.
- **Deferred dividend shares** are those where due dividend payments can only be received after a specified period or after a certain level of dividends have been paid to ordinary shareholders.
- **Company options** allow the holder to take up new shares in the company in a specified period and at a fixed price (the 'exercise price'). There is no obligation to exercise the option, but it will lapse and be worthless if it is not exercised by the expiry date. You usually pay a low premium for options.
- **A bonus issue** is a free issue of new shares to existing shareholders, often made as a result of an improvement in the value of a company's assets and therefore to keep the share price affordable. The bonus issue is done on a ratio basis, e.g. 1:3 – one new share for every three shares already held. Therefore if the original shares were worth $10 each, after the bonus issue the value of each share would be $7.50 ($30 ÷ 4).

GOING INTERNATIONAL

Thirty years ago, few people thought of investing in international markets – indeed, for most of us it wasn't even a possibility. Today, however, as the result of both financial deregulation in 1983 and developments in computer technology, the world markets are literally at our fingertips.

So why invest overseas? Well, for a start, it's a good way to diversify your portfolio. And when you consider that Australia is a fairly small market, representing less than 2 per cent of the world market, limiting yourself to local shares is likely to mean that you miss out on some good investment opportunities. Offshore you have the chance to invest in emerging markets such as Latin America and parts of Asia, which are growing faster than Australia, or in important industries or companies which are only listed on overseas exchanges.

There are, however, a few extra risks attached to international investments. Perhaps the most important of these is that as you buy the shares in the currency of the country where the company's shares are listed, any movements in that currency will affect the Australian-dollar value of the investment. (This can, of course, also work to your advantage if the exchange rate is in your favour.) There may also be tax implications, such as tax being payable on unrealised capital gains in certain circumstances.

THE TAX BENEFITS: FRANKED DIVIDENDS AND IMPUTATION CREDITS

Income from Australian shares is very tax-effective: if a company has paid tax on its profits at the full company tax rate, any dividends received by shareholders are classed as 'franked' dividends – and if your tax rate is lower than the company rate of 36 per cent you will get the dividend tax-free. Even better, you will receive a tax credit, which can be used to offset tax payable on other income. This is a 'use it or lose it' credit, so it can't be carried forward to another financial year, nor can you take it as a cash payment.

Have a look at the table on page 124 to see how this system (known as dividend imputation) works for two investors, one on a low marginal tax rate of 20 per cent and the other on the highest rate (47 per cent). The example assumes that they both hold shares in an Australian company which makes an annual profit of $100 per share and distributes these profits after the company tax has been paid. As you can see, fully franked dividends are especially valuable if you are on a low personal tax rate, provided you can use the credit to offset tax payable on other income in the same year.

Companies may also pay 'unfranked' dividends, which means that no Australian company tax has been paid on the dividend, owing perhaps to previous losses or to the fact that the earnings originated overseas and are subject to tax in that country. In this case you can't claim a tax credit and the dividend is fully taxable at your marginal tax rate. Some shares are offered for sale 'ex-dividend', which indicates that the seller has retained any dividends declared thus far.

Some companies offer a dividend reinvestment plan, which gives you the opportunity to reinvest any dividends, by buying more shares instead of receiving a dividend cheque. If regular income is not important to you, this can be a good option. The main advantage is that you get additional shares

THE VALUE OF FULLY FRANKED DIVIDENDS

• Taxpayer personal tax rate	20%	47%
• Dividend received (after company tax paid)	$64	$64
• Add tax paid by the company	$36	$36
• Total assessable income	$100	$100
• Tax (at personal tax rate)	$20	$47
• Tax credit for company tax already paid	$36	$36
• Tax payable/Tax credit	$16 credit	$11 to pay
• After-tax value of fully franked dividend	$80	$53

Source: BT Funds Management Ltd

at a discount, so you get more for your money. Also, it is done automatically and no commissions are paid. You will still, though, pay tax on the dividend (as you would if you received it as income) and the extra shares will be a new investment as far as the Tax Office's calculation of capital gains is concerned. Also, of course, consider the company's prospects before you go ahead: if they don't look all that good, why buy more shares?

SHOULD YOU BORROW TO BUY SHARES?

Most of us are prepared to borrow money to buy a car or a house, but are less likely to do so to buy shares. Yet it is worth considering if the expected returns are good, particularly if your income from other sources is high, if you are comfortable with a certain level of debt, or if you can use your investment portfolio, rather than your home, as security for the loan.

The main advantage is in tax relief, because the interest on the loan is tax-deductible if it is for earning income. And the tax benefits are even greater if you receive franked dividends from your shares. One warning: if you

WHAT A RELIEF!

Stephanie paid tax at the highest personal rate. She had very few investments, so her accountant suggested that she borrow to buy a portfolio of Australian shares. She borrowed $50 000 at an interest rate of 10 per cent and invested a further $30 000 of her own money to buy $80 000 worth of shares. On average, they paid a franked dividend yield of 4 per cent. After five years, she sold the shares and repaid what she'd borrowed.

If the shares had increased in value by 5 per cent each year and Stephanie had only invested $30 000, at the end of five years her investment would have been worth $43 624 (after tax). Because she borrowed $50 000, at the end of the same period her profit was $22 103 (i.e. $8500 more than if she had not borrowed to invest).

If, on the other hand, her shares had fallen in value by 5 per cent each year, she would have lost $18 098 of her initial $30 000; if she hadn't borrowed, her loss would have only been $2418. So be warned: borrowing works to your advantage if you make a profit on your shares, but any loss you make will also be bigger.

do borrow to buy, a fall in the value of your shares may significantly increase your loss.

How Do You Go About It?

The two most common ways of borrowing to buy shares are by using a 'margin loan' facility (where the shares themselves are used as security for the loan), or by using your home as security. You can apply for these loans though sharebrokers, banks and fund managers.

Margin lenders usually lend money only against selected shares and only lend 50–75 per cent of the value of each. The main risk with a margin loan is that if your investments fall in value you may trigger what is known as a margin call, whereby the lender asks you to either repay some of the loan or provide additional security. If you can't do either, you will be forced to sell some of your investments, possibly at a loss. One way to reduce the chances of this happening is to borrow less than the allowed maximum or make sure you have cash in reserve.

For the same reason, think hard before mortgaging your home to purchase shares: if the value of your shares is down when you need to sell them, you may be forced to sell your home in order to repay the loan.

Another way to borrow to buy a limited range of shares, but protect yourself against a drop in their value, is to organise a 'secure equities loan'. The interest on such loans can be double the usual rate (up to 20 per cent per annum), as the lender takes on the risk of any fall in the value of the shares (which is not the case with a margin loan). Thus you get the benefit of any profits over and above the cost of the loan.

Some Special Investments

Derivatives

Derivatives are a form of investment which take ('derive') their value from commodities and securities such as gold, shares or wool. They are primarily used as a tool to manage risk, because commodity and share prices are so volatile. Essentially, through investing in derivatives an investor locks into a commodity at a fixed price and thus is protected from a future fall or rise in the market price.

Derivatives can also be traded: traders accept the risk deliberately, in the hope of making a profit. In this market, both the profits and the losses can be large. Derivatives are sometimes used, typically by portfolio and fund managers, to increase or reduce their exposure to a specified asset (such as shares) without having to buy or sell the asset itself.

There are many types of derivatives, but the two best known are options and futures. An **option contract** provides the investor with the right, but not the obligation, to buy or sell a particular commodity or security. A **futures contract** binds the investor to buy or sell a particular commodity or security at an agreed time in the future, at a fixed price.

Gold and Other Precious Metals

Gold has traditionally been regarded as an international currency – and of course, it has aesthetic value too. The problem with buying gold bars as an investment is that they don't give you an income and can be difficult to store safely. Alternatively, you can invest in gold by buying shares in a company which explores for and mines gold: particularly where companies have established mines, this can give you an income as well as allowing you to share in new finds.

SHARE INVESTMENTS: KEY POINTS

- Shares usually provide the best investment returns over the long term.
- Shares generally perform best in times of low to moderate inflation.
- Shares provide income by way of dividends, the amount of which will vary according to the company's earnings.
- Industrial shares typically pay higher dividends than resource shares, as resource-based companies often retain a higher proportion of their earnings to fund exploration.
- Shares are less accessible than cash and fixed-interest investments, but generally more so than property.
- Investing in shares can have some tax benefits, particularly in the case of Australian shares.

MANAGED FUNDS

The investments available in the marketplace are probably far more numerous than the dollars in your bank account. As we pointed out at the beginning of this chapter, you can invest directly, as when you buy a parcel of shares or a property, or you can invest indirectly, in a managed fund. With a managed fund, your money is pooled with that of hundreds or even thousands of other investors, which gives you added buying power and access to a broad range of investments which are managed and monitored by professionals.

If you have superannuation you may already be investing in a managed fund, and a financial adviser may well recommend that you invest in one, so it's a good idea to familiarise yourself with what's available. Novice investors are often a bit wary of managed funds, because their performance can fluctuate in the short term – a reflection of price movements in the underlying investments. As funds with volatile investments are more appropriate for the medium–long term, it shouldn't be of too much concern if you have an ordinary year once in a while. Of course, if a fund or investment performs poorly for several years running there may well be some cause for concern: this is why it's so important to put some time into choosing the right fund and the right investments.

HOW TO INVEST

There are many different managed funds, but the two main vehicles through which your money is likely to be invested are unit trusts and insurance bonds. Some managed funds, notably property and share trusts, are listed on the Stock Exchange and you buy and sell them through a stockbroker. Most, though, are unlisted. Cashing in your investment can be easier with listed trusts, because the stockmarket matches buyers and sellers for the 'units', without having to sell the assets themselves. The box on page 129 gives a snapshot of the main features of the most common managed funds.

THE MAIN TYPES OF MANAGED FUNDS

- UNIT TRUST: *diversified portfolios (a balanced trust), Australian or international shares (share trust), range of property (property trust), mortgages over residential or commercial properties (mortgage trust), fixed-interest (bond trust) or cash (cash trust).*

  All income (including realised capital gains) is generally distributed, and is taxed at your personal tax rate. Capital-gains-tax indexation is available, which means that any profit on the value of the investment is tax-free up to the rate of inflation (provided it has been held for at least twelve months).

- INSURANCE BONDS: *diversified portfolios, shares and fixed-interest are most common.*

  All income is retained within the fund. The earnings (including any capital gains) are taxed at a maximum rate of 39 per cent. No capital-gains-tax indexation is available. Bonuses (after fees and taxes) are declared at 30 June each year. Withdrawals made after ten years do not incur any additional tax.

- FRIENDLY-SOCIETY BONDS: *generally limited to fixed-interest securities, although some invest in a restricted number of shares.*

  All income (including any capital gains) is retained within the fund, and is taxed at a maximum rate of 33 per cent. No capital-gains-tax indexation is available. Bonuses (after fees and taxes) are declared at 30 June each year. Withdrawals made after ten years do not incur any additional tax.

- SUPERANNUATION FUNDS: *all investment sectors.*

  All income is retained within the fund, and is taxed at a maximum rate of 15 per cent. Special tax rates apply when you withdraw your money.

What Does It Cost?

Entry fees for managed funds can range from 0 to 5 per cent of your initial investment, some of which may be paid to your adviser by way of commission. Financial advisers referring clients to managed funds may instead charge a fee for their service and refund any part of the entry fee which represents a commission.

There are also management fees, which can amount to 0.5–2 per cent of the value of your account balance. If you are paying higher than average fees, you could reasonably expect above-average performance and service.

Some funds (particularly those which do not charge entry fees) may charge exit fees, which can be up to 5 per cent of the value of your investment depending on when you withdraw it.

Unit Trusts

To invest in a unit trust, you fill in an application form, which is available from the fund manager or a financial adviser. Because most trusts are public trusts (i.e. they raise money from the public), their prospectuses must follow stringent rules set by the Australian Securities Commission. Do take time to read any such prospectus before you commit any money.

When you invest in a unit trust, you are allocated a number of units according to the amount you wish to invest. Of course, the unit price can go down as well as up, because the price reflects the current market value of the investments. All unlisted trusts must have a 'repurchase' or redemption provision, which means that the fund manager has to buy back from you any units you wish to sell, subject to certain conditions, usually within a maximum of sixty days (although in practice the majority of funds would not keep you waiting this long). With a unit trust, the income is generally distributed and you pay tax on this at your marginal tax rate.

Insurance and Friendly-society Bonds

These investments come into their own if you are on a high personal tax rate, because the earnings are taxed within the fund at a rate of 33 per cent (for friendly-society bonds) or 39 per cent (for insurance bonds). If, for example, you pay the highest personal tax rate and invest in an insurance bond, you will save about 9 cents in the dollar. On the other hand, these bonds are only suitable if you don't need a regular source of income and are investing over the long term: the entry fees typically of about 3–5per cent, make an investment of one or two years uneconomical.

If you want to withdraw money from an insurance bond within ten years of making the initial investment, you must include some of the earnings in your tax return. If your personal tax rate is less than 39 per cent, you will receive a tax rebate: if it is higher, you will have to make up the difference. If you hold the bonds for ten years, you don't have to pay additional tax on the bonus earnings. If you withdraw after eight years, only a portion of your bonuses are included as assessable income, along with the respective rebate. Another plus is that each year you can increase the previous year's contribution by 125 per cent without affecting the ten-year rule, because each such 'top-up' is considered as part of the initial investment (although earnings only accrue from the actual date of the top-up).

MANAGED FUNDS: KEY POINTS

- You can begin with a relatively small amount of money: the minimum investment required is usually $1000–$5000.
- You benefit from professional expertise and research.
- You have access to investments which may not ordinarily be available to you as a direct investor. These include overseas investments and commercial properties.
- Your risk is reduced because you can choose to spread your money across a number of investment sectors, and to diversify within sectors.
- As with shares and property, over the long term a diversified managed fund should give you a better rate of return than a normal savings account.
- Some funds offer the facility for regular automatic debits from your bank account, which can be an effective way to increase your investment balance.

CHOOSING A FUND

The performance of a fund is only ever as good as the investments which the fund manager chooses. So once again, it's essential to check the track record and credentials of any organisation you are considering putting your money with. Different fund managers have different investment philosophies, so it's important you understand their objectives before you invest. Are they looking to buy undervalued shares which are expected to appreciate over a few years, offering slow and steady growth, or are they trading aggressively with greater risk? You may prefer one approach to another.

SUPERANNUATION

'A LARGE INCOME IS THE BEST RECIPE

FOR HAPPINESS I EVER HEARD OF.'

— JANE AUSTEN

Superannuation is simply another form of investment, but one in which we are all encouraged (and many of us are required) to take part so that we can support ourselves, as far as possible, when we are no longer working.

In Chapter 6 we look at the reasons why you should think as early as possible about your likely income needs when you retire. Not least of these is that it has been estimated by the government that, over a working life of forty years, you would need to put aside an average of 12 per cent of your yearly income to give yourself a retirement income equal to 40 per cent of your pre-retirement salary. The following section looks mainly at the structure of existing superannuation arrangements, and offers some practical tips on how to make the most of them.

WHY SUPER IS GIVEN SPECIAL TREATMENT

As we are constantly reminded by the press, our population is ageing and the proportion of workers to retirees is diminishing. And as the government funds the age pension from the taxes we pay, it stands to reason that there simply may not be enough money to go around in the future.

So, many of us have had to think seriously about where our retirement money will come from. As late as 1994, fewer than 5 per cent of retired women nominated superannuation or life assurance as their main source of income, and nearly 60 per cent were relying mainly on pensions and other government benefits. It is to encourage us to provide for our own retirement that the government offers special tax concessions for superannuation investments, in the hope that far fewer of us will rely totally on the age pension.

Certainly superannuation is now very much a part of any employee's life, and today 86 per cent of female employees in Australia have some superannuation cover. Often this consists mainly of the Superannuation Guarantee (a minimum percentage of your salary which employers must contribute each year to a fund if you earn over a specified amount a month): this is gradually being increased from the current 6 per cent and will reach 9 per cent by 2003. In addition, of course, you can make your own contributions – and if you are not doing this already it would be sensible to start thinking about it, as 'member' contributions (which come out of your after-tax salary) will soon be compulsory for any employees covered by an award or enterprise agreement, and will increase to 3 per cent by 2000. The good news is that the government proposes matching such contributions up to a certain limit, or providing other financial incentives which will also be extended to those outside the award/enterprise system or self-employed.

WOMEN AND SUPER

Superannuation is a crucial issue for women. On average we live longer than men, and therefore need to accumulate enough capital to support ourselves further down the track. Yet our opportunities to contribute to superannuation are often not as great as they are for men: the system is geared to those who work full-time and take no career breaks. But for anyone who works part-time or on a casual basis, is self-employed, or does not work at all – situations which affect far more women than men – it can be difficult to build up adequate super. If, for example, you are self-employed, superannuation is not compulsory, and as late as 1993 only 23 per cent of self-employed women did have superannuation cover. This figure is disturbing – after all, self-employed people have the same need for money when they retire. Even if you think that the investment you have in your business is the solution, it is worth considering superannuation for the tax savings it offers and to give you some diversity.

WHAT MAKES SUPERANNUATION DIFFERENT FROM OTHER INVESTMENTS?

Superannuation differs from other investments in the tax treatment it receives and in the restrictions on withdrawing the money (generally until you are at least 55 and retired). You can also buy life insurance as part of the package.

How Super Is Taxed

While there is no doubt that the tax concessions make superannuation a pretty attractive investment, they are of greatest benefit for high income earners. And if you earn less than the average wage, the tax on your super contributions may be only marginally lower than your personal tax rate. The government has, though, put in place some protection for people with low superannuation balances, to prevent them being eroded by fees, and if your balance is less than $1000 the fees cannot exceed your earnings.

As things stand, superannuation is taxed at three stages: when contributions are paid, on earnings of the fund, and when money is withdrawn.

Stage 1

Your employer's superannuation contributions are taxed at 15 per cent. Any after-tax contribution you make to the fund is not taxed, and you can claim a rebate of 10 per cent of your contribution up to $1000 (i.e. to a maximum of $100) if you earn less than $27 000 (the rebate continues for incomes up to $31 000, but on a reducing scale).

Stage 2

The earnings on your superannuation investment are taxed at a maximum rate of 15 per cent.

Stage 3

When you withdraw your superannuation benefits, the rate of tax you pay depends on the components that make up your payout amount. Only 5 per cent of any portion relating to service before 1 July 1983 is included as assessable income, while the tax on any portion relating to service after 30 June 1983 depends on both your age and the amount you withdraw.

Keeping It Locked Away

To encourage us to use our superannuation as retirement income, the government has made it increasingly difficult to access the money until we reach 55 and are retired. There are, however, some conditions under which your super is not preserved (i.e. locked up in this way).

▲ Your member (after-tax) contributions are generally available when you leave a job, provided your employer has also contributed to the fund.

▲ Your employer contributions can sometimes be withdrawn if your company's superannuation fund was established before December 1986 (when preservation was introduced).

▲ You can access your super if you are leaving Australia permanently.

▲ You can apply for access to some of the money if you are suffering severe financial hardship.

THE ADDED BENEFIT: LIFE INSURANCE

You can buy life insurance within most superannuation funds, which is more tax-effective than paying for it separately. While premiums for death and disability insurance cannot be claimed as tax deductions by individuals, they are deducted from pre-tax employer contributions to a super fund. If you're on the highest personal tax rate, this can halve the cost of such cover. You can, however, claim a personal deduction for premiums for temporary disablement cover, because it is an expense incurred in earning income. The pros and cons of insurance such as this are covered in Chapter 2.

What are the extra advantages of buying life insurance through your employer's super fund?

▲ You may not need to provide evidence of your level of health .

▲ The insurance premiums may be cheaper because you get a group (rather than an individual) rate.

▲ The response to claims may be better, because the insurance company will not want to risk losing your employer as a client.

The main disadvantage of insuring through an employer's fund is if you leave the company but still need insurance: if your health has deteriorated and you need to provide evidence for your new policy, you may be denied cover. So make sure your company's insurer has a 'continuation' policy which enables you to keep the same amount of cover (though the premium may increase) when you leave the company, without having to provide medical evidence. Alternatively, you could take out personal life cover which is 'guaranteed renewable' (that is, once you have provided initial medical evidence the cover continues each year). This will give you more flexibility, though it will be more expensive than the group rates offered to super fund members.

How Much Super Will You Need?

In Chapter 6 we look in detail at your likely income needs when you retire. The table on page 137 provides a quick guide to the amount you would need to contribute if you plan to rely on superannuation alone for a retirement income of $20 000 a year (in today's dollars). If you think you will need more than this – say $40 000 – first calculate the contribution level you'd need to achieve the first $20 000 (taking into account any super you already have), then calculate the contribution required for the additional $20 000 (but this time assume zero existing super); finally, add the two contribution amounts together.

As an example, if you are 35 and already have $25 000 in benefits, you will need to contribute $3900 a year to provide $20 000 a year throughout your retirement. And if you want an annual income of $40 000 you will need to contribute $3900 plus $5600, or $9500.

HOW MUCH WOULD YOU NEED TO CONTRIBUTE TO GIVE YOU $20000 A YEAR IN RETIREMENT?

CURRENT AGE	YEARS TO RETIREMENT	YOUR EXISTING SUPERANNUATION ASSETS					
		$0	$10 000	$25 000	$50 000	$100 000	$150 000
50	15	$16 000	$15 000	$13 500	$10 900	$5 700	500
45	20	$10 700	$9800	$8600	$6400	$2100	$0
40	25	$7600	$6800	$5700	$3800	$100	$0
35	30	$5600	$4500	$3900	$2200	$0	$0
30	35	$4200	$3600	$2600	$1000	$0	$0
25	40	$3200	$2 600	$1700	$200	$0	$0
20	45	$2500	$1900	$1100	$0	$0	$0

These figures apply for females only. The annual interest rate used (taking superannuation tax of 15 per cent into account) is 8.5 per cent. Inflation is assumed to be 4 per cent.

So Do You Have Enough?

The above exercise should give you an idea of whether you are accumulating enough superannuation or are likely to have a shortfall and need to contribute more. If you would like to increase your contributions, how do you do so?

Topping Up Your Super

If you can afford to direct a bit more money towards super, it is worth considering 'salary sacrifice' where you forego some take-home pay (which is normally taxed at your personal tax rate) and put it, before tax, into superannuation. As a result, it is taxed as an employer contribution (i.e. at 15 per cent).

To know whether this is right for you, consider whether you may need

WAYS AND MEANS

Kate is working part-time three days a week and she plans to go to university in six months' time. She has saved a few thousand dollars and decides to use these savings to make an after-tax contribution to her employer's fund. She does this for two reasons. First, she expects to earn more than $5400 each year while at university, so the 15 per cent tax rate on her earnings from the fund will be lower than her personal tax rate. Second, she can access her undeducted contributions at any time after she leaves her current job, whereas her employer's contributions are preserved until she retires. In addition, if her income is less than $27 000, she will be entitled to a tax rebate of $100.

to access the money before you retire, because in most cases you won't be able to do so. Also do your tax sums, because the higher your personal tax rate the more you will benefit from contributing the money to superannuation instead of taking it home. Salary sacrifice is thus a better option for people in their middle to later years; a time when (hopefully) your other financial commitments are lessening.

You can also top up your super with personal (after-tax) contributions, which are referred to as undeducted contributions. The value of this is that the maximum tax rate on earnings in the super fund is 15 per cent. And if your employer is contributing to the same fund, at present you have the added advantage of generally being able to withdraw your personal after-tax contributions if you leave your job. The tax rebate on after-tax contributions is means-tested: it starts to reduce once you earn over $27 000 and cuts out completely once your earnings reach $31 000.

There is no limit to the amount you can contribute from your after-tax income, but there is a limit (based on your age) on the pre-tax contributions which can be claimed as a tax deduction – this is known as your MDC (maximum deductible contribution). If you are self-employed or are not covered by the Superannuation Guarantee, you can contribute as much super as you like but you can only claim a tax deduction for the first $3000

MAXIMUM DEDUCTIBLE CONTRIBUTIONS (1996–97)

under 35 years of age $9782

35 – 49 years $27 120

50+..$67 383

These figures are indexed to the average wage

---

of your contributions, plus 75 per cent of any contributions over this amount, up to your MDC.

Your maximum contribution may be increased if you belong to a company with more than ten employees, as such employers can instead choose an average MDC of about $27 000, averaged across the number of employees. Speak to your employer if you want to increase your superannuation contributions significantly.

Even if you can increase your deductible contributions, there is a limit to the amount of superannuation you can withdraw and still gain the full tax concessions. This is called your 'reasonable benefit limit' (RBL), which varies greatly depending on whether you take a lump sum (in which case the limit is around $435 000) or take half in the form of a complying lifetime annuity (in which case the limit increases to almost $900 000). Yes, confusing isn't it? It's worth discussing your situation with an accountant or financial adviser.

Using Non-super Savings

If you think you need more money for your retirement but don't want to lock too much money away in superannuation, you could build up your savings outside the super system, which will certainly make it easier to access the money if you need to. Non-super investments are discussed earlier in this chapter: whatever vehicle you choose, the key is to commit money on a regular basis so that you benefit from compounding interest (see Chapter 2).

Q *I'm taking maternity leave next year. How will this affect my super?*

A Although your employer contributions stop if you take maternity leave, your superannuation balance continues to be invested (and, hopefully, the earnings continue to increase). You can make personal contributions for up to two years while you are on leave, and in some cases for up to seven years provided you have a contract to return to the same company. If your superannuation package includes insurance benefits, find out whether any of these cease while you are off work. It's common practice for employers to suspend payment of premiums for disability cover during this time, but you can arrange to pay these yourself.

CHOOSING A FUND

Although there are lots of different super funds, in reality your options can be limited. Unless you are self-employed, it is most commonly your employer who selects the fund into which your company contributions are paid. Even if your employer allows you to choose another fund, always consider your employer's fund first. This is because the fees associated with employer funds are typically lower, particularly if the company is of a reasonable size. In many cases, some of the administration costs are also subsidised by your employer.

Industry Superannuation Funds
These were developed to provide for members who worked in one industry for most of their working lives, so that they could stay in the same fund even if they moved between employers within the industry. If you work under an award, your superannuation contributions have traditionally been directed to your industry's fund. But with the introduction of the Superannuation Guarantee, in certain states you now have the choice of contributing to a non-industry fund. Speak to your employer if you need more information on the options available to you.

Personal Superannuation Plans

For small to medium companies, for individuals, and for women going into business for themselves, a personal super plan is worth considering. This is a type of managed fund offered by financial institutions such as insurance companies. The main advantage of personal superannuation plans is that they are both portable and flexible. If you are with such a fund and you leave your job, you don't have to transfer your superannuation, as the account is set up in your name rather than being linked to a specific employer. Personal superannuation plans also give you some say in where your contributions are invested. They do, though, tend to be more expensive than an employer or industry fund, a direct reflection of the cost of running an individual account. Entry fees are generally 0–5 per cent, and annual management fees around 1.5–2 per cent. One thing to watch for with such funds is that the policy does not bind you to contribute a regular amount over a set period: you pay very high commissions with such policies, and if you don't continue to make the regular payments the commissions can increase further. It is worth discussing the options with an accountant or financial adviser.

Just as you would rate any investment on its performance record, so should you rate a super fund

Self-managed Funds

Setting up your own superannuation fund gives you absolute control over where your money is invested. At the same time you are responsible both for operating the fund and for how well it performs, so you should weigh the benefits of personal autonomy against the ongoing cost, time and responsibility involved. Some industry experts suggest that a self-managed fund needs to be worth more than $200 000 to justify the costs involved.

In addition, the penalties are fierce if your fund does not comply with legislation: the contributions and the investment earnings can be taxed at 47 per cent instead of 15 per cent throughout any period of non-compliance. Self-managed funds, like all super funds, are also legally required to have an investment strategy: this must take account of risk, diversification and liquidity, and the fund's ability to pay out members when they leave.

So Which Fund is Right for You?

Although the tax treatment of super sets it apart from other investments, super funds are essentially managed funds where your money is pooled with that of many other investors. Just as you would rate any investment on its performance record and its risk and reward factors, so should you rate a super fund. What, then, should you consider when choosing a fund?

How Your Money Is Invested

Superannuation contributions can be invested in any of the four broad investment areas (cash, fixed interest, property and shares), both within Australia and overseas. Therefore the general principles of investment discussed at the beginning of this chapter apply equally when looking at superannuation funds.

The distinguishing feature of superannuation, though, is that it is a long-term investment and you should consider putting some of your money in riskier areas (such as shares) which will give you long-term growth. That said, it's important to balance the long-term view with your risk profile (see page 95). If you want to feel confident that your investment will not fall in value, you may be more comfortable with a capital-guaranteed fund: offered by life-insurance companies, this type of fund guarantees that your investment will not fall in value. At the same time, though, the lower risk over the long term usually means a lower rate of return over time than you could expect from a similar market-linked portfolio (the value of which fluctuates in line with the market value of the investments held in the fund).

Super funds usually offer a range of investment portfolios. To find out more about the options, check with the administrator of the fund. Switching fees may apply if you transfer from one portfolio to another, and these are usually most severe in the case of capital-guaranteed funds.

Performance of the Fund

By law, you must receive details of the performance of your superannuation investments at least once a year. Independent surveys of all wholesale funds are published monthly, and these should be available from your employer or financial adviser. The performance histories of other types of funds are published regularly in finance magazines such as *Personal Investment*. In the end, your aim should be to find the best-performing fund (after costs) which operates at a level of risk that you find acceptable.

Fees

When selecting a fund, look at the administration and management fees to make sure you are getting a fair deal. Unfortunately it can be difficult to compare fees between organisations, as administration fees can be deducted in a number of ways, including one or a combination of the following:

▲ entry fees (on initial contributions)
▲ ongoing administration/account-keeping fees
▲ ongoing fees charged for funds management
▲ exit fees

These fees can also be deducted from your account or from your investment earnings before they are added to your account, which can make it even harder to compare different funds. Rather than selecting the fund with the lowest fees, consider the investment return after fees, as your aim is to get the best overall result. It is false economy to compromise the potential for earning a higher return simply to save costs. Most fees are now disclosed in the documents you receive on joining a fund and on your annual benefit statements.

Portability

The ability to transfer your superannuation benefits without penalties is an important consideration. If you are with an employer fund, you are usually required to withdraw your benefits within ninety days of leaving that job, though it's unusual to be penalised if you don't do so. You may, of course, be up for entry fees when you invest the money in another fund.

If you are in an industry fund your superannuation is not affected if you move between employers within the industry, and any contributions from your new employer can continue to be made to the same fund. If you leave the industry, the money can remain in that fund or you can transfer into another one.

Personal superannuation funds, as we said earlier, are very portable (provided you don't contract to pay a regular amount over a set period and then incur penalties for failing to do so). You should, though, always check whether any fees are payable when you leave such a fund.

Q *I keep reading about 'vested' superannuation contributions. What exactly does this mean?*

A The 'vested' contribution is the amount of super contributions (and any earnings on them) you are entitled to if you leave the company. Contributions made under the Superannuation Guarantee or an award are fully vested, which means you will always be entitled to this money and the earnings on it. Your ability to cash in the money will depend on whether it is preserved or not.

If your employer contributes more than is required by the Superannuation Guarantee, they may have a 'vesting' scale for the additional contributions, which sets out how long you must work there before you are entitled to the extra benefits. So if you are considering leaving your current job and your present fund has a vesting scale, consider the financial repercussions. Your annual statement will show (as 'Partially Vested Amounts') any contributions which are subject to such a formula and will also state the total benefit you are entitled to if you resign from the company at that time.

CONSOLIDATING YOUR SUPERANNUATION

If you've had more than one employer in your career – and most of us have – your superannuation contributions could well be spread around more than one fund. Presently, about $250 million dollars worth of super sits in hundreds of thousands of small and unclaimed superannuation accounts around

> ### SUPERANNUATION: KEY POINTS
>
> - Ensures you have savings available for your retirement, as your access to the money is generally restricted until then.
> - There are tax concessions on both contributions and earnings.
> - Personal super plans are portable and flexible, and give you some say about where the money is invested.

Australia. If you do have small amounts scattered around, you should try to consolidate them in one fund; the Insurance and Superannuation Commission is establishing a register of 'lost' fund members.

WHEN YOU HAVE A COMPLAINT

Australia's superannuation system is highly regulated and fund trustees are liable if they act outside the best interests of fund members. If you wish to dispute anything to do with your superannuation entitlements, the trustee of your fund should have in place some means for considering your inquiries and dealing with the matter to your satisfaction within ninety days. If you can't reach agreement, you can submit your complaint to the Superannuation Complaints Tribunal, which is an independent body and may conciliate or review the fund's decision.

ONE THING ABOUT THE RULES – THEY ALWAYS SEEM TO CHANGE!

The superannuation system has undergone seemingly constant changes since the early 1980s – and it has become more complicated as a result. And there is no guarantee that the situation won't change yet again in the future: indeed, the Coalition Government elected in 1996 foreshadowed further modifications. These include proposals for people with small superannuation balances and for small-business owners, and for widening access to superannuation (for non-working spouses, for example).

The greatest potential for changes to the system centres around its tax treatment. As long as superannuation investments receive tax concessions, governments will be faced with the temptation to raise revenue simply by increasing the tax on the growing pool of super funds. There may also be changes in your ability to take your super as a lump sum: it is always possible that in the future some percentage of your benefits will have to be taken in the form of income (a pension or annuity). At the very least, it is likely that an increasing proportion of your super will be locked away until you retire.

TWO STEPS FORWARD, ONE STEP BACK?

Investing some of your spare money is the key to financial independence and security. This is fine in principle, but there are lots of situations in life – and many things we need or want to do – that affect our finances. If we take a new job or start up a business, if we decide to buy a new car or a house, we inevitably have to go back to the budget and reassess our priorities. So the next chapter looks at exactly these things, with some tips on how to get the decisions right.

4

GETTING THE
BIG DECISIONS RIGHT

There are lots of times when we have to make decisions that directly affect our finances. Being armed with the right knowledge greatly increases our chances of getting those decisions right. This chapter looks at the main situations you're likely to encounter that involve financial decision-making – starting or changing a job, buying and selling a home or a car, going into business – and what you need to know to get the best out of each.

You've Got the Job!

'IF A WOMAN CAN FIGURE OUT

WHICH ONE GETS THE LAST TOFFEE

— THE FOUR-YEAR-OLD OR THE

SIX-YEAR-OLD — SHE CAN NEGOTIATE

ANY CONTRACT IN THE WORLD.'

— Anita Roddick

For many of us, the income we earn from our job is our chief concern, but there are a few other things to consider as well, depending on your circumstances. If you sat a group of women around a table and asked them what aspect of their working conditions was most important to them, you'd undoubtedly get a wide range of answers: a career path for one, job training for another, and flexibility to fit in with family commitments for yet another.

When you get a new job, or you're reviewing your existing one, it's worth taking some time to get your thoughts together about what you expect from your employer (just as they, no doubt, will expect certain things from you), so that you can try to negotiate the best deal possible.

It's not really advisable to lay detailed demands on the table before you've been offered the job. But once that's happened (and before you accept), it's an ideal time to discuss the terms and conditions that matter to you. Remember that at this point in the negotiations you've been chosen above the other applicants and you're in the driver's seat. Use this to your advantage – you're unlikely to have a better base to work from again. Don't rush in and agree to their offer if you want time to consider your future needs.

THE BIG PICTURE – AGES AND STAGES

What you want from your job will, of course, depend to a large extent on your age and your stage of life.

When you start out (for most of us, this is in our twenties), your career has begun and you're seeking fame and fortune! Look for companies which offer a broad range of experience and training, and the opportunity to build your career – perhaps through study programs. You may also be interested in how the company designs your job (team or individual work? job rotation? lack of hierarchies?).

When you want time out to start a family (anywhere from your twenties to your late thirties), flexibility in the form of staggered starting and finishing times, part-time work, job sharing or working from home is likely to be all-important. If you take extended time off to have children, try to stay visible in your field by working part-time, by joining a professional organisation or by upgrading your skills through study.

A NEW JOB: WHAT YOU NEED TO CONSIDER

- What will your take-home pay be? Are there automatic deductions (such as superannuation contributions) which will reduce the quoted figure?
- Is there any flexibility to package your salary? Are there any benefits (a company car, a work-based gym or child care, or other 'perks') available?
- Is there scope to progress to more senior (and more lucrative) positions?
- Does the company offer ongoing training or the opportunity to upgrade your skills?
- How flexible are the working hours and conditions? Can you start and finish earlier (or later) than the set hours if you want to? Could you work a four-day week? Could you use your sick leave to look after your sick child?

Your mid-career (your thirties and forties) is likely to be your most productive and influential time. For some of us this is a period in which we re-examine our skills and experience with a view to a change of job or career. If this appeals, go for training and skills development, or consider packages which allow you time out.

This is also 'make or break' time as far as the corporate ladder goes, so if your ambitions run that way you should negotiate with promotion prospects in mind: if you feel you aren't going to get due recognition in the future, consider taking your talents to another employer. If you've been with the same employer for ten years, you may be due for long-service leave, in which case you should know how this will affect your job status.

When you're starting to think about retirement (around your early fifties onwards), keep your options open. This may be a time when you consider a lifestyle change and want to work fewer hours. It's certainly a time to look to your future needs, in particular what you do with your earnings, so superannuation or health insurance may become priorities.

WAYS OF WORKING

'DON'T COMPROMISE YOURSELF.

YOU'RE ALL YOU'VE GOT.'

— JANIS JOPLIN

There are many ways of working (and getting paid), and there is always room for negotiation. If you know your entitlements, you'll be in a far stronger position.

Working Under an Award

Currently 80 per cent of Australian workers are covered by an award, which may be state-based or federally based. Awards set a minimum hourly rate of pay, plus other entitlements such as holiday and sick leave, and employer

---

AT THE BARGAINING TABLE

- **Understand your minimum entitlements.** These should be the starting point from which to negotiate.
- **Understand the employer's viewpoint.** If you've thought through how the business operates and your role in improving it, you have established a good basis for co-operative negotiation.
- If pay increases are based on productivity, **establish what will be expected of you** and how this will be measured.

---

superannuation payments. You don't have to be a member of a union to be covered. If you do work under an award, technically you have to negotiate anything over and above the minimum rate of pay, although many companies pay 'over-award' rates. (You can find out the latest minimum rates from the Department of Industrial Relations.)

Enterprise Agreements

Some employers have moved towards 'enterprise agreements', where minimum rates of pay for ordinary hours and for annual and sick leave are regulated, but everything else is open to negotiation. The Department of Industrial Relations has produced a booklet called *Why Women Should Play Snakes and Ladders: The Enterprise Bargaining Game*, which is designed to guide you through the intricacies of this system. New South Wales has developed the only state-based version: for free advice and assistance, you can phone the Workplace Agreements advisory service on 1800 803 836 (NSW only); they also provide training workshops for employees and employers.

One of the advantages of enterprise bargaining is that you have more chance to negotiate flexibility in your job. You could, for example, arrange to work a set number of hours over the year but have the flexibility to choose *when* you want to work them: this approach, known as 'annualised hours', could be useful if you're a working mother with school-aged children and would prefer to work longer hours during term-time and fewer hours during school holidays.

Under enterprise agreements, pay rises are usually linked to productivity. More and more women are working in service industries, where productivity can be difficult to estimate – but it's not impossible, so ask your employer how such measurements will be made. Many government bodies and unions now have experience in these matters and it may pay to contact them for advice.

Working Under Contract

Contract-based work is increasingly common as governments and companies try to reduce their overheads, and it can be a good opportunity to negotiate terms that suit you.

Under a contract you agree to work for a set term at a set rate of pay: this may be a PAYE position, or you could be self-employed. Superannuation and paid leave are not automatically included as part of the agreement, so if you are considering a contract position, remember to take this into account and increase your hourly or weekly rate accordingly.

WHAT MIGHT BE IN YOUR PACKAGE?

Before the fringe-benefits tax (FBT) was introduced in 1986 and began to bite, many salaried staff took some of their package in the form of benefits which were paid for out of their pre-tax salary, thus reducing their taxable income. FBT has dramatically reduced this option – and the 'business-lunch' trade for restaurants!

Employers must now pay FBT (which is calculated at the highest personal tax rate) on any cash or non-cash benefits they give their employees, and increasingly they are charging this tax back through our salary packages. For this reason, think long and hard about taking a benefit which is subject to FBT rather than taking it in salary. Also bear in mind that accepting such benefits will reduce both the amount of holiday pay you get and your employer's base superannuation contribution, as these are calculated on your taxable income and not your total package.

But don't despair, there are still ways to improve your overall package.

OPTIONS FOR WORKING MOTHERS

If you have children, flexible work arrangements can mean the difference between continuing to work and opting out. The following approaches offer some modern answers to an age-old problem.

Job Sharing

Here two people are responsible for one position, dividing the work, pay and other benefits between them according to the hours they work. The three common methods of job sharing are:

- **shared responsibility for the same job**, where the tasks are not divided and each sharer simply takes over where the other leaves off. This can be suitable for ongoing work.
- **divided responsibility**, where the sharers have their own projects or clients and provide mutual back-up when required.
- **separate responsibility**, where the sharers perform quite unrelated tasks as if they hold two part-time positions.

For job sharing to be successful, the arrangements must suit you as well as meeting your employer's needs. Be as flexible as possible.

Working From Home

Thanks to modern technology, setting you up in a home office is now a relatively cheap option for your employer. It's likely to suit you if your job is pretty autonomous or is project-based. The things you need to think about are covered in the section 'Going into Business' later in this chapter, but there are a few extra considerations if you are answerable to an employer. Make sure that your wages and conditions are equal to those of office-based employees. Also give some thought to communications, training and promotion opportunities, as there could be a tendency to overlook you if you are not in the office regularly.

Superannuation

It can't be stressed too often that superannuation or some other form of retirement savings should be near the top of every woman's list of financial priorities. And clearly the message is getting through: ten years ago, fewer than 25 per cent of working women had any form of superannuation, while today the figure is closer to 86 per cent.

Investing in super funds, and how the superannuation system works, are dealt with in greater detail in Chapters 3 and 6 respectively. But how (and how much) superannuation your employer contributes on your behalf also directly affects your job package in a couple of ways. First, your employer may offer to pay more super than is required by the Superannuation Guarantee. If so, you should seriously consider this in the light of your income needs when you retire. Second, many employers are encouraging the principle of 'salary sacrifice', where you pay more superannuation yourself and your take-home pay is reduced accordingly. The best course for you will depend on your personal circumstances: if, say, you are in your forties or fifties and are on a reasonably high income, salary sacrifice may be a sensible option.

What If I Change Jobs?

When you change jobs, you have to decide what to do with any superannuation benefits you may have accumulated thus far. If you transfer straight into another fund, you continue to receive tax concessions on the earnings. You can cash in any part of your super which is not preserved (i.e. cannot be accessed until you're at least 55 and retired), but remember that you may pay tax of up to 20 per cent (depending on your age) on it if you do so. You have to roll over the preserved part: ways of doing so are discussed in Chapter 3.

Child Care

Child-care facilities provided by your employer at your place of work are exempt from the fringe-benefits tax (FBT). This is intended to encourage companies to provide such facilities for their staff, but it is worth noting that according to the Australian Bureau of Statistics, only 4 per cent of employers do provide work-based child care.

So if you're one of the lucky ones, make the most of it. You can arrange to have the costs deducted from your pre-tax salary. If your company does not offer this facility, it may be worthwhile doing some research around the office – if there is a need, take this up with your employer. A word of warning, though. As of late 1996, employer-sponsored child-care facilities located outside your place of work may be subject to FBT. This is likely to mean that the tax will be passed on to employees and that there will be a big jump in the amount you pay for this form of child care.

Employers' Rolls Royce child-care facilities are likely to have a matching price tag

Whatever the case, always compare cost of work-based care relative to the other options available, as some employers provide 'Rolls Royce' facilities which are likely to have a Rolls Royce price tag. And don't forget that the government refunds a percentage of the costs of child care outside the workplace: child-care options are discussed in more detail in the section 'Having a Child' in Chapter 5.

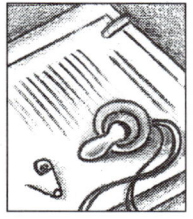

'BE DARING ABOUT NEW IDEAS FOR

WORK/FAMILY BALANCE.'

— SKYE ROGERS AND CARO LLEWELLYN,
JOBS FOR THE GIRLS

A Car

A car funded by your employer can be a definite plus, but as this can be subject to FBT you should do your sums. If you use your car for work purposes, it may prove cheaper in the long run to pay your car costs yourself and claim them as a tax deduction.

If your car is financed through your package, there are two ways of calculating the FBT. The **statutory method** is based on the value of the vehicle and the number of kilometres travelled, regardless of whether or not these are for business. Because this is the simplest calculation, it is the only approach offered by some employers. The statutory method could work for you if you travel significant distances (as FBT reduces the more kilometres you drive), if you have a low-priced to middle-priced car (as FBT is directly related to the value of the vehicle), or if a high proportion of your travel is for business purposes.

The **operating method** is essentially the same as claiming a tax deduction for business use: you calculate the costs of running the car and FBT is payable at the highest tax rate on the proportion of those costs associated with private use; any FBT not paid by your employer is charged to your package. To determine the proportion of business and personal use, you must keep a log-book over a twelve-week period and this is used as a guide for all subsequent years unless your business use changes significantly. The operating method may suit you if you travel a small number of kilometres, if you have an expensive car, or if a high proportion of your travel is for business purposes.

Profit-sharing Schemes

Some employers offer shares in the company to their staff. This may be a straight bonus (i.e. free), but more commonly the shares are offered for sale at a discount. Obviously you should take a dispassionate view of such an offer. Are the shares a good investment even at the discounted price? Is the timing right to consider investing in this industry? At the same time, buying shares in your employer's company could have some tax advantages, so it's worth discussing any such offer with an accountant or financial adviser.

Low-interest Loans

The offer of low-interest loans by employers (particularly financial institutions) was once quite common, but again FBT has made this less attractive. The main danger here is if you plan your finances on the reduced interest rate but later leave the job and find that you need to refinance at a higher rate. So, look carefully at the figures.

CLAIMING WORK EXPENSES AS A TAX DEDUCTION

There are quite a few tax deductions you can claim in relation to your job, though in recent years the Tax Office has clamped down and made very specific rulings for different professions. The expenses you can claim must relate directly to earning an income: you may not claim anything which is deemed to be a personal cost, and this includes travel to and from work, and special clothing (unless it is a uniform). You should claim any allowed expenses on your tax return: the government's Tax Pack booklet includes a general list of claimable expenses, but consider seeking professional advice at least once to make sure you are claiming what you're entitled to. Also, do keep all relevant receipts and records for five years.

BUYING A HOME

'HOME IS THE PLACE TO DO THE

THINGS YOU WANT TO DO.'

— ZELDA FITZGERALD

The availability of plentiful and relatively cheap land in Australia has made owning a home an affordable dream for nearly three-quarters of the population.

Owning your own home can satisfy some deeply rooted psychological needs, not least of which are the emotional security of having paid for the roof over your head, and the independence this brings. There are also sound financial reasons for owning your own home, even though there is less guarantee than in the past that property will significantly increase in value.

That said, the following pages look mainly at the things you need to think about if you decide to buy. There are plenty of good books around on how to buy real estate and it's not our aim to reproduce them here, but we do point out the ways in which buying or selling a house will impact on your financial health. Whether you're a first-time buyer, or whether you're trading up or down, there are thousands of dollars to be made – and saved – if you go the right way about acquiring a property. It's also worth noting that, in terms of money management, it is probably better to direct any spare savings towards reducing your mortgage to a manageable level, rather than try to build up other investments.

To Buy or Not to Buy?

There is no simple answer to this question: the decision will depend on both your lifestyle and your financial circumstances.

The fact that the housing market today may be less attractive than it once was has led many people to begin to question how much of their wealth should be tied up in their home. And there's no doubt that buying will bite into your disposable income. Of course, the security of owning the roof over your head may be more important to you than any possible financial gain if and when you sell, but most of us aim for both.

The Advantages of Buying

If you have a mortgage, you can look on it as an enforced form of saving. It is also true that (assuming that mortgage repayments are higher than rent payments) if we rented and then invested the difference between the rent and mortgage payments we might be better off renting than buying. But if you've ever said 'I had $100 at the beginning of the week – I don't know where it's gone', you'll be all too aware of the capacity of money to evaporate if you're not forced to put it away – which is what a mortgage does for you.

Another benefit of buying is that if your home is in a desirable location, or you improve or develop the property, the odds are still on your side to make money if and when you sell. And even if the real value of the property (taking inflation into account) doesn't rise much in the time you own it, you will at least have paid off some of the principal and this will mean you have a larger deposit available for your next house.

Then there are the tax benefits. Provided that this is your principal residence, any profit you make when you sell it is yours tax-free – the only investment for which this is the case. (By the same token, if you make a loss when you sell, this can't be offset against any profits you make elsewhere.) And if you want or need to move, or to travel for an extended period, renting out your home while you do so will not affect your exemption from capital-gains tax provided you're absent for no more than six years. Of course, any rent you receive in such an event would be taxable, so look at the sums very carefully.

IT'S NEVER TOO LATE

Jean was 60 and close to retiring when she bought her unit – the first property she'd ever owned. She used her superannuation payout to buy it, knowing that a twenty-five-year mortgage was out of the question, and she took up casual work to supplement her pension. She's happy with her decision because she feels secure, can't be uprooted by a landlord and won't have to worry about rent rises now she's living on a small income. She also feels that she has an asset which may appreciate and be of benefit to her children when she dies.

Last, but by no means least, owning a home is a tangible sign of your independence and financial achievements, and this has financial as well as emotional rewards. Lenders, for example, may regard you as a better risk than a non-home-owner, which means that other financial doors may start opening: such benefits can include exemption from having to lodge a deposit when you want gas or electricity connected to your property.

And the Disadvantages ...

Getting together the deposit for a house is hard work and should never be under-estimated. Unless you have a windfall, you'll need every spare cent for between two and five years to save for a deposit. There's not much reward in that kind of discipline – until, of course, you turn the key in your own front door.

And however scary your mortgage payments may seem in the beginning, there's no guarantee that they won't get worse – much worse! Anybody who was paying off a mortgage in the eighties will shudder at the memory of 18 per cent interest rates – but it just goes to show that it can happen. So when you're working out what you can afford, take into account what can go wrong. There are ways of managing the situation, such as locking into a fixed level of repayments. And if you get into financial difficulties as the result of being overcommitted, there are some solutions in the section 'Help, I'm In Trouble!' in Chapter 2.

Beyond the actual cost of buying, there are expenses associated with ownership that a renter never need consider. Stamp duty, legal fees, loan-establishment fees when buying, and advertising and the agent's commission when selling: these and other up-front costs can alone total 5–7 per cent of the purchase price. *And* you have to budget for ongoing expenses such as rates and (if you buy a strata-title apartment) maintenance levies.

In addition, it's rare to find that the house you want is in perfect condition, let alone decorated to your taste. While renovating can be a great hobby (and judicious alterations can increase a property's value), it all costs money. The same goes for any additions you choose to make as your needs change or your family grows, let alone the seemingly constant repairs. In other words, more for your budget to cope with.

Renting: the Good, the Bad and the Ugly

Some people rent because they haven't got sufficient funds for a deposit and for ongoing mortgage repayments. Some rent because it gives them mobility, allows them to make quick decisions about moving if they are changing jobs, and can free up income for other things. And others, particularly in more recent times, have decided to rent rather than buy until the property market shows signs of picking up.

The Positives

Certainly you don't need a huge amount of money to begin renting. You do usually have to pay a bond when you first sign a lease – typically four weeks rent for an unfurnished property and six weeks rent for a furnished place – but this is nowhere near the thousands required for a home deposit.

It's often said that rent money is 'money down the drain'. On the other hand, when you rent you don't have to worry about unexpected or unmanageable maintenance bills, all of which makes it easier to budget and can give you more disposable income.

... And the Negatives
There are, of course, some major down sides to renting. Obviously, it will never make you money. In addition, your weekly rental bill is likely to increase over time, which could be a major issue if your salary is not rising at the same rate or if you're likely to be on a fixed income at any stage. In addition, your landlord can ask you to leave whenever the lease is up. And while you don't have to pay for maintenance and other regular costs, you may have an agent or landlord who is tardy or difficult about organising repairs when you need them. Furthermore, you will probably have to put up with those lime-green cupboards!

There can also be disputes about the return of bond money. In most states, landlords are required to lodge your bond with an independent body, and this money is returned to you when you leave, provided the premises are deemed to be in reasonable condition. Always confirm the condition of the property when you first move in (the agent will usually provide a checklist for this purpose) and inform the landlord of any damage. You can't be held liable for any reasonable wear and tear, but 'improvements' like unauthorised paint jobs or picture-hooks can pose a problem; cleaning the premises properly is the best way to pre-empt any problems. You can take disputes up with the Department of Consumer Affairs in your state (usually through their Tenancy Services section): requests for mediation must be in writing, and both parties must agree to this approach. If mediation fails, you can take the matter up with the Residential Tenancies Tribunal (application forms are available from the Department of Consumer Affairs Tenancy Service).

SO YOU'VE DECIDED TO BUY?

If you want to increase your chances of buying well, and of making a profit when you sell, real-estate agents suggest there are a number of things you should think about. Most of them can be summed up in three words: position, position, position.

▲ Aim for a property that is close to amenities such as public transport, schools and local shops (within walking distance) and within fifteen minutes' drive of a major shopping centre or supermarket.

▲ Buy in areas experiencing population growth, which should ensure demand when you sell. At the same time, check out future development plans for the area with the local council: a great deal of development could lead to an oversupply of properties, which will suppress prices.

▲ And while you're at the council offices, investigate the zoning regulations. Future plans for road-widening or new power-lines will affect property values, and you don't want to pay a premium for a wonderful view if there is a chance your outlook could be shut off by a new block of units. Similarly, choose a property which is as free as possible from air and traffic noise, as these can affect property prices.

▲ Buy the worst house on the best street rather than the best house on the worst street, especially in run-down areas which are being 'gentrified'. This gives you plenty of scope to improve the property without over-capitalising.

▲ Look for street appeal. Are there trees? Are the houses relatively well kept?

▲ Make sure the house has enough storage space. If there are no built-in cupboards, especially in the bedrooms, is there enough space to build some?

IT'S ON THE MARKET! HOW MUCH WILL YOU NEED?

There is little more exciting (and more nerve-racking) than the moment when you find the house you want. It's nerve-racking because you don't know whether the vendor will accept your offer, or you may have to compete with others at auction – and, of course, you have to get finance approved.

Even if you think the house you want will go for a price you can afford, it's important to realise that you will be dipping into your pocket for more than the purchase price. In other words, you need to plan for a whole range of extra costs, which fall roughly into two camps: those associated with the purchase itself and those associated with getting a loan (see the figures on page 168).

The first thing to know is that lenders generally provide only 85–95 per cent of the value of the property. Be realistic about the cost of financing the loan: if you borrow $100 000, for example, your interest repayments alone could be around $10 500 a year.

And when you finally take possession of your new home, you'll still need more in the kitty for removal costs, utilities connections, home and contents insurance, and miscellaneous requirements such as new locks.

THE HOME-LOAN HEADACHE

Borrowing to buy a home is so easy, yet so confusing. Financial institutions offer a dazzling array of loans, interest rates and extra 'features', while all most of us really want to know is how much we can (and should) borrow, which type of mortgage we should choose, and how to get the best deal.

You will be dipping into your pocket for more than the purchase price

How Much Should You Borrow?

As a general rule, lenders prefer your repayments not to exceed 30 per cent of your gross monthly income, although they will look at your total financial picture, including your other commitments. You'll also find that different lenders often have differing views: some may ask you to show that you could pay them back at a higher interest rate if necessary, while others will let you be the judge. Making an assessment when interest rates are low can be dangerous, though: if you are in any doubt, ask to see the (free) computer program that most banks now run, which shows you the figures for different loan amounts, interest rates and loan periods.

You may be tempted, when interest rates and inflation are low, to take out the largest mortgage possible. Before you rush out to do this, remember that your other costs such as stamp duty and legal fees, can add quite a few thousand dollars to the cost of the property. So if you prepare a budget for the lender, make sure it is accurate and that you've taken into account all the costs. And never talk up the state of your finances to persuade them to give you a larger loan. They'll catch you out anyway when you have to provide proof of your income, and you'll catch yourself out – and suffer the financial consequences – if you cannot really afford the repayments.

Types of Home Loans and how They Vary

Banks, building societies, credit unions, insurance companies, solicitors, housing co-operatives, finance companies, mortgage originators and some superannuation funds will all lend you money if you want to buy property, and many of the loans are packaged along similar lines. The add-ons and the service may vary, but basically you'll get a fixed or a variable rate of interest on the loan, or some combination of the two.

Fixed-rate Mortgages

As the name suggests, with a fixed-rate mortgage you borrow at a fixed rate of interest over a set period of time. Because interest rates are so volatile, borrowers and lenders alike tend to be cautious about fixing the rate for more than a few years. The great advantage with a fixed rate is that you are protected should interest rates rise, which is particularly important if your budget is tight.

With fixed-rate mortgages, timing is critical. If you manage to lock in when interest rates are at the bottom of the cycle, you could save thousands of dollars. But how do you know when you have reached the bottom of the cycle? This is pretty difficult to pick, because interest rates are affected by so many variables, but you can start by considering the direction in which interest rates have been going until now and by finding out what the 'experts' are saying, reading the business section of your daily paper and listening to the news.

The greatest risk with fixed-rate mortgages is that you will miss out should interest rates fall. In addition, they are less flexible than variable-rate mortgages: there may not, for example, be any provision for you to pay extra amounts off the loan if you're in a position to do so.

Variable-rate Mortgages

With a variable-rate mortgage, the repayments on your loan rise and fall in line with interest rates. The advantage here is that a fall in interest rates reduces your repayments, which means that if you keep repaying at the original rate you can reduce the period of the loan. Also you have the flexibility to pay additional money off your loan and have the interest automatically recalculated on the new balance.

Of course, there are down sides too, not least that if interest rates rise and rise, so will your repayments. And there are problems from a budgeting point of view, as the variable rate means you can't be sure how much your repayments will be in the future. Most mortgages are, though, taken out on a variable rate.

Cocktail or Combination Mortgages

These mortgages are just what they sound like – a combination of fixed and variable rates, giving you the flexibility to increase repayments on the variable portion while protecting you against interest-rate rises with the fixed rate portion. Some lenders have a minimum amount you can allocate to each section ($25 000 is not unusual) but after this, choosing the mix is up to you. If you think the variable rate will go higher than the fixed rate during the loan period, if it's important to you that your repayments stay the same, or if you are likely at any stage to have some spare cash to put towards paying off the loan, a cocktail loan is well worth investigating.

Other Options

With lenders fighting to retain or build market share, you're likely to see lots of special offers, such as discounts on interest rates if they're fixed for one year. 'Capped rates' (where you pay no more than the agreed interest rate for a specified period, which is often lower than the current variable rate) are also common. In the finance trade these are sometimes referred to as 'honeymoon' loans, as they all revert to the standard variable rate at the end of the agreed period.

Also available, though a little out of favour at the moment, are high-start and low-start loans. The monthly repayments on high-start loans are initially higher than is required to service the current variable interest rate, which allows you to pay the loan off more quickly at the start, thus saving you interest and giving you some flexibility to make lower repayments later. They are a good choice for double-income couples who plan to start a family at some later date.

Low-start loans achieve the opposite result. The initial repayments are lower and often don't cover the interest, so the loan balance actually increases in the first few years. The advantage is that you can borrow more, because you are not at first paying interest: this may suit you if your current earnings won't support full loan repayments but you expect that your future income will. On the other hand, if your income doesn't keep rising, or if property prices are flat or falling, low-start loans can spell big trouble.

Shopping for the Best Deal

Here are a few tips to help you cut through the lenders' promotion and get the best home-loan deal. As ever, it pays to shop around; remember that preliminary interviews with lending institutions are free of charge.

▲ **Get some advice**, if you feel you need it. Several organisations offer free advice on a selected range of mortgages available in the marketplace, although your choice is limited to the loans they are selling. One such group is Lawfund Australia, which comprises around 160 firms of solicitors and operates in all states except Western Australia. It may be worth investing in a copy of the magazine *Your Mortgage*, which independently rates all the mortgage options on the same basis so that you can compare costs.

▲ **Don't just consider the interest rate**. Also examine the lender's terms and conditions, and any other charges.

▲ Although you can't do much about mandatory costs such as stamp duty, **try to negotiate** everything else, and this includes interest rates and loan-establishment fees. Lenders who advertise the lowest interest rates may not be offering the cheapest deal: check their fee structure, as by the time you add this to the advertised interest rate the 'effective' rate could work out much higher (see 'When You Want to Borrow' in Chapter 2 for more details on these sums). Don't be afraid to play one lender off against another.

▲ **Make sure you won't be penalised if you want to pay out the loan early.** Also find out what happens if you are late with your repayments. Similarly, what will it cost if you want to switch from a fixed-rate loan to another type of loan if interest rates come down? A high refinancing fee could negate the benefits of switching.

▲ **If you think you might want to vary your repayments, choose a loan which gives you this flexibility** (such as a variable or cocktail mortgage). You may find yourself in a position to increase your payments at some stage, or you may need to reduce them if your income drops for a period.

▲ **If you opt for a fixed-rate loan, make sure you know what your options are at the end of the period**: will it revert to a variable rate? And when the term expires, don't be afraid to ask for a better rate if the competition is offering one.

Getting Your Loan Approved

Once you have established the amount you can borrow and have chosen your lender, you need to make a formal application to have your home loan approved by the lending institution. For this you need to provide proof of your income (if you're self-employed, you will need statements of past and expected future earnings), preferably through your accountant, plus evidence of all your debts and assets. You may also be asked to sign a consent form allowing the institution to check your credit rating.

Request all costs in writing from the lending institution, and be wary of any unusual clauses in the contract. Read the fine print very carefully: this may be the most important financial contract you will ever sign, so please give it serious consideration.

It is at this point that you pay loan-establishment and other fees. If you decide against taking out the loan before it is approved, you are entitled to have all your money, except fees paid to third parties such as valuers, returned to you.

If you are borrowing more than 75 per cent of the value of your property, the lender will probably ask you to take out mortgage guarantee insurance: this protects the lender in case you default on the loan and the proceeds from selling the home don't cover what you've borrowed. It involves a one-off payment (which can be around $800–$900 on a $100 000 loan) which is determined on the ratio of the debt to the value of

Don't Put Away that Chequebook

The following is a rough guide to the expenses you're likely to face when buying a home. The fees quoted are based on a Sydney home with a purchase price of $200 000 and a mortgage of $100 000.

Buying the Property

CONVEYANCING FEE   **$1197**

This is the fee charged by the professional who undertakes on your behalf all the legal paperwork associated with the purchase. Conveyancing is an optional cost, as you can do it yourself (see page 174).

DISBURSEMENTS   **$334**

These are the various expenses incurred during conveyancing, such as fees for title searches and the cost of obtaining certificates from the relevant government authorities.

PEST AND BUILDING INSPECTIONS   **$850**

Such inspections are optional, but a good idea. (Use an architect or builder, or the Housing Industry Association's inspection service.)

STAMP DUTY   **$5490**

This government duty, which may be calculated on the purchase price or on the figure at which the property is valued, must be paid within two months of exchanging contracts.

STRATA-SEARCH FEE   **VARIABLE**

These searches, which are optional, apply if you buy a strata unit or townhouse. They involve checking the records of the block or body corporate for solvency and any major building problems. The cheaper option is to do it yourself through the managing agents, although a small fee will still apply. Alternatively you can engage a specialist: see 'Title Searchers' in the Yellow Pages.

INSURANCE $550

Insuring the contents of your home is optional, but building insurance is mandatory if the property is mortgaged (in the case of strata-title properties, it is paid by the body corporate).

SETTING UP THE LOAN

LOAN ESTABLISHMENT FEE $500

This is usually a flat fee which you pay to the lender in order to open the loan account.

LEGAL FEES $233

STAMP AND REGISTRATION FEES $400

VALUATION FEE   VARIABLE

This is payable if the lender requires a professional valuation of the property. It may be included in the loan establishment fee, or charged separately.

the property. The terms vary between lenders: some allow you to add the amount to the loan, while others may ask you to pay it up-front. Mortgage *guarantee* insurance should not be confused with mortgage *protection* insurance, which provides for your repayments to be met if you become ill or lose your job. If you need mortgage guarantee insurance, ask whether you will get a refund if you pay off your loan before the term expires.

Tips for Reducing Your Mortgage

Once you have a mortgage, there are ways to reduce the total cost.

Make Larger Repayments

If you have a variable-rate mortgage and can afford to increase your regular repayments, even by a little, you will be surprised at the difference it makes to the total cost of the loan. For example, if you take out a $100 000 loan over twenty-five years at an interest rate of 10 per cent, your repayments each month will be $909 and the total cost to you will be $272 610. If you could increase your repayments by just $50 a month, you would pay off the loan in twenty years and the total cost would be $235 035, saving you $37 575. And paying an extra $100 per month would save you $59 936 and allow you to pay off the loan in little more than seventeen years. The benefits can be seen even more clearly when you consider that if you invested the $50 monthly, instead of putting it towards extra repayments, you would have to be earning 10 per cent interest (after tax and charges) to get the same results. That's a pretty good rate of return in anyone's language.

Another way to reduce both the amount and period of the loan is to put towards it any lump-sum payments you may receive (tax refunds, bonus payments from work, or inherited money).

Pay Fortnightly Instead of Monthly

This is one of the biggest discoveries of the last few years, so approach your lender with the idea. Unless your budget is very tight, you won't notice the difference if you make your repayments fortnightly instead of monthly, but by doing so you are making the equivalent of thirteen monthly repayments over a year instead of twelve, which leads to significant savings and cuts years off the loan. If, for example, you have a $120 000 mortgage at 10 per cent over twenty-five years and pay on a fortnightly basis instead of monthly, you would save $57 855 in interest repayments and reduce the period of the loan to nineteen years.

Use an Offset Account

Many lenders now offer this facility, and it's well worth considering. When you deposit an amount of money in an offset account (which you open with the institution providing the loan) the interest earned on that account is automatically offset against the amount outstanding on your loan. There are two main benefits of this system:

▲ If you are continuing to make your usual interest repayments, anything from your offset account will go towards reducing the principal of your loan. This, in turn, reduces your interest costs and therefore the number of years it will take to pay off the mortgage.

▲ Because the balance in your offset account is used directly against the home loan, you don't earn interest on the account and therefore no tax is payable.

Or, Even Better...
Some lenders will allow you, once you've repaid some principal, to borrow back up to the original approved amount without paying any additional fees; others charge a small fee. This is useful if you want to 'park' some money for later use and at the same time reap some mortgage benefits. Either way, don't treat this like a transaction account.

Now You're Ready to Buy

The house you're after may be offered for sale at a public auction or privately. The first rule, whichever way you buy, is to negotiate where possible. Look for all the property's faults or, better still, bring the building inspection report into play and use this to negotiate the price down. Make sure that you are clear about which items in the house – curtains, light fittings, and so on – are included in the price.

You should also obtain a copy of the contract and have your solicitor check it out before you sign anything. If you buy privately rather than at auction, you usually have the benefit of a cooling-off period – ranging from two to five days, depending on the regulations in your state – which means that you can withdraw from the sale without losing your deposit.

Tips When Buying at Auction
Buying at auction has some advantages, not least that once the hammer falls the property belongs to you if you are the final bidder. For this reason you have to have your finance arranged before the auction, including the 10 per cent deposit (which you pay on the day).

You need to be very clear, before the bidding starts, about the price you are prepared to pay. Above all, don't let yourself be tempted into a bidding war: if the reserve price is fanciful and the property fails to sell, the owner will negotiate afterwards with the highest bidder. Also be sure that you really want this property – unless it has a serious fault which has not been disclosed in the contract, there is no cooling-off period when you buy at auction.

For most homes, the auction is usually held on-site, in the hope that the charms of the property will push bids up. If the auction is off-site, there is usually a reason (excessive traffic, perhaps, or factory noise), so visit the property at different times of the day and night, and try to keep its short-comings in mind when you bid.

Buying at auction can be a nail-biting experience. If you haven't been to an auction, go to a few before the day so that you are comfortable with the proceedings. And if you are not confident about the process, or you are very attached to the house and fear you might bid more than you can really afford, organise a trusted friend to bid for you. (It's a good idea to put any such arrangement on paper, to cover both of you.) Tell your proxy the price limit, then keep right out of the action.

Reducing the Costs of Buying

As well as trying to negotiate the purchase price down and shopping around for the best home-loan deal, there are a few ways to reduce the cost of buying.

Buying at the right time is, of course, a bonus. Although it is not always possible, try to buy when the market is down owing to either economic or seasonal factors: as an example, prices for properties on the coast may vary considerably between seasons. If you buy in a down market, not only are you in a better position to haggle over the price but every dollar saved there can be doubly saved on associated costs such as stamp duty and legal fees as these are often calculated as a percentage of the purchase price.

If you happen to be a first-home buyer, there are a couple of concessions you can take advantage of. These may include deferred payment of stamp duty on the contract, or (depending on your income) a discount of up to 30 per cent for stamp duty paid up-front. Contact the Real Estate Institute in your state for further details.

If you're already a home-owner and you've sold your existing property in order to purchase the new one, try to co-ordinate the exchange to your best advantage. Depending on your circumstances, you may wish to or-ganise things so that settlement of both properties occurs on the same day.

Finally, when the house is yours and you come to insure it – shop around for the best policy at the best price: see page 175 for some tips.

WAYS OF BUYING

Sale by private treaty simply means the property is offered through a real-estate agent. As agents receive a commission on the price obtained for the house, they are usually keen to sell its merits and minimise its faults. For the same reason, an agent can be used to your advantage: if the vendor is unrealistic about the value of the property, the agent can often talk them round. Buying through an agent also has the benefit of keeping you and the vendor at arm's length, which is particularly helpful in cases where there is a forced sale.

A **private sale** means that the owner is organising the sale, usually as a means of saving on an agent's fees. This could give you some room to negotiate the price. (On the other hand, in the absence of professional advice the owner may ask a fanciful price.) Do your homework to ascertain if the price is realistic; ask local agents for a report on sales of similar local homes over the last year, or look for publications which detail the results of home sales area by area (you may have to pay a small fee for this service).

When you have come to an agreement with the vendor, have a solicitor draw up a contract and make sure you fully understand it before signing. You may be able to negotiate for the seller to pay the cost of drawing up the contract; if not, at least share the costs. With a private sale, 'gazumping' (which means that someone else's later and higher bid is accepted over yours) is not unknown. In some states 'gazumping' is outlawed – check with the Real Estate Institute in your state.

Sale by auction puts you in a good bargaining position, because the vendor faces further expense if the house fails to sell on the day. For some tips about buying at auction, see page 171.

Bridging Finance

If, as sometimes happens, you find and buy the home you want before you sell your old one, you may need a short-term loan (known as bridging finance). In such cases the repayments meet the interest only and the principal must be repaid at the end of the term. Bridging finance is available from most of the large financial institutions who offer home loans: the interest rates on this kind of loan are usually high, so it's worth avoiding if possible. If you have no choice, it's worth shopping around for the best rate, as there can be a large difference between the terms offered by different providers. Also take out the loan for the shortest term possible, and ask if there will be any increases in the cost of the loan after a particular period (e.g. three months) or if you require the loan for longer than you expected.

IT'S YOURS! NOW FOR THE PAPERWORK

You've paid the deposit and the loan has been approved. What happens next?

Conveyancing

This is the general term for the legal paperwork associated with the transfer of property from one owner to another, such as making sure that all the proper searches are done and that the lender's requirements are met. You can use a solicitor or a licensed conveyancer to do this work on your behalf, for which service you pay a fee plus associated costs. There is a government schedule of fees (which varies between states) based on the value of the property, but as there is quite a bit of competition it's definitely worth shopping around for the best price. For conveyancers, see 'Conveyancing Services' in the Yellow Pages: it is advisable to only use a conveyancing company which has professional indemnity insurance.

You can do the conveyancing yourself, and this is the cheapest method, but you are responsible for any mistakes and you don't have the security of professional indemnity. DIY kits are available (for around $125) from specialist stationers.

Settlement

The exchange of contracts (called 'settlement') on homes usually occurs four to eight weeks after the sale, though you can negotiate a longer period.

Because of the time lapse, it's a good idea to check the condition of the property before you pay the balance of the purchase price, particularly if the property has tenants. You can also exchange contracts via the real-estate agent, which may be attractive if you want to effect a speedy deal. The balance of the purchase price is paid directly to the vendor by the lender, and you don't have to attend settlement unless you are doing the conveyancing work yourself.

What Happens to Your Deposit?
Between the time you lodge the deposit (usually 10 per cent of the purchase price) and pay the balance, there is the question of what should be done with your deposit. If the house is sold through a real-estate agent, the deposit is usually placed in the agent's trust account and no interest is earned. If it is a private sale, the deposit is often placed with the seller's solicitor and again no interest is usually paid. Both parties can agree to invest the deposit somewhere where it will earn interest – such as a cash-management account – in which case they usually split the interest. This may be the best option where the deposit is large and at times when interest rates are high; if you do so, make sure that both your signatures are required for the money to be withdrawn. The Home Purchase Advisory Service advises against releasing the deposit directly to the seller.

And Now It's Yours, Insure It!

Your home is a big investment, so it pays to protect it with insurance. As a home-owner, there are two kinds of policies you are likely to need – cover for the *building* (also called home insurance) and cover for its *contents*. If you have a mortgage on the property, building insurance is mandatory (unless it's a strata property, in which case the insurance is paid by the body corporate). If yours is a strata property, make sure you have a Certificate of Currency confirming the level of cover, to make sure the property is adequately insured: the lender will want to see details and proof of this on or before settlement.

The responsibility for insurance differs from state to state. In some states the buyer is responsible for the property from the date the contract is signed and you should therefore take out insurance at that point. Elsewhere (in New South Wales, for example), the vendor is usually responsible until the settlement date, after which insurance is the buyer's responsibility.

Whether or not you take out contents insurance is your decision, but as it also covers fixtures such as carpets it goes some way towards protecting your new asset. Insurance companies offer both types of cover, often as a package, or you can ask an insurance broker to source the best policy for your circumstances.

Is Not Being Insured Worth the Risk?

Most people hate forking out for insurance premiums. A survey taken just before the disastrous New South Wales bushfires in 1994 showed that a third of homes in the state were not insured, and that a significant portion of the rest were under-insured. The bushfires graphically showed the hardships faced by people who under-insure, yet for many of us the 'I can't afford it and I'll take the risk' philosophy is hard to shake.

Putting a Premium on It

While the policies offered by insurance companies are generally similar, the premiums can vary significantly as they are based on the risk factor and how much the company wants this type of business. But no matter which company you choose, the cost of your cover will depend to a large extent on where you live, as some areas are 'riskier' than others. This is particularly relevant for contents insurance, because the majority of claims are for theft – so if you live in an area with a high crime rate you can expect to pay more. You'll also pay more if you've made similar insurance claims in the past.

Other than risk, there are several factors that affect the cost of insurance cover. With contents insurance, you can choose between a 'new for old' policy (also known as 'R and R', for reinstatement and replacement), which replaces your lost possession(s) with a brand-new equivalent, or an 'indemnity' policy which deducts money for wear and tear in the event of a payout on items over a certain age. Despite the extra cost, most people go for the 'new for old' option, and with good reason, but even here some items (like clothing, videos, and fitted carpets) over a certain age will only be covered for the depreciated value. The insurer may have the right to replace the item rather than pay you the money, so check the policy carefully.

You can arrange cover for just about anything and anywhere – lost keys, perished food in the freezer, injury to someone in your home, or temporary accommodation should your home be uninhabitable. In general, the more comprehensive the policy, the higher the premium.

The other issue which will affect your premium is the 'excess'. Most companies allow you to choose, within a range, how much you'll pay out of your own pocket should you make a claim. The excess amount you choose should be a direct reflection of the value of the goods: if an item isn't worth much, there's no point having to pay $350 excess and then lose your 15 per cent no-claim bonus next year.

With all contents policies, it's important to know exactly what and whose possessions are covered, and also where they are covered. Valuables not listed separately on the policy may only be covered to a certain amount, for example, and de-facto partners' possessions may not be covered unless their presence is noted on the policy. Also, some of your possessions, such as jewellery, and computer and sports equipment, may have only limited cover outside the home ('portable' cover isn't cheap, and can add on up to 3 per cent of the value of the specified item a year).

Building insurance usually covers the residence, and associated structures and fixtures against a list of defined events such as fire, rain and earthquake. There are policies which cover all damage (with some specific exclusions), and these are more expensive. The Insurance Act prescribes a 'standard' level of cover, but insurers are free to offer more or less cover as long as they inform you. As with contents insurance, always query any aspect of the policy you're not sure about.

How Much Cover?

Nothing is easier than to under-estimate the amount of cover you need – and nothing is more painful should you have to make a claim. Also, many policies have an 'average' clause which kicks into action if you are under-insured by more than 20 per cent, in which case they can scale down the amount you receive. It's therefore wise to check your cover amount every year, and add to the policy any new valuables or structural improvements.

Contents insurance is best determined by walking from room to room in your house, noting what's there. If you have a 'new for old' policy, check the value of the equivalent new model of major items. If you own works of art, antiques, jewellery or other valuables which need to be noted separately, make sure you have a recent valuation to attach to the policy – and while you're about it, photograph or video them and leave the film with a friend for safe-keeping.

The level of your building cover should equal the cost of rebuilding your home to its present standard, and this includes all associated costs (for having debris removed, drawing up plans, temporary accommodation if necessary, and so on). To work this out you should ask the insurer, as many companies produce tables of building costs based on the type of construction and the floor area. But remember that this will only be a guide, as your home may be worth more (or less). Alternatively, you could consult an architect, builder or property valuer (listed under 'Valuers – Real Estate' in the Yellow Pages).

Saving Money When You Buy Insurance

Insurance is one area where you can save a lot of money if you are prepared to do some legwork. There are ways to lessen the size of the premium without skimping in the amount of cover.

As the premiums on similar policies from different insurers can vary greatly, the first golden rule is to shop around. Before you start ringing around, make sure you are comparing apples with apples by defining the type and amount of cover you want.

There are also a few bargaining chips you can throw on the table to sweeten the deal and reduce the premiums. Putting all your insurance with one company, installing a smoke alarm, burglar alarm, window locks or other security devices, and having an active Neighbourhood Watch will all help induce the insurer to offer discounts on your premium. Many companies also have better deals for the over-55s.

SELLING WELL

If the time comes when you want or need to sell your home, there are a few ways to improve your chances of getting the best possible price. Of course, the procedures for buying and selling a house have many similarities, particularly when it comes to the legal paperwork involved, but as a vendor you have a few extra things to consider.

The Three Ps: Presentation, Presentation, Presentation

When selling, it's not a bad idea to think like a prospective buyer and take an objective look at your home. First impressions are important, so once you've decided to put your home on the market cast an eye around and see if there are any improvements you could make: tidy up thoroughly inside and outside, fix the leaking roof, and touch-up any cracks and tired paintwork. At the same time, it's rarely worth redecorating on a major scale – after all, prospective buyers may not share your taste.

Using and Choosing an Agent

As a seller, you are probably best advised to use a professional to do the work for you. After all, real-estate agents know the market and they have greater access than you do to a wide range of possible buyers. In most cases it's best to use one agent only, as it's in their interest to sell the property; if they are competing with other agents, and may or may not make the sale and get the commission on it, they're likely to treat you as a lower priority. Large agencies with offices in more than one suburb or region will, of course, give you the greatest exposure.

When looking for an agent, do your homework. Ask around and read the papers to get an idea of the agents with the highest profile (and highest sale results) in your area. Contact several agents and ask them what they think is an appropriate asking price. If their opinions vary dramatically, don't necessarily go for the one who cites the highest figure: they should be able to verify the estimate with sales figures for comparable local properties. It's also important that you are comfortable with the agent and his or her style.

Unless you feel strongly one way or the other, be guided by the agent as to whether you sell privately or by auction. And if you sell by auction, ask the agent's advice on whether to hold the auction on-site or elsewhere, as they are probably the best objective judge of the charms (or shortcomings) of your home. In general an auction is likely to get you the best price, as interested buyers (and you only need two) are likely to bid each other up. Experienced sellers suggest that once you have decided on a reserve price (the minimum price you'll sell for) you should keep this to yourself until the auction is well under way, as the agent may otherwise 'stop trying' once the bidding reaches that figure.

The Costs of Selling

If you use an agent, you will pay them a commission on the sale (typically around 2.5 per cent on the first $100 000 and reducing on a sliding scale thereafter). You may be able to negotiate who pays the advertising costs.

You should also budget for any repairs and/or facelifts you and the agent consider necessary – but don't invest too much if it's unlikely to make more than a few thousand dollars' difference to the price you get.

In addition, if you are selling one home and buying another, you will also be up for stamp duty and conveyancing fees (see page 168) and extras such as removal costs. All this, particularly if you are 'trading up', can make quite a dent in your budget, which is why it's preferable to sell your old home first so that you know what you've got to spend on the next one.

WHEN YOU NEED TO BUY A CAR

'WE LIVE IN A MIXED-UP WORLD.

NOW A CAR IS THE NECESSITY AND

WALKING IS THE LUXURY.'

— MONTA CRANE

After a home, a car is the second most expensive purchase you are likely to make – and just like a home it keeps on costing you. Add to this the fact that a car is a depreciating asset – the moment you drive a new car from the showroom, its value can reduce by nearly a third – and you'll realise that it's worthwhile making sure you buy well. And as cars do depreciate so much, ask yourself whether you really need to buy one or whether you could use the money elsewhere, perhaps to pay more off your home loan. The answer is obvious: if you can do without a car, don't buy one.

Try to buy the cheapest safe car your ego can bear

But if you don't feel the alternatives (walking, public transport, taxis, cycling, or a car pool) are realistic, at least try to buy the cheapest and cheapest-running safe car your ego can bear. If you must have a new car, you can reduce the amount of instant depreciation by purchasing a demonstration model or superseded model (though, of course, you'll still be up for stamp duty). On balance, a secondhand car that's two or three years old may be the best bet in both financial and safety terms.

Raising the Finance

If you need to borrow money to buy a car, it's wiser to organise the finance before you start looking, so that you know exactly how much you can afford. Knowing the limit (and your repayment amounts) also means you won't be tempted to spend beyond your means.

If the car is for business use, remember that you may be able to claim your interest repayments and depreciation costs as a tax deduction. We discuss financing your car through your salary package in the section 'You've Got the Job!' earlier in this chapter.

Don't Forget the Additional Costs

The hidden extras can total hundreds or even thousands of dollars, depending on the price of your car.

▲ New cars: stamp duty, registration, insurance, delivery charge (negotiable). If a dealer quotes a drive-away price, these charges are included.
▲ Used cars: stamp duty, registration transfer fee, insurance.

Increasing Your Mortgage

Tacking your car loan onto the back of an existing home loan can be a relatively cheap way of financing a car. The interest rate is likely to be lower

---

GOLDEN RULES WHEN BORROWING FOR A CAR

- Always finance the car at the lowest possible interest rate for the shortest period of time.
- Shop around for the best rates and terms. Always ask what the annual interest rate and the repayments are, as this helps you to compare costs on an equal basis.
- The more you can save, the less you need to borrow – and thus the lower your overall costs. The one exception is if you're in business and can claim these expenses as a tax deduction.
- As with any large purchase, the interest you have to pay on the loan will add to the total cost, so look carefully at the options available. The ins and outs of different loans are covered in more detail in the section 'When You Want to Borrow' in Chapter 2.

---

than for a personal loan and your track record with the bank may speed up the process. If you are merely using equity you have built up in your home, you may not have to pay further fees and charges. If, on the other hand, you increase the amount of the initial mortgage, you may be up for additional stamp duty.

As with anything you finance through your mortgage, set a reasonable time limit for paying back the loan: work out what you'll need to pay each week and stick to it. Borrowing $30 000 for a car and then taking twenty-five years to pay it back is no bargain.

Personal Loans
You can pre-arrange finance from a bank, credit union or building society and draw this as a personal loan once you have chosen the car and negotiated the deal. But bear in mind that personal loans offer less flexibility than drawing on your mortgage or using an overdraft, as the repayment period is usually fixed.

As with any borrowings, ask whether the loan will be secured or not.

With a secured loan the loan is guaranteed ('secured') by the asset you are borrowing for, and the lender has the right to repossess the goods should you default. If your loan is secured, you may have to pay stamp duty to register the mortgage over the item, which adds to your costs

Obviously, it's wise to shop around for the best interest rate, but how the interest is calculated will also have a big impact: it's usually preferable to choose a variable rate (see the section 'When You Want to Borrow' in Chapter 2).

Consumer Finance

Consumer finance, formerly known as hire purchase, has tradit:onally been a popular means of financing a car because it is usually available through the dealer and the agreement can be finalised at the showroom. But do your sums carefully, as this type of loan can be relatively expensive.

When you finance a car in this way, you will be the owner but it is a secured loan and the lender thus has a legal interest in the car. If you default on your repayments, the lender can take legal action to recover the debt. If they wish to repossess goods, they *must* first give you one month's notice in writing that you are behind in your payments, and (if you have repaid more than 75 per cent of the loan) have an order from the Commerc:al Tribunal.

The repayments for this kind of loan are often expressed as a dollars-per-week figure, which can sound very affordable, especially if the time-frame is several years. This method can be helpful for budgeting purposes (although no more so than a personal loan), but offers little flexibility if ever you want to increase your payments. Also, you need to be clear about how much interest you will be paying over the full period. Some states require dealers to include the schedule of repayments in their advertisements. If this is not the case in your state, make sure you find out exactly what you'll be up for, which depends on the price of the car and on the repayment system.

Borrowing $30 000 for a car and then taking twenty-five years to pay it back is no bargain

Finance companies are the major providers of consumer finance, and often the car dealer is paid a commission for arranging the loan. This may increase the cost to you, so if you consider this option find out before you commit yourself. You can, of course, deal directly with a finance company yourself: if so, always include any fees, charges and commissions in your calculations and ask what the resulting 'effective' interest rate is. Also shop around on interest rates – they do vary, and you can negotiate.

Finance from a Motoring Organisation

Motoring organisations can offer competitive finance, so this is worth investigating. Also, if you are a long-term member or already have a loan with the organisation they may offer a further discount on interest rates.

Using Your Credit Card

If you only require a small loan and are confident of repaying it quite quickly, putting the car purchase on your credit card may be an option. And with the rewards schemes now attached to credit cards, you could earn significant points. If you have the cash, you may be able to deposit it against the card (in fact you may be asked to do so by the credit-card company) and still pick up the points.

Q *I am considering leasing a car instead of buying it. Is this a good idea?*

A The main advantage with leasing is that you don't need money up-front for a deposit (and if the car is a lemon you can usually just hand the keys back at the end of the term!). Also the lease payments are tax-deductible if you use the car for business – but then so are financing costs and depreciation if you buy rather than lease. If, however, you need to quit the lease for any reason you may find that you have not paid much off the loan principal and still have to pay the difference. Also, if you choose to pay out the residual when the lease expires and then sell the car, any profit you make could be taxable. All in all, if the car is mainly for private use and you have a reasonable sum saved for a deposit, buying is the better option. If you do consider leasing, discuss the arrangements with an accountant.

DO'S AND DON'TS WHEN BUYING A CAR

- *Do* thoroughly research the make and model you want.
- *Do* check that the chassis number matches the one on the registration papers.
- *Do* contact the Register of Vehicles in your state to make sure the car isn't stolen or still has money owing on it.
- *Do* organise a mechanical inspection by a professional (e.g. your motoring organisation) before you buy. Test-drive the car for twenty minutes or so, and try out all the accessories.
- *Do* be aware of tricks of the trade, such as a paint touch-up hiding crash damage, or an unusually low kilometre reading which could signal that the clock has been turned back.
- *Do* check what the warranty covers, if you're offered one: some cover parts but not labour costs, which are often expensive. Be particularly careful if you're paying for a warranty (extended or otherwise), as you may be paying a lot for very little.
- *Don't* be afraid to negotiate. Sellers usually ask a higher price than they expect, so offer 20 per cent less than the asking price and they may meet you half-way.
- *Don't* fall for the 'bait and switch' ruse. This is when the advertised car is of lesser quality than you expected and the dealer shows you another which is in better condition – and, of course, it's more expensive.
- *Do* consider the resale value of the car with a view to minimising your depreciation losses.
- *Don't* overlook running costs. Ask the price of a typical 'basket of parts' for the car, including oil, air and fuel filters and brake pads, and also find out the cost of a typical service. If the car is second-hand, ask for log-books or copies of receipts of any mechanical work which has been done.

WHERE TO BUY A CAR

You can buy a car from a dealer, privately, or at an auction or car market. Which approach you choose really depends on your knowledge about cars, and the sort of car you are buying.

Buying Through a Dealer

Shopping around is essential, even if you're buying a new car, as dealers are always prepared to negotiate, especially if you are paying with cash. If you are buying a used car, expect to pay more to a dealer than you would privately or at auction, but this may be offset by better legal protection, including a warranty. You're not in any way bound to accept dealer finance or insurance offers as part of the package.

Buying Privately

Buying a car privately is usually cheaper and there's more scope for negotiation, but you don't enjoy as much consumer protection. The bottom line is 'Buyer beware': before you buy, arrange for an expert mechanical inspection and make basic checks to establish the authenticity of the vehicle. In some states a road-worthiness certificate must be provided by the vendor, so check with the motoring organisation in your state.

Buying at Auction

Auctions are a wholesale market, so the going prices are generally cheaper than you'll get through a dealer, and may or may not be cheaper than buying privately. There are regulations governing auctions, so you will have some protection, but judging the mechanical condition of the vehicle is difficult as you may not get the chance for a test-drive. Again it's advisable to thoroughly research any vehicle you are interested in, or take along someone who has a good knowledge of cars. As the atmosphere at an auction makes it easier to get carried away, have a price limit firmly in your mind and if the car you want goes over that limit, let it go.

Buying at a Car Market

Car markets may have the merit of convenience, but again offer little in the way of consumer protection. So apply the same rules that you would for an auction or private sale, as you'll have little redress if you do buy a lemon.

SIGNING THE CONTRACT

Once you have agreed on the price of a brand-new car, you will be asked to sign an order form. This is a legally binding agreement and you should read it carefully before signing: make sure all the additional costs such as optional extras and on-road costs are listed clearly. Never sign a form which has not been completed, or which does not guarantee a delivery date.

Whether the car is a showroom model or a secondhand beauty, be very careful about leaving a deposit. If you can't avoid doing so, make sure you get something in writing stating that you will get the money back if the inspection report is not satisfactory.

INSURING YOUR CAR

Make sure your car is insured before you drive away: the chance of having an accident as you drive home is a chance not worth taking. Third-party insurance (covering injury to passengers, other drivers, and pedestrians) is compulsory and the cost is included in your motor-registration fee. Cover for damage to your own and other vehicles is optional: it pays to shop around for the best rates and to make sure you use an insurer you're confident will promptly and fairly settle any claims.

Some insurance companies recognise the statistics showing that young men (under the age of 24) are almost three times more likely than young women to be at fault in accidents, and have therefore waived the age excess for younger women drivers. It is worthwhile phoning around to check

MAKING MONEY WHEN YOU SELL

A few people are lucky (or smart) enough to make a profit when they sell their car. Most of us feel satisfied if we can just contain the amount of loss.

Some vehicles do hold their value more than others. Before you sell, check the going price for similar vehicles in newspaper ads or used-car

Ways to Reduce Your Insurance Premium

- Shop around: there will be a difference in basic premiums.
- The type of car you buy will affect the insurance rates (the more expensive or sporty the car, the higher the premium). Motoring organisations publish theft and insurance ratings.
- Limiting the number of people who drive the car – particularly younger, higher-risk drivers – will also reduce the premiums. Some companies have family schemes which reduce the excess usually payable to cover younger drivers.
- Consider a no-frills policy, as feature-laden ones may include a number of options you have little use for (e.g. overnight accommodation if you're away from home when you have an accident).
- Some companies will reduce the premium if you have an approved security alarm on the car. Others have 'gold customer' or 'safe driver' schemes, rewarding long-term, non-claiming customers with discounts on premiums. These could amount to substantial savings over time. If you consider yourself eligible for such a scheme, speak to the insurance company.

guides, or ring your motoring organisation. Selling the car yourself will probably get you the best price; selling through a car market also allows you to negotiate a reasonable price. A dealer, while convenient, will usually give you the lowest price, to allow for a mark-up when reselling.

Trading in your vehicle on a more expensive one will seem to improve the price, but it is usually a false economy, as it's unlikely to match what you could get by selling privately.

When you sell, you're unlikely to recover the cost of 'optional extras' on a new car, especially if these are only cosmetic: purchasers tend to value air-conditioning, and safety features such as ABS brakes, over design details like alloy wheels. At the same time, never under-estimate the value of a little spit and polish. It pays to keep your car in good mechanical and cosmetic condition over the period you own it.

GOING INTO BUSINESS

'WOMEN ARE GOING TO SPIN OUT OF THE LARGE CORPORATIONS AND ARE GOING TO INVENT NEW BUSINESSES... THEY'RE REINVENTING THE WAY WORK IS ORGANISED.'

— SUSAN OLIVER IN *GOOD WEEKEND*

Running a business is a dream for many of us. If you have a good idea and the persistence to keep going when the going gets tough, if you have the personality to be your own boss and are realistic about what it will mean financially and personally, there's no need to stay one of the dreamers. And if you decide to work for yourself, you'll be joining an increasing number of women who have made the same move.

Women, it is said (and not only by women!), have many of the qualities needed to run small businesses. We tend to plan thoroughly, we are mindful of risks before committing too much capital, and we tend to be realistic about what we expect to gain. And funnily enough, these qualities are thought to result from women having relatively low self-confidence – a good case of a negative being turned into a positive.

Women go into business for many reasons. These seem to include a desire to be independent and the key decision-maker, flexibility to fit in with child-care and/or family commitments, a desire to capitalise on an idea or entrepreneurial flair, the 'glass-ceiling' syndrome, the appeal of forming a family business, or early retirement when an income is still needed.

THINKING IT THROUGH

If your business is successful, the rewards are obvious. But you need to consider whether you are prepared for the substantial commitment involved in running your own business – you could find yourself working seven days a week, with very little time off or flexibility. And, from the outset, be prepared for the fact that the business may not in the end provide the financial security you were seeking.

This section looks mainly at the things you need to think about when starting up a business. Once it's a going concern, there will be many more questions you need to ask, and the answers are beyond the scope of this book. Seek advice from the organisations and professionals mentioned in the following pages.

GETTING PROFESSIONAL

'TO SURVIVE AND PROSPER IN BUSINESS

YOU NEED THREE ACCOMPLICES: A GOOD

ACCOUNTANT, A GOOD SOLICITOR AND

A GOOD BANK MANAGER.'

— ANON.

If you're ready to go into business for yourself, you will certainly need good advice, but more than this you'll need a good attitude. Above all this means being professional. So many people start with high hopes and end with dreams of dust because they didn't quite make the leap from amateur to professional. For a professional, near enough isn't good enough, excellent customer service is a byword, and you never forget you're in it to make money. You also need to recognise that there will be good times and bad, and plan accordingly.

▲ **Do your homework.** Get to know thoroughly your market, your competition and your product or service. Also, do as much research as possible on how to operate a business: attend workshops and seminars, and contact the small-business advisory association in your area for information.

▲ **Prepare a business plan** (see page 201 for some suggestions) setting out how and where the business will operate, the equipment and supplies required and how much they will cost. This will be essential if you need to borrow money.

▲ **Make sure you have enough capital,** be it through using savings, borrowing, or taking a partner. (According to research, most female owners of small businesses start out very small, 40 per cent opening up shop with less than $5000 of capital.) Cash flow can be a real hurdle in the first year or two, and you need to be able to weather this period as well as have money to expand.

▲ **Purchase the right equipment:** you'll probably need at least a telephone, answering machine and fax, computer and photocopier, plus any specialist tools of your trade.

▲ **If you work at home,** keep regular office hours and a professional environment. Use properly designed stationery and business cards.

▲ **Recognise that time is money.** Use your time efficiently and recognise that chores like shopping or a dental check-up are 'time out' and should be accomplished, if possible, in non-working hours. On the other hand, don't beat yourself for not accomplishing the impossible. Keeping time sheets or day schedules will help you discover what is realistic.

▲ **Don't go too far too fast,** by moving into luxury offices or buying the most expensive gadgets in town before your business justifies it.

▲ **Be realistic about the need to take on staff,** and recognise the responsibilities that this entails (e.g. holiday pay, Workcare, superannuation, fringe-benefits tax).

▲ **Remain open to new ways of keeping costs under control and dealing professionally with suppliers.** If you're not confident about your financial expertise, take a course or get professional advice.

▲ **Never sign anything you don't understand,** never 'hope for the best' or take someone's word for it.

▲ **Never allow your business to jeopardise your other assets without deep consideration.** If you need a loan or an overdraft to expand your business, you will probably have to put up your home or other assets as collateral. Realise that the loss of your home may be a consequence of the business going sour, so don't hang onto a disastrous business venture past the point of no return.

Getting Help

'No business plans to fail — they simply fail to plan.'

— Anon.

Much about surviving and prospering in business will depend solely on your own will and wit, so don't be shy about seeking help where it's appropriate. In addition to legal and financial advice, there are other kinds of assistance you could consider.

First, find out about any professional or industry associations and networking groups relevant to your field, or you could consider starting your own. In New South Wales, the Office of Small Business runs a Women in Business Mentor Program which gives access to a mentor for fifty hours of help in any six-month period. This scheme has not yet been picked up by other states, but why not adopt your own mentor – someone you admire and who may have the time and expertise to be a sounding board? A retired businessperson may be a suitable candidate. In Victoria, the Victorian Women's Trust runs a networking group called the Women's Enterprise Connection which can be contacted on (03) 9670 3674.

Government Assistance

The government offers a range of services designed to promote and support small business. Contact your local Office of Small Business or the state Small Business Centre for a list of the workshops, grants and other assistance on offer. (Workshops include such topics as record-keeping and financial management, marketing, importing and exporting, and running a business from home.) The Office of Small Business can also refer you to suppliers and other professionals such as accountants and solicitors in your area.

If you are unemployed, a sole parent or a widow, and are receiving social-security benefits, the New Enterprise Incentive Scheme (NEIS) can help you set up your own business. If you meet the eligibility criteria (for example, the business should be a new enterprise and you must work full-time), they will provide training, business and income support for up to fifty-two weeks at the same rate as a Jobsearch Allowance.

WHAT TYPE OF BUSINESS WOULD SUIT YOU?

Although the industry you choose will reflect your taste and talent, you'll also have to give due consideration to the form of business which would best suit you.

Starting a New Business

Statistics show that women most commonly create a new business rather than buy an existing one. And whilst success stories abound – we've all heard about Poppy King, who with no formal training went into business at 19 developing her own range of lipsticks and three years later was turning over $8 million a year – if you choose to start up a new business you should weigh up the pros and cons carefully before you open up shop.

The Advantages

▲ You can start with a small capital outlay.
▲ There is no goodwill to pay for (and if you create your own goodwill, you can sell it later for a fortune!).
▲ You can build the business in line with your own ideas and aspirations.
▲ You may face less competition if your idea is original.

The Disadvantages

▲ You'll need to build up customers, supplies and possibly staff.

▲ If you have no previous experience in business, this can increase the chance of failure (60 – 70 per cent of businesses fail in the first three years).

▲ It may take a number of years of blood, sweat and tears before you show a profit.

▲ Loans are more difficult to obtain for a start-up business, and lenders often prefer you to have substantial financial input to illustrate your commitment to the venture.

Buying an Existing Business

Buying a going concern can be one of the easiest ways to get started in business. But you should still do your homework.

Above all, try to find out if there is a genuine reason for the sale: if the seller has nothing to hide, he or she may be prepared for you to trial the business for a couple of weeks before you commit yourself. Speak to other business-owners about the pattern of customers' purchases: Are they seasonal? Are they based on the state of the economy? Beware of tricks a seller may use to inflate the value of the business, such as stacking the till with personal cash. To prevent this, have an accountant analyse the books going back over a period of time. And last but not least, do seek professional advice, particularly before signing a contract.

The Advantages

▲ You have more chance of success, because the business is already a going concern.

▲ Stock, equipment and lines of credit with suppliers are established.

▲ You should receive immediate income from existing customers.

▲ Obtaining finance is easier because the business has a track record.

▲ You gain valuable experience and knowledge from existing employees.

▲ You can improve and develop the business according to your own ideas.

The Disadvantages

▲ You pay a premium for goodwill.

▲ There may be a reason for selling which is not immediately apparent (for example, the stock may be unsaleable or the equipment obsolete).

▲ The recent results of the business may not be be a true reflection of its longer-term history.

Buying a Franchise

Franchising is one of the fastest-growing areas of business in Australia. Some 4000 franchise outlets opened in Australia in 1995, and this field is expected to account for half of our gross national product by 2020.

When you buy a franchise you are purchasing the right to sell, distribute or market the owner's product or service: examples range from retail outlets such as McDonalds, Pizza Hut and The Body Shop to services such as lawn-mowing runs. The cost of buying in can range from a few thousand dollars to half a million or more. As with any existing business, do seek professional advice, particularly before signing a contract.

The Advantages

▲ You may require little business experience, as training is usually provided.
▲ It's easier to obtain finance because the business has an established name.
▲ You receive continuing assistance in marketing and developing products.
▲ You benefit from the goodwill attached to an established brand name.
▲ Your costs can be reduced through bulk purchases and group discounts.

The Disadvantages

▲ The up-front financial commitment can be significant, which may strain your resources.
▲ You have to pay a share of your profits to the franchisor.
▲ The franchisor determines the procedures and standards for running the business, so there's little scope to introduce your own initiatives.
▲ You pay the price if the franchisor makes a bad decision in marketing or managing the business.
▲ You are very reliant on the promises made by the franchisor.

Multi-level Marketing

Multi-level marketing means you become part of a network, which usually involves either buying stock to sell or placing orders for products on behalf of yourself or clients. In exchange you receive a discount on any purchases you make, and/or receive a percentage of the profit made on your sales. This system is more commonly known as 'network marketing' or 'party plan': the best-known examples are Tupperware, Amway and Nutrimetics.

You may alienate friends and family if you rely on them to buy products

Some people cringe when multi-level marketing is mentioned. This is probably because some companies have developed a reputation for training their salespeople to use high-pressure techniques to recruit new members or sell the products. But for everyone who has a bad experience, there's another who swears by the system.

Multi-level marketing is particularly suited to those who want to be self-employed and work part-time. The financial rewards increase if you sign up additional people to join your sales team and as a result move higher up the network. The financial rewards come as you reap the commissions paid on sales made by those you recruit.

The Advantages
▲ You need little or no capital to get started.
▲ There is a low risk of losing money, and you have low overheads.
▲ As the business is home-based, it offers both flexibility and mobility.
▲ The marketing company develops the products and provides all marketing material.
▲ You can increase your sales team without incurring the costs associated with hiring staff.

The Disadvantages
▲ You may alienate friends and family if you rely on them to buy products.
▲ It can take some time to establish a client base, which in turn may make it difficult to establish the business as your primary source of income.
▲ Sales presentations are usually held at a time to suit others, which is likely to involve you in evening and weekend work.

Which Business Structure?

Before you launch into any business, you should also give careful consideration to which business structure might best suit your particular needs. This decision should be based on tax and liability considerations, and the costs involved: seek advice from an accountant or solicitor. The three most common business structures are outlined below.

Sole Trader

If you set up a business on your own without any formal arrangements, and without a partner, you are classified as a sole trader. This is a simple and inexpensive structure. However, you carry full responsibility for the business and any debts incurred, which means that your personal assets (including your home) can be sold to meet any debts.

The Tax Considerations

As a sole trader you pay tax at your personal rate, which may be higher than the company rate of 36 per cent. Also, if you make a profit you may have to pay provisional tax, which means that you pay tax in advance to cover the following year's anticipated earnings – this can be a real killer if you haven't planned for it.

Q *I started business as a sole trader six months ago and my income is uncertain. What is the best way to provide for my tax?*

A If you're self-employed and don't have tax deducted from your pay, you may be liable for provisional tax (where you pay tax not only for the current year but also for the following one) if you make a profit over the year. It's advisable to discuss the tax implications of your business with an accountant to get an idea of how much you may have to pay, and open an account (perhaps a cash-management account or a redraw facility on your mortgage) into which you put 30–50 per cent of your earnings regularly throughout the year. It's important to do this, as if you owe less than $8000 in tax you may not have to pay it for quite a few months and it's all too easy to lose track and eventually find yourself caught short. If you owe more than $8000, you have to pay it in quarterly instalments throughout the year. If you believe your earnings will be less in the coming year, you can apply for a variation of the tax you're deemed to owe; but if you under-estimate by more than 15 per cent you will have to pay additional tax as a penalty.

Partnership

A business partnership is another simple and inexpensive structure, as it can also be set up without any formal arrangements. Any profit or loss is shared equally amongst the partners, but at the same time you are liable not only for your own actions but also those of any partners. Partnerships are notorious for becoming unworkable, and ruining family relationships and friendships – so enter any such arrangement with due caution.

▲ A formal agreement between partners is advisable: it should document the amount of time and money each partner will put into the business, split the equity of the business accordingly, and formalise arrangements in the event of the departure of one of the partners. Seek advice from a solicitor.

▲ Agree upon authorised signatories for company cheques (this could pre-empt misuse of funds).

▲ Choose your partners carefully – being great friends (or lovers) is no indication that your relationship will work in business.

Being great friends (or lovers) is no indication that your relationship will work in business

The Tax Considerations

One advantage of this structure is that tax can be minimised, particularly where members of the same family are included in the partnership. However, the Tax Office requires that all partners have 'real and effective' control over the assets and liabilities of the partnership.

Limited Company

This business structure is the most complex of the three, and the most expensive to set up and maintain. The advantages are that the liabilities of the shareholders are limited to the amount of capital they have invested in the business, and that additional cash can be raised for the company by issuing shares. Also, the business name continues after the departure or death of the original owners and management.

The disadvantages are that costs of complying with relevant legislation (in areas such as workers compensation) can be significant. Also, there can be enormous legal obligations, as directors are becoming increasingly liable for their actions. Directors of small companies may also be asked to provide personal guarantees when borrowing money for the business.

The Tax Considerations

This business structure has a tax advantage where the shareholders' tax rate is higher than the company rate of 36 per cent. This is because any earnings within the company are taxed at a lower rate until dividends are distributed, and if company tax has been paid the dividends will be 'franked' (tax-paid) to shareholders (this system is discussed in more detail in the section 'Investing in Shares' in Chapter 3). One warning, though: any losses remain within the company structure, and while they can be carried forward to offset future income they cannot be used by shareholders to offset their other income.

The Tax Office takes a dim view of people setting up a company solely to minimise their tax, and there are fairly strict criteria involved, so it's definitely advisable to discuss all the issues with an accountant or solicitor.

Trusts

The advantage of operating your business through a trust is that it enables you to distribute income amongst members of your family. The other side of the coin is that trusts can be complicated to set up and administer, and family disputes over allocation of profits are not uncommon. Family trusts are dealt with in more detail in the section 'Marriage and De-facto Partnerships' in Chapter 5.

GETTING FINANCE FOR A BUSINESS

This used to be the most heartbreaking and humiliating hurdle for women going into business. We've all heard stories of plucky businesswomen being denied finance or, worse, being asked if a man was going guarantor. Those days, mercifully, are long gone, thanks largely to the proven success of women in business in recent decades.

One option is to use your own equity and money from investors. This means you won't have to pay interest on a loan, but of course the shareholders will have a right to a proportion of any profit your business makes (and similarly, will have obligations as far as any losses are concerned).

Borrowing Funds

There are many possible sources of loan finance, most of which are covered in detail in Chapter 2. These include bank overdrafts, fixed-term loans and personal loans. Debtor finance (or factoring) is also an option for short-term finance: here a finance company provides a cash advance on the basis of sales already made and you repay the loan when your invoices are paid. Leasing is a further alternative for medium-term finance: the financer purchases the equipment you require and then leases it back to you; at the end of the lease term you can purchase the equipment at an agreed residual value.

It is worth investigating whether your potential lending institution has a business section, as lenders experienced in this area will be better equipped to understand your needs.

As with any loan, shop around to find the best terms and interest rates, bearing in mind the needs of your business and the timing of the finance required. The lender will probably want to see your business plan, and evidence of your credit rating, net worth and professional expertise. They may require some security over the loan. It helps if you have a letter from your accountant or are already a customer of the institution.

BUSINESS PLANS AND OTHER SCARY MONSTERS

You've got a great business idea, but now your bank manager wants to see your business plan. You've never done one before, and you freeze. But they aren't really that scary once you've done one.

The point of a business plan is to show potential backers, lenders or partners that you really understand your business and its potential. After you've drafted your plan, get someone you trust to evaluate it. How easy is it to read and understand? After all, if you lose your test audience, you'll probably lose the bank manager.

A Business Plan: What to Include

1   Contents Page

2   Executive Summary
Put this at the front, but prepare it last. It summarises your plan and what you hope to achieve. Keep it to less than one page.

3   Business Objectives
Describe what your business does and how you plan to achieve this.

4   Product or Service Profile
Describe in detail what your business offers. If any specialist equipment or machinery is needed, include it here.

5   Marketing Plan
Detail your marketing strategies and sales projections. Include information about the market you are entering (historical trends, the segment you are aiming for and its growth potential) and your competitors.

6   Organisational Plan
Detail the structure of your business, including the responsibilities of the main office-holders. If possible, list existing and planned staff, and their areas of expertise.

7   Financial Plan
Include a detailed plan for the short (one to two years) and longer (three or more years) terms, including projected cash flows. Be conservative about any projections. If possible, include a detailed profit-and-loss statement and balance sheet: consider consulting an accountant or book-keeper.

8 FINANCIAL REPORTING
Outline the accounting procedures you will follow (i.e. quarterly reports or yearly balance sheets prepared by a professional accountant or auditor).

9 LOAN REPAYMENT DETAILS
Show how and when you can repay any loans. Indicate how the regular repayments will reduce the principal, and include any expected lump payments which could be put against the loan. Detail any assets you plan to use as security, and include any encumbrances such as mortgages and recent valuations (remember that the financial institution will value property conservatively).

10 PERSONAL FINANCES
List your personal assets, liabilities and income.

DO YOU WORK FROM HOME OR LEASE PREMISES?

There are some good tax reasons for working from home

For women with children, working from home can be a way to balance family commitments and income needs. You save on travelling time and have the flexibility to work when you like. Working from home also saves you having to commit yourself to a lease – which you might find difficult to pay if your business hits a rough patch. It must be an attractive option, because in 1994 around 43 per cent of women (compared with 23 per cent of men) had home-based businesses.

People who work from home say that the main drawbacks are the problem of self-motivation and the feelings of isolation. Certainly you have to be highly disciplined, and it's important to establish your working routine with the rest of the household so that they know you are not to be interrupted except in an emergency. To stave off feelings of isolation, you could consider networking or attending courses to improve your business skills, or meeting your clients at their premises. Also consider whether the layout of your house is suitable for your business needs and whether local zoning regulations might restrict your operation in any way.

How the Taxman Will View This

There are some good tax reasons for working from home. You can claim deductions for the proportion of services (electricity, phone/fax, etc.) which relate to business use, and you can claim depreciation costs on office furniture. Establishing an office at home also means that you can claim a proportion of your mortgage repayments as a business expense.

There is, of course, a catch, so do your sums carefully. If you have a room set aside exclusively as an office, you may forfeit some of the tax-free capital gain when you sell your home. It's worth getting advice from an accountant about this and other considerations.

For and Against Leasing Premises

Going to an outside office imposes a discipline on your work pattern, and removes you from the distractions found at home. Having business premises also promotes a more professional image. Leasing also makes it possible for you to sublet or share with others running complementary businesses. This gives you a social environment and the potential to pick up new work. And, of course, the costs associated with leasing and running business premises are entirely tax-deductible.

On the other hand, the cost and fixed term of a lease can be a problem if money is short. As lease contracts are complex, it's advisable to seek legal advice before signing.

MOVING ON

This chapter has looked at some of the situations we come across where our choices and decisions are largely financially based. The next chapter concentrates on some of the crucial events in life, which can have major financial implications even though money may not, on the face of things, seem to be a paramount consideration.

5

GETTING THE MOST OUT
OF LIFE'S EVENTS

This book is about getting your financial affairs in order – and keeping them that way. It's also about living your life the way you want to. But life is rarely a simple journey from A to B (let alone from A to Z): lots of things happen along the way which may affect the best-laid financial plans. So, in this chapter we look at the events – the highs and the lows – which tend to have the greatest impact on women and their finances.

Being married or in a de-facto relationship is a great chance to work together for what you both want. So what ways are there to make sure you do this, yet still maintain your financial independence? And if the worst happens and things go wrong, what are your rights and responsibilities, and how can you protect your interests in the event that the split is less than amicable?

There are lots of great books around on the joys of birth and motherhood, but few of them deal with the financial realities. What exactly will you be dipping into your wallet for, and when? And if you find yourself juggling motherhood and a career, what ways are there to save both money and your sanity?

Finally, a couple of inescapable realities. Fact One is that many women find themselves carrying the main responsibility for ageing parents or other relatives. Fact Two is that many people leave their financial affairs in less than perfect order when they die. So, what can you think about and do to lessen the grief for all concerned?

But – on with life! Hopefully, the suggestions which follow will help make sure you get the most out of the happy events, and get through the difficult ones, at the least possible cost.

MARRIAGE AND DE-FACTO PARTNERSHIPS

'IF THERE'S TROUBLE IN A HOME, IT ISN'T ALWAYS IN THE BEDROOM — IT'S QUITE OFTEN IN THE BUDGET.'

— SHIRLEY CONRAN

If you are in a relationship, you'll know how much strength you can draw from having two on the team. Working together to achieve your goals can also be very productive financially.

Of course, when you first become a couple there are also great adjustments to be made. You may have been used to having your own money to spend as you choose, but circumstances may dictate that your income becomes 'our' income; or you may find you have differing goals and spending patterns.

It is vital to understand each other's financial expectations

A 1996 marketing survey by *Family Circle* magazine revealed that more than a third of all domestic arguments are about money. Yet, while today we don't mind asking our partners about their sexual history and insisting on safe sex practices, many people are still wary of discussing money. Why is this? Do we assume true love will find a way? Will our partners think we don't trust them? Are our attitudes so disparate that we are scared we won't find any common ground?

It really is vital that you understand each other's financial expectations and keep those communication lines open.

You're in This Together

You'll already know quite a bit about your partner's attitude to money. But don't assume anything: discuss your money habits. Many couples find that it strengthens their relationship if financial issues are dealt with openly and fair solutions are agreed to before they become a source of friction. And it's important to establish these financial ground rules as early as possible.

Having different money styles is a common point of difference in relationships, so try to focus on your mutual goals. It may be a useful exercise for both of you to write down your financial goals (personal and collective), and see how they compare. Are you both saving for different things? Does he like to spend and you like to save? By talking things through, you should be able to agree on some common goals, and even come up with a financial plan.

You should, in other words, treat your financial relationship a little like a partnership in a small business. Make sure you always understand what is going on financially, and this includes knowing your partner's assets and debts: a good way to keep informed is to prepare your tax returns together. And try to make all financial decisions jointly, regardless of which one of you is the major breadwinner. Don't fall into the trap of believing that if you earn less, or nothing at all, you're not making any contribution.

BUT DON'T LOSE YOUR INDEPENDENCE

This sounds like a contradiction of the comments above, but it's not. While as a couple you will have joint goals that you want to work towards together, you should both retain a measure of financial freedom.

First up, work out an amount which you can each keep for your own personal use. It's prudent to have your own bank and/or credit-card account: this will give you access to funds at all times and allow you to build up your own credit history, which could be vital should you ever need to apply for a loan in your own right.

WIN / WIN MONEY MANAGEMENT

Even when your relationship is thriving, there are a few basic things you can do to keep the financial side of things on an even keel.

▲ Set limits on the amount of money that can be drawn from joint accounts without both your signatures.

▲ Agree on the credit limit available for your credit cards.

▲ Make investment decisions jointly. Think twice about having joint investments in one partner's name: this leaves the other with little evidence of their financial contribution through the years, should the relationship end less than amicably.

▲ Keep records and receipts (it's good practice in any event).

▲ Keep an up-to-date list of your assets and liabilities, both joint and individual. This is important should something happen to either of you, or you need to access the information quickly.

▲ Always read carefully anything you are asked to sign, including agreements to act as a partner's agent, to be a guarantor, to appoint a power of attorney, or to be a co-borrower.

▲ Think carefully before putting inherited money or property, or assets gained prior to marriage, in a joint account. In the event of problems in the relationship, these assets could be in dispute.

SHOULD YOU HAVE A MARRIAGE CONTRACT?

While 65 per cent of Australian marriages remain happily intact, some 35 per cent end in divorce. So perhaps a financial agreement to complement your vows may not be a bad thing. Bear in mind, though, that while such agreements are on the increase they may not be binding in court.

Whether binding or not, such contracts can be a good way to establish some financial ground rules on a more formal basis. If you go this way, take care that the agreement is as fair as you can make it, and that there is some mechanism for review should circumstances change. Don't sign away established rights such as the inheritance of property in the event of your partner's death, or an equal distribution of assets if you divorce.

A MARRIAGE CONTRACT: WHAT TO INCLUDE

- The assets and liabilities each partner brings to the marriage.
- How you will split household expenses, including day-to-day bills and any loan repayments.
- For any joint assets, who will receive what proportion when they are sold.
- What financial responsibility you will have to each other for your separate assets and liabilities.
- How you will rearrange your finances if your circumstances change (for example, giving up work for the birth of a child, caring for a parent, illness).
- What will happen in the event of a break-up, with regard both to assets and the financial support of any children.
- An agreed process for terminating the marriage contract.

Marriage agreements are useful if:

▲ one of you has money and assets you wish to protect

▲ one of you has children from a former relationship, whom you wish to benefit or protect

▲ you are joint shareholders or partners in a business

▲ one of you expects to inherit substantial amounts of money from a relative

While such agreements are most commonly drawn up before marriage, it's perfectly possible to introduce one after you are married. These post-nuptial agreements are often harder to negotiate, though, because they are usually instigated only when one partner feels there is a circumstantial change in the offing (such as inheriting money, embarking on a business, or trouble in the relationship).

MAXIMISING YOUR JOINT FINANCES

There are quite a few ways in which being a couple can be financially bene-ficial. And, of course, working as a team can help you reach your financial goals much quicker.

Sharing Day-to-day Living Costs

There's an old adage that two can live as cheaply as one. While this is not completely accurate, when you move in together you'll undoubtedly find yourself better off financially, as many of your daily living expenses (for example, rent or mortgage, electricity and food bills) are shared. Couples also tend to spend less on going out than single people do.

Once you have drawn up a budget, you can divvy up responsibility for the various bills (which will ensure, amongst other things, that both of you remain financially involved). For this purpose you could perhaps set up a 'household' bank account, to which you both have access. If at any stage you find you're having trouble sticking to your budget (or one of you is questioning where the other's money is going), try trading responsibility for paying the bills and expenses or doing the shopping, and compare notes afterwards.

If you find you have some money left over every week or month, it could be divided into three portions: one for you, one for him and the third for a joint investment or savings plan. This system can be particularly useful if you have only got together recently and one of you already had debts, as it gives that person access to independent money to pay them off.

You may, of course, find that you both have different priorities, and the division could reflect this. The main thing, though, is to try not to let any spare money just disappear, but rather make it work for you: perhaps invest it or, if you have a mortgage, use it to increase your repayments. If you find you don't have any savings left over, it's back to the budget!

Your joint budget may well have to take account of your differing spending patterns. A good way of preventing budget blow-outs (and a few disagreements) is to set a limit on how much can be spent on any single purchase without consulting the other partner. This can also help if one of you is a credit-card addict.

AN ADDED BONUS

After going out for nearly a year, Sally and Simon decided to move in together. While the last thing on their minds was the effect this might have on their living costs, they agreed from the outset to divide the main bills in half. After a time, Sally was surprised to find that she seemed to have an unusual amount of spare money at the end of each month. She sat down and worked out that for every bill they were sharing – rent, car repayments, petrol, insurances, and gas and electricity – she was spending almost exactly half what she had spent when living alone. The result? She was saving about $1000 a month. Simon did his sums too, and the figures were similar. They gave themselves a celebratory present, then they opened a high-interest account into which they each put $200 a week to go towards a house deposit.

Make Sure It's a Fair Share

If you are both earning, it's likely that one of you will earn more than the other. Many couples choose to keep their finances completely separate, each paying fifty–fifty as if they are flatmates. There is a danger, though,

What a Difference a Name Makes

Dudley is an actor, but roles are few and far between. His wife Kerri has a successful naturopathic business and is the main breadwinner. They plan to put $10 000 into a three-year fixed-interest investment earning about 8 per cent a year: Dudley is earning $16 000 a year and his tax rate is 21.5 per cent (taking the Medicare levy into account), while Kerri pays the highest rate (48.5 per cent). For this reason they have decided to invest the money in Dudley's name and reduce the amount of tax they pay on the income from their investment. If they invest in Dudley's name rather than Kerri's, over three years they will save more than $700 in tax.

that the lifestyle of the higher earner comes to set the pace, and the other partner ends up behind, in debt, or dipping into savings to keep up. So if you choose this method, perhaps suggest that the higher earner pays proportionally more.

And if you are not working at all, you're still entitled to know how money is being spent. If possible, try to have some money placed regularly in an account for your own use.

If serious financial problems do come up – be they irreconcilable differences as far as your attitudes to money are concerned, or your finances are in a bad way – consider getting professional advice. In the first instance, phone the Credit Helpline or the financial counselling service in your state.

Income-splitting – Worth Getting Married For!

Income-splitting simply means that, if one of you is earning much less than the other, you put any investments in that person's name and thus reduce the amount of tax you have to pay. Note, though, that with assets or investments bought before 20 September 1985, it is usually better to keep them in the name of the original owner: if ownership is transferred, they will be subject to capital-gains tax when they are next sold.

Family Trusts

Another way for couples to minimise tax is by setting up a family trust. Discretionary family trusts, where you can vary the distributions of investment income each year and direct these to different family members, have long been popular as a means of reducing tax bills. The main advantage is that you can make payments to family members paying lower tax rates, without having to transfer the asset on which the income is earned.

Remember, though, that family trusts are subject to the same tax treatment as any investment income. For example, a child under 18 can still only receive about $640 (which includes a low-income rebate of $150) tax-free before penalty tax rates apply. And if you do distribute income to a child, the child can legally claim the money as their own. Also, if the trust makes a loss, this loss cannot be distributed to the members to offset any gains from investments outside the family trust, though it can be carried forward in the trust to be offset against gains in subsequent years.

Setting up a trust through a corporate trustee costs about $1500. Then there are the ongoing costs which (depending on the complexity of the trust) could amount to about $400–$1000 each year. If you are considering a family trust, first weigh up the costs against the benefits – including any tax savings.

When One of You Is Supporting the Other

If one of you is the main breadwinner, even if the dependent partner works for part of the year, you can claim a tax rebate. The amount you can claim depends on how much the dependent partner earns (currently the cut-off point is around $5000 a year) and whether or not you also have a dependent child. The maximum rebate is about $1200 (if you have no dependent children), and there are a few other conditions: for more information, contact your accountant or the Tax Office.

WHEN YOU OWN THINGS TOGETHER

Having joint accounts and assets can be convenient and reduce costs, but there are a few things you should consider before committing yourself. First, remember that you are jointly responsible for any debts, which means that if one of you leaves or dies the other may be liable. Also, joint accounts can be problematic if you have different attitudes to money and how to spend it. If this is the case, consider having a joint account only for those expenses you want to share, and keep individual accounts for the rest of your income.

How your joint assets are registered will affect your position should one of you die. Where you own things as *joint tenants*, if one of you dies the survivor will automatically own the asset irrespective of the terms of the will. This is the way that most long-term partners prefer to hold assets.

Where you register as *tenants in common*, if one of you dies that person's share is paid according to his or her will while the surviving owners retain their holding. As this enables you to choose your beneficiaries, it is the best approach if you are in a second marriage and want to leave assets to children from a prior marriage (or if you wish to hold assets with friends and/or siblings). The drawback is that, if one partner dies, the surviving partner (and this could be you) may have to buy out the beneficiaries, or even sell the asset unless the will gives you a life interest in it (as is often the case with the marital home).

For more information about the operation of joint accounts in the event of the death of one partner, see the section 'About Death' at the end of this chapter.

OTHER THINGS TO CONSIDER

De-facto Relationships

If you are in a de-facto relationship, make sure that you are aware of your entitlements. The legal situation varies from state to state: in New South Wales and the Northern Territory, for example, if you live together for more than two years both partners are entitled to make a claim on property should you split up. New South Wales is currently the only state with legislation specifically covering de-facto relationships, so seek the advice of a solicitor if you are concerned about your rights.

Have You Made a Will?

When you marry or set up house with your partner, it's an ideal time to review your wills (only in some states does marriage automatically revoke any previous will). Even if you have everything in joint names, what is the situation for any children you may have from a previous marriage, or if you both die? These and other considerations are discussed in the section 'Where There's a Will' on page 239.

Review Your Insurance Needs

Your insurance needs will change once you are in a permanent relationship, particularly if you take on debt or decide to have children. This can be the time to take out life and/or disability insurance: for a guide to insurance cover, see the section 'Insurance – Protecting What You've Got' in Chapter 2.

HAVING A CHILD

'THE THING ABOUT HAVING A BABY

IS THAT THEREAFTER YOU HAVE IT.'

— JEAN KERR

Having a child is one of life's most rewarding experiences. But while the pluses of being a parent far outweigh the financial costs involved, there *will* be new and ongoing demands on your financial resources.

Amidst the exhilaration and exhaustion of your baby's first months – particularly if you're a first-time parent – it's often difficult to appreciate the extent to which this little bundle will tug at your purse-strings as well as your heart-strings. But, according to the Institute of Family Studies, a baby costs plenty – upwards of $190 a week in the first year alone for food, transport, clothes and medical bills. And what's more, by the time he or she reaches the age of 18 you will have spent around $200 000 on clothes, food and education, excluding private-school or university fees. Last but not least, there are the hidden costs, particularly in the early years when the greatest impact on your finances can be the cost of child care if you return to work, or the loss of income should you or your partner choose to stay at home or to work part-time only.

So it makes sense, if it's possible, to do some financial planning ahead of the event, leaving you free to enjoy your new offspring.

THE BIRTH: HOSPITAL AND MEDICAL EXPENSES

Many of us, given the option, would like as much comfort as possible – our own doctor in attendance, the hospital of our choice, perhaps a private or semi-private room – when we give birth. If this is the case, you need private health insurance.

Even with private cover, you may have to meet some of the costs yourself. For prenatal check-ups, you may have to pay the difference between what your doctor charges and the Medicare refund (the difference may be as much as $20–$30 per visit if your doctor charges the Australian Medical Association's recommended fee), particularly if the visit is outside the hospital. You could also have to pay as much as $1000 out of your own pocket for the costs of the delivery and postnatal care.

So if you consider private insurance, check the policy. What is the qualifying period (for a birth, it's usually nine months)? What exactly does the policy cover? Does it meet the costs of a home birth or a midwife, if this is your preferred approach? If your doctor charges more than the Australian Medical Association's recommended fee, how much will the fund pay?

If you elect to be covered only by Medicare, you are entitled to accommodation in a public ward or birth centre of a public hospital and you will be treated by the obstetrician on duty. Prenatal visits are currently free, providing you attend a public health centre or use a GP who bulk-bills. Pharmaceuticals are free while you are in hospital, but you must pay for any obtained from an outside chemist.

In the end, of course, it's a matter of personal choice, but it is worth taking time to research some creative ways to obtain what you want at a price you can bear. See the box on page 217 for some ideas.

Furnishing the Nursery

This is where the budget can really blow out, especially if it's a first child and you want the best for baby! Parents can easily outlay $2000 on basic equipment (car capsule, bath, pram/stroller, bassinet/cot, bedding, nappies)

CHOICES, CHOICES, CHOICES

- If your GP is qualified in obstetrics, you could choose to use her or him instead of a specialist for your prenatal visits.
- If you're happy to share a room during your hospital stay after the birth, you may only need middle-level private cover. And you might enjoy the company and moral support.
- Even if you are admitted to a public hospital under private health insurance, you can elect that you or your child be treated as a public patient. This may be worth doing if you find there is a significant gap between the hospital costs and what your policy covers, and it should not affect the quality of care you receive.
- If you have private insurance, make sure that you swap to family cover before the birth, so that your baby is included too. Check your policy in case there is a waiting period.
- Some private hospitals allow you to transfer to a separate wing soon after the birth, where you largely look after the baby yourself rather than relying on nursing staff. This allows you to enjoy a private room for the cost of a shared room. You will, of course, need to check with your doctor first, but most obstetricians are amenable to this idea if you and your baby are in good health.

and clothing before the baby arrives. And you'll have some ongoing expenses like feeding equipment (even if you breastfeed, you may find the odd bottle handy) – and then, of course, there are all those toys.

Obviously the cheapest option is to beg, borrow or rent as much as possible, particularly nursery furniture, as baby will grow out of most of it in a nanosecond – ask at your local council or baby health centre. Otherwise, do consider buying at least some of the equipment secondhand, and try not to reject castoffs out of hand.

SOME MONEY-SAVING TIPS

- Aside from its other benefits, breastfeeding is, of course, the cheapest option. If you are able to breastfeed, you'll save a minimum of $10–$15 a week in formula, plus the cost of bottles, teats and sterilising equipment.
- As clothes, equipment and toys are outgrown, consign them to recycle shops or organise a garage sale to boost your finances. These outlets are also an excellent source of cheap toys and books, as is your local library.
- Babysitting fees can make regular evenings out prohibitively expensive. Consider joining or establishing a babysitting pool with other parents in your area.
- Shop around if you're considering a nappy-wash service, as prices can vary. Or, better still, convince a loving relative it would be a much appreciated present.

WHAT THE GOVERNMENT OFFERS

Through the Department of Social Security (DSS), the government provides some financial assistance for the support of children. This depends on your financial circumstances, though, and currently if the combined income of you and your partner is more than about $61 000 you won't qualify.

If you are eligible, the benefits include a one-off payment of about $800 for a first child born or adopted after February 1996. There is also a small fortnightly payment, the Family Payment, which is means-tested: the basic payment is currently around $22 per child per fortnight, increasing (depending on your income) up to a maximum of about $93. If you are eligible for any such assistance, you have to provide regular proof of your financial situation.

If you work and have to pay for child care, you can get some of this back through the Childcare Cash Rebate, which is not means-tested but requires regular review of your work situation. You can apply for this on the same form used for Family Payment applications, and the rebate is available through any Medicare office.

A pension is also available for single parents who are unemployed; this varies according to the amount of support you are receiving from the other parent. The government also pays an allowance (to a maximum of about $62 a fortnight) in cases where one parent remains at home to look after the children; again, the amount varies according to your income.

To find out more about Family Payments, the Childcare Cash Rebate and other DSS payments and services, phone the Family Hotline on 131305.

WORKING MOTHERS

'TOTAL COMMITMENT TO FAMILY

AND TOTAL COMMITMENT TO CAREER

IS POSSIBLE, BUT FATIGUING.'

— MURIEL FOX

Even if you plan to return to work after your baby is born, you will inevitably have at least some time off. Whilst some companies are prepared to subsidise a number of weeks maternity or paternity leave, this period is usually one in which your income will be reduced, even if you use up some annual leave. And if you have received paid maternity leave but change your mind about returning to work, you may have to pay the money back: check your employment agreement, as the conditions vary between industries and individual employers.

Flexible working hours can be important, so don't be afraid to approach your employer to negotiate for more flexibility in your job. (Possible approaches are covered in the section 'You've Got the Job!' in Chapter 4.) If you are feeling tired towards the end of your pregnancy, you may be able to negotiate with your employer to go part-time without affecting your legal entitlement to return to your previous position (or one of comparable status) on a full-time basis after the birth.

Whatever you negotiate with your employer, have the terms put in writing. Finally, even if you are not planning to return to work, try to keep up to date with developments in your field. It's important to remain competitive and employable in case circumstances change and you do return to the workforce.

CHILD CARE

Women still take on greater responsibility for child care than men do. So if you are planning to return to work after having the baby, or simply want to organise some time out, you really should begin to think about the options available as early as possible in your pregnancy – not least because there tend to be long waiting lists for day care.

You can get information about local child-care centres from your local council or the Yellow Pages. As you need to feel totally happy with the style and quality of care, you should investigate all the options thoroughly yourself: ask other parents, and above all drop in to any centre you're considering (preferably do this unannounced, so that you see how the centre functions on a 'typical' day).

Anyone operating a child-care service for children for non-family members must have a licence, which is issued by the Department of Health and Community Services. To find out whether any centre you are considering is licensed, contact the department's office in your area. Note, though, that some outside-school-hours care services are not currently regulated.

What you will pay for child care varies dramatically (from $3 to $15 an hour), depending on which option you choose.

Good Relations

Having a relative or friend who can care for your child is the most inexpensive and flexible option, and usually less of an emotional wrench. At the same time it can create guilt feelings if you are putting too much burden on the carer. Grandparents today may be less willing to act as carers – paid or unpaid – as they are often still active and have their own lives to pursue, so make sure this is a realistic option for you.

Day-care Centres

These centres (also sometimes referred to as pre-school centres) offer all-day care on a full-time or part-time basis, and are in ever-increasing demand as more and more mothers are returning to work before their children start school. Many such centres are open for a minimum of eight hours a day, and weekly fees typically range from $90 to $360. Some centres provide meals and others don't, and this may be a time–money issue to consider.

Family Day Care

Under this system, which is usually cheaper than centre-based care, several children are looked after together in an authorised carer's home. The conditions are regulated by the local council, which is where you should go for more information.

Occasional Care Centres

These centres cater for those who only require child care occasionally – for example, when you want to go shopping unhindered. They are council-run and charge on an hourly basis. Occasional care does mean just that: there can be restrictions on the number of hours per week you can use such

---

SCHOOL'S OUT!

It's worth pointing out that, contrary to the expectations of many new mothers who work, the early school years can make life more, rather than less, difficult. As the school day averages six hours and there are upwards of eleven weeks of holiday each year in most states, if you're planning to work you may find yourself up for the costs of before-school and after-school care and for holiday programs. Alternatively you will need to work part-time – or, if possible, marry a school-teacher!

---

centres on an hourly basis, so it's not usually an option for working mothers unless you're only working a few hours a week.

Company Child Care

Some (but not many) employers provide child-care facilities for their staff, either at the workplace or at a local licensed centre. The ins and outs of this are discussed in the section 'You've Got the Job!' in Chapter 4: the main catch is that from the end of 1996 only on-site child-care facilities are exempt from the fringe-benefits tax (FBT), and if this tax does apply the cost may well be passed on to users, which is likely to make it prohibitively expensive.

Nannies

Although nannies were traditionally the preserve of high-income families, it is becoming increasingly popular for couples who both work to have someone living in or visiting daily to look after their children. If you only have one child, this is undoubtedly the most expensive option, but if you have more than one it can be cheaper – in fact it's likely to be very cost-competitive. And the value of coming home from work to a bathed and fed child or children is incalculable!

The cost of a qualified nanny ranges from $350 to $600 a week; if you are comfortable about employing an unqualified nanny, you'll pay less. Sharing a nanny with another family is one way to cut costs and has the added benefit of providing a playmate for your child. Hiring a nanny means you have certain obligations as an employer, and there are tax implications: as these can be quite complex, it would be wise to consult an accountant.

Another thing worth thinking about: a live-in nanny means another household member – and it's often hard enough to live with the foibles of existing ones!

YOUR CHILD'S EDUCATION – WHO'S GOING TO PAY?

Educating a child is one of the largest single outlays families face. And the spiralling costs of both public and private education at every level – primary through to tertiary – make it a goal definitely worth saving for.

If you are considering private schooling, you can expect to pay $3500–$9000 in tuition fees a year (and the same again for boarding fees). And in private schools there are always additional costs, from uniforms and equipment to excursions and fundraising levies. Even in government schools there are usually quite a few extra expenses in addition to the basic levy and the cost of uniforms, though government assistance is available for low-income earners (see page 224). And if your child goes on to tertiary education, the fees can range from $2000 to $5000 a year, depending on the course and the institution.

What you can afford will, of course, be a factor in your choice between private and state schools. The reality is, though, that most of us want 'the best possible' education for our children, and more often than not this is perceived to occur within the private system. So what ways are there to subsidise the costs?

There are many scholarships available from middle primary school onwards, which offer full or part remission of fees. Understandably, there is a lot of competition for these, so the alternative is to set aside money specifically to cover education expenses.

Special Investment Plans

A number of organisations have set up investment plans specifically to encourage and help parents provide for the cost of their children's education. All of these plans involve putting money regularly into an investment pool operated by a funds manager. The amount you need to put away each month will, of course, depend on the annual school fees and how early (i.e. how many years before your child begins school) you start saving. The types of investments involved include unit trusts or friendly-society or insurance bonds: these are discussed in more detail in the section 'Managed Funds' in Chapter 3. Your earnings on the money are continually reinvested, with the intention of building up enough savings to cover all future education costs.

In the case of at least one friendly-society fund (the Australian Scholarship Group), the earnings are tax-free because it is geared specifically to meeting education costs – but your access to your money is restricted and you can forfeit earnings if your child does not complete his or her education. So, as with any managed investment, you should read the fine print very carefully and compare the performance history of the port-folios being offered.

Savings Accounts

You can, of course, set up a bank account in which you regularly deposit a sum of money (such as the government's Family Payment, if you're eligible for it). But while this is a flexible and relatively low-risk method of saving, the rate of return may be comparatively low.

Government Assistance

In some states the government gives an allowance to low-income-earners, primarily to help meet the costs of books and other equipment in govern-ment schools. Elsewhere, the basic levy may be waived. Such arrangements are organised through the school, so for more information contact the school principal.

If your child is over 16 and studying for at least 75 per cent of a full-time course, he or she may also be eligible for financial assistance. AUSTUDY, as this assistance is known, is means-tested: contact your local Common-wealth Employment Office (CES) for further information.

Q *I and my husband earn good salaries, so we're on the highest personal tax rate. Should we consider putting investments in our three-year-old daughter's name?*

A The Tax Office is not at all happy about adults diverting income to their children purely to minimise tax, and actively discourages this. You can, though, set up an account which is genuinely used for the benefit of the child (such as your daughter's education) without being penalised. Currently the first $416 earned on such an investment is tax-free and a rebate for those on lower incomes, including children, increases the tax-free amount to $643. But any earnings over this amount are taxed: a penalty rate of 66 per cent is applied to any income between $416 and $1445, and all earnings over $1446 are taxed at 47 per cent. So it's sensible to talk to an accountant before making your decision.

All in all, the most tax-effective way to make an investment for your child's education – depending, of course, upon your family situation – is to put it in the name of a non-working spouse. In this way you can take advantage of the $5400 tax-free threshold for adults, and any income between this figure and $20 000 will be taxed at the lowest rate of 20 per cent. Also, of course, it means that you keep control over the money.

CARING FOR OLDER RELATIVES

'WOMEN NO SOONER FIND THE PRESSURES OF RAISING A FAMILY EASING THAN THEY ARE ONCE MORE LEFT WITH THE RESPONSIBILITY OF PROVIDING CARE.'

— HAZEL HAWKE, *MY OWN LIFE*

Today we are living much longer, and one of the growing concerns in our society is how we will care for elderly family members. In Australia, people aged 75 and over make up the most rapidly growing age group, and by 2000 about one in five of our population will be 60 or more years old. So even with the dramatic improvements in health care and, as a result, in the health of the aged, there is a good chance that someone in your family will need assistance in their later years.

Statistics show that the responsibility for caring for a parent, or later in life for a disabled or ill partner, largely falls on women. It is also a fact that, as many women are choosing to start a family later in life, we can find ourselves still looking after young children at the same time. Whatever our situation, there will be significant financial, practical and emotional matters to deal with.

WHAT YOU NEED TO THINK ABOUT

The help needed may be assistance with tasks such as weekly shopping or occasional home maintenance, or it may extend to full-time care. How you meet the person's particular needs will depend on the circumstances – both yours and theirs. Try to assess the situation as rationally as possible:

▲ What assistance is needed?

▲ How can this best be provided?

▲ Do you need to give up work, or work part-time only, or could you enlist the assistance of a professional carer?

▲ What financial assistance is available?

▲ What community services are available?

▲ If you become the full-time carer, what will this mean in financial terms?

▲ Are there support groups available?

The thing to remember is that there are many options available to you, and you should explore every avenue if you are making decisions that will affect your way of life and that of the rest of your family. If, for example, you have a job, perhaps you can negotiate more flexible working hours and/or utilise the services of the Home and Community Care (HACC) program in the area. If you wish or need to continue working full-time, consider engaging the services of a carer.

It is also worthwhile speaking to a solicitor about being given an enduring or protected power of attorney, so that you can make financial decisions on your relative's behalf if their mental or physical health deteriorates.

WHAT HELP IS AVAILABLE?

The HACC provides a range of services, which are not means-tested (though a small fee may be charged if the recipient has the ability to pay). This assistance includes:

▲ home help such as cooking, cleaning, washing, ironing and shopping

▲ home maintenance (lawn-mowing, fixing taps, changing light-bulbs)

▲ occasional or regular home nursing

▲ assistance with personal tasks such as showering and dressing

▲ food (such as Meals on Wheels)

▲ respite care (to give carers a break)

Financial assistance is also available if you are providing full-time care. Some people are reluctant to ask for this, perhaps because they see the care they're providing simply as an extension of a close relationship, and as an obligation – but close family ties should not stop you applying for any such benefits. There are conditions, however: a carer's pension, for example, is means-tested and is only available if the dependent person receives a social

Don't overlook the emotional back-up you may need

security or service pension. The domiciliary nursing care benefit is not means-tested, but it is relatively small (currently around $55 a week). If you receive a carer's pension, you are also entitled to concessions for things such as health and dental care, car registration, and so on. For more information about all these benefits, contact your local Department of Social Security.

HOME ALONE

Most aged people prefer to stay in their own homes for as long as possible, and the different forms of government assistance described above do make this feasible as long as the person is able to look after himself or herself.

Obviously, you must jointly decide whether staying at home is a sensible option, and what practical help you may be able to get. There are, for one thing, various ways of financing house modifications, such as government-subsidised loans. These and other options are considered in the section 'There's No Place Like Home' in Chapter 6.

I'M FINDING THIS HARD TO DO ON MY OWN

The dependency of a parent or a partner – whether this happens suddenly or has been expected – can cause much anguish for everyone concerned, so don't overlook the emotional back-up you may need. There are support groups which can help: in the first instance you could discuss the available options with your local doctor or council (via the health centre or social-work section), or the hospital if applicable. There is also a 'carer support' information kit which is available from the Department of Health and Family Services.

Separation and Divorce

'MONEY IS ALWAYS THERE BUT THE POCKETS CHANGE; IT IS NOT IN THE SAME POCKETS AFTER A CHANGE, AND THAT IS ALL THERE IS TO SAY ABOUT MONEY.'

— GERTRUDE STEIN

In four out of five divorces, women are the initiators – and this is despite the fact that women are more likely than men to suffer a drop in living standards afterwards. It is also evident that women aged 25 – 35 who have no children tend be in the best position to recover financially, and far more so than mothers who have been principally home-makers.

If your marriage does come to an end, hopefully it can be ended amicably. But even if this is the case, it pays to be clear about your rights and to be financially prepared, because although divorce may be instigated for emotional reasons the battlelines are often drawn around matters financial. So what do you need to know so that you don't end up with 'empty pockets'?

Some Hard Facts about Divorce

Today one in three marriages in Australia ends in divorce. The Family Law Act of 1975 revolutionised divorce by removing the notion of 'fault'. The only ground for divorce is an irretrievable breakdown of the marriage, the evidence for which is a separation of at least one year (conduct is only examined where there are serious financial consequences).

A few more revolutionary changes have also been set up as regards divorce settlements: account should be taken of a spouse's non-financial contribution to the marriage; a defined standard of living should be maintained by the disadvantaged partner; children are the financial responsibility of both parents, whether married or not, and assets should be split with a bias (usually an additional 10–15 per cent) towards the custodial parent; and it is assumed that women can and should support themselves if at all possible.

While this system tries to be fair, the results are sometimes less than equitable. This can work both ways, of course, but it does reinforce the importance of taking equal financial responsibility within the marriage from the outset.

WHEN YOU SEPARATE

You don't have to go through the divorce process to agree on a financial settlement. In fact, when a couple separates is usually the time when these arrangements are made, even if divorce follows. So the comments and advice which follow are equally applicable in either situation.

The Family Court offers a number of ways to resolve family differences, including counselling and mediation (which is confidential and free of charge). Do note, though, that mediators cannot give legal advice and may not have the know-how to resolve complicated financial situations equitably. If you are interested in counselling or mediation, contact your nearest Family Court registry.

A marriage breakdown is almost always painful. In addition, especially if you were not the breadwinner, you may find the first few weeks or months after separating financially difficult. This is a good reason for having safeguards in place throughout a marriage, such as keeping some financial independence and having limits on the amount of money that can be withdrawn from joint accounts by individual signatories. If money is a problem in the short term, there are ways of dealing with this. You can, for example, apply through the courts for interim maintenance so that you have access to funds prior to the financial settlement (at which time an adjustment will be made for the money you have already received). Alternatively, you can continue living under the same roof with your spouse and still be separated for the requisite year. Doing so can, though, make the divorce process more difficult, as you will have to prove that you lived separate lives during that time, so it's worth consulting a solicitor if you consider this. If, however, this situation is intolerable (for example, where the tension in the household is having an adverse effect on children), you can apply for exclusive occupation of the house immediately, rather than waiting for the case to be heard.

Once a split has occurred, consider cancelling any joint accounts or credit cards, as you can be liable for joint debts even if they are incurred after separation. You may want to consider putting a caveat on the property to prevent your partner doing anything with it, and check with any institution with which you have a mortgage that it cannot be increased without both your signatures. While courts may take account of any recent debt built up by one partner, or of conduct deliberately designed to 'dilute' assets after the marriage breakdown, once the money has gone it's difficult to get compensation.

PROTECTING YOUR INTERESTS

'SINGLE WOMEN HAVE A GREAT

PROPENSITY FOR BEING POOR.'

— JANE AUSTEN

If you believe separation or divorce is inevitable, there are some preliminary steps you should take to safeguard your interests. Contact your family accountant as soon as possible, and begin gathering together and making copies of any financial information which may be relevant (see box on page 231): if you decide to adopt legal proceedings and don't have this information, you may have to pay for a court order to get it (and this process, known as 'discovery', can be expensive).

If getting the information is difficult or if you suspect your partner is hiding assets or income, you can employ financial detectives to collect the information for you. Although it sounds sordid, it could save you a lot of money in the long run. A solicitor should be used to hire the detective, however, as the information may then be protected under client–lawyer privilege.

Divorce does not automatically revoke a will in every state, so contact the Law Society in your state to find out how the law stands. In any event, one of the first things you should do if divorcing is review your will and, if necessary, make a new one to ensure that there is no doubt about your intentions. (Wills are discussed in the section 'About Death' at the end of this chapter.)

INFORMATION YOU'LL NEED

Make sure you have the following information:

- a list of all assets, from household goods to investments
- copies of all bank statements and investment accounts
- copies of any title deeds and contracts
- details of all outstanding debts, including home loans, car loans, credit cards
- copies of tax returns for the last few years, including those for any business in which you or your partner have an interest
- copies of life or other insurance policies
- copies of your partner's remuneration statement, superannuation entitlements, and any associated schemes
- a copy of any pre-nuptial agreement detailing who will receive what assets and income
- documentation of your non-financial contribution to the marriage (this could include care of children, home improvements, and any involvement you have had with your partner's career, such as entertaining clients, making suggestions for business presentations, etc.)

WHO GETS WHAT?

In the event of separation or divorce, many women take less than they are entitled to, often because they can't afford the legal fees, or want to avoid the emotional drain of a prolonged process. But if you compromise too much you may regret it later on, not least because you might find yourself in straitened circumstances.

There are two separate aspects to a divorce: legal confirmation that the marriage has ended, and the settlement (which includes the division of property and assets). Where both partners are able to come to an agreement, the starting point for any such arrangements should be a fifty–fifty split (but see 'When There are Children Involved' on page 234).

The Settlement

Here any official division is based on both partners' financial and non-financial contributions to the marriage and their ability to support themselves and any children. Thus you should seriously decide, and sooner rather than later, what you will need in order to maintain a reasonable lifestyle: to do this, the courts usually require you to prepare a budget. While you're not entitled to *claim* this amount from your partner (in fact, the awarding of spouse maintenance is increasingly rare), it does provide a basis for negotiating matters such as child support.

Once a divorce becomes final, you only have one year to apply for settlement, so it is usually advisable to do so before the divorce takes place.

What are the Tax Implications?

It's important to be aware that the settlement has tax implications. Where assets are transferred between partners through a court order or maintenance agreement, stamp duty can be avoided and capital-gains tax may not be payable at the time of transfer. You may have to pay tax, though, if you later sell an asset (other than the family home) on which tax relief was granted, so it is important to understand how this may affect the value of what you receive in the settlement.

Considerations When Dividing the Major Assets

The longer the marriage, the greater the likelihood of a fifty–fifty split starting point when dividing the assets. The first steps in determining a settlement are to identify the assets and get an independent valuation (the latter can cause much angst for both parties, particularly the valuation of the family home if one partner is still living in it). The next move is to assess each partner's contribution to the assets: this takes account of both direct and indirect contributions, including who bought, maintained and improved them. Solicitors often advise their clients to put on paper a chronological history of the marriage, including information on what things were purchased and by whom, family events such as the birth of children, and both partners' occupations and earnings throughout that time. The aim in determining a settlement is to provide as clean a break as possible for both partners.

The Home

Many of us feel that we would like to stay in the family home at this time of upheaval, particularly if we have children, as this could give them a sense of security and continuity. But, as one financial adviser commented, 'You can't eat the house', so try to be realistic and consider all the options. Can you afford the mortgage payments, rates and maintenance, particularly if your income is reduced and/or you have to buy out your partner? Could you take in a boarder to help reduce your living expenses? Would you be better off selling the house and splitting the proceeds with your partner?

Other Goods and Belongings

In divorce, everything is up for grabs: this includes property and goods acquired before you were married, inherited assets, and all personal possessions – an insurance policy is a good guide for the purposes of making an inventory. Even professional goodwill and celebrity status (or a professional degree) can be considered divisible assets.

Superannuation

Any accumulated superannuation is generally considered as a financial resource rather than an asset, because the money may not be accessible for some time. Unfortunately there is no hard and fast rule about the allocation of superannuation, although one of the following methods is usually used:

▲ The financial settlement is adjusted in favour of the spouse with less superannuation.

▲ A set formula is used to determine the amount payable to each spouse, based on the years in the superannuation scheme and the years of marriage.

▲ Settlement is postponed until the superannuation is accessible (which is often at retirement). This is the least favoured option, as the courts prefer a clean break.

Family Business

Where there is a family business, an independent valuation should be made by an accountant. A spouse can usually claim a share in the other partner's business assets, even if he or she has had no legal involvement in it or has made no direct contribution. Businesses can, however, be hard to value and it must be said that in some cases (where relations have become adversarial), they have been used to hide assets or understate income.

A court will take into account the continuing viability of the business and usually loads the settlement of this asset in favour of the person running it, so that he or she can continue earning a living. If you're not a director of a private company, you cannot demand to see the books. However, if one partner refuses to provide evidence of the value of the business, the Family Court can order a 'statement of financial circumstances' which would include providing two years of balance sheets and profit and loss accounts of the company.

WHEN THERE ARE CHILDREN INVOLVED

A century or so ago, children were owned by their father 'as of right'. Later, it came to be expected that women would automatically have custody of any children in the event of a divorce. Today, both parents have equal right to seek custody, and both are expected to contribute financially to their children's upkeep to the best of their ability. The courts have the discretion to increase the settlement in favour of the parent who has custody of the child(ren).

Sadly, custody and access are too often used by one or both partners as a weapon during divorce negotiations. This is, of course, a pretty powerful bargaining tool, so it should always be made clear from the outset that access and money are not linked.

If you come to an amicable agreement about child support, you don't need to involve the courts or any other authority. If you cannot agree, the Child Support Agency (which is part of the Tax Office) can, according to a set formula, assess how much should be paid by the non-custodial parent and will, where possible, enforce this. Such payments are tax-free.

Despite the government's efforts to enforce the payment of child support, evidence suggests that many women who have daily care of children are still not receiving these payments; obviously they are at risk of suffering financial difficulties. Where child support cannot be enforced, you may be entitled to extra social-security benefits: contact the Child Support Agency or the Department of Social Security for more information about this.

What if the Financial Situation Changes?

If your financial circumstances change (for example, your former partner remarries and wishes to reduce his payments because he has new financial obligations, or if you have a new job), a review of the situation can be requested from the Child Support Agency.

There may also be unforeseen financial difficulties if your former partner dies. In most cases the situation will depend on the quality of your relationship after the divorce: if it is good, chances are that you will have discussed how any children would be provided for in the event of his death. Provisions through a will could include the bequest of an outright sum of money or of some or all life insurance or superannuation, or a 'testamentary trust', whereby an independent trustee could allocate money to the child each year until he or she is financially independent.

If your relationship after the divorce is not good, there is less that you can set in place whilst your former partner is alive. If no provision is made for a child, you can either challenge the will in court or make a direct claim to the trustee of the father's superannuation fund, as the trustee often has discretion to allocate the benefits according to the needs of any financial dependants even where no provision has been made in the will.

For more detail about such considerations, see 'Where There's a Will' in the section 'About Death' later in this chapter, and the section 'Superannuation' in Chapter 3.

GETTING A LAWYER

The financial outcome of a divorce will have a significant impact on your future lifestyle. Getting legal advice,. although often expensive, can save you literally thousands of dollars if the lawyer can negotiate a more advantageous settlement.

Whether or not you need legal representation to help with financial and custody matters will depend on both the degree of goodwill between you and your partner, and your financial situation. If your finances are uncomplicated or you have no major assets, you may not need a solicitor to do the negotiating, but even if you want to settle out of court it is still advisable to get separate and independent legal advice, and to have any agreements enshrined in a court order, particularly if there are major assets (such as a property) involved.

It is relatively simple to file for divorce. If you file for divorce yourself, it costs about $300. This is the cheapest method and is common when there are no children involved; the fee may be waived in cases of financial hardship. A divorce kit containing the application forms is available free from any Family Court registry. Another fairly cheap option is to seek advice from a citizens advice bureau or community legal centre, which again is probably more suitable where there are no children and the financial arrangements are uncomplicated. Legal Aid may be available, but this is usually only the case where children are involved: to find out if you're eligible, contact the Legal Aid Commission in your state, your nearest community legal centre, or the Family Court.

Using a Lawyer: Weighing up the Costs

Always compare the costs of using a lawyer against what you will gain financially. Is it worth fighting for $12 000 if it will cost $10 000 in legal fees? And don't let the lawyers be the only winners: if assets are whittled away in legal fees, this will have a direct effect on your own financial future.

TIPS WHEN CHOOSING A DIVORCE LAWYER

- Choose a family-law specialist, rather than a general practitioner. Ask for referrals from people who have been through divorce and were happy with their lawyer, or from a solicitor if you know one. If you don't have any contacts, get in touch with the Law Society in your state for a list of practitioners in this field.
- Find out how often the solicitor has represented women and what the outcomes were.
- Make sure you have a good rapport with your solicitor, that you trust his or her judgement, and that he or she will be accessible out of office hours if necessary.
- Get an idea of the likely fees and whether payment will be ongoing or payable at settlement. Of course, your costs will escalate the more complex or time-consuming your case: the Family Court can order one spouse to pay in certain circumstances.

In short, if you have a clear picture of what you are entitled to, try not to let emotions deter you from knowing when to settle.

Lawyers charge by the hour (or part thereof) and will tell you up-front about the estimated costs involved. Even with a good practitioner and a good case, you can contain costs by jotting down before a meeting or a phone-call the points you want to cover, and by always being as succinct and as constructive as possible.

But We're Only Living Together!

When you separate from a de-facto relationship, you do not always have the same legal entitlements as a married person. (This is another good reason for keeping financial records.) Your status and entitlements will depend on where you live, as the situation varies between states: to find out about your rights, contact the Law Society in your state.

In New South Wales, Victoria and the Northern Territory, each partner's financial and non-financial contributions are, in theory at least, taken into account. In the other states, de-facto partners must look to the Law of Trusts for a property settlement: this considers the intentions and the contributions of both parties when property was acquired.

If, however, there are children from the relationship, matters of custody, access and financial support are treated as if you were married: such issues are dealt with in the Family Court, and child maintenance can be assessed and collected by the Child Support Agency (see 'When There Are Children Involved' on page 234).

STARTING OVER

However painful the end of a marriage, it inevitably signals a new beginning. There will be many adjustments to make, emotionally, practically and financially, and even if you initiated the break it may take time to get used to living without your partner. It may also be a time when you want or need to reassess some aspects of your life, including your personal and financial goals. You will come through it, though, and you may even discover new talents and resources that you didn't know you had.

ABOUT DEATH

'THINGS HAVE A TERRIBLE PERMANENCE

WHEN PEOPLE DIE.'

— JOYCE KILMER

There is an old saying that the only two certainties in life are death and taxes. Yet while most of us make time at least once a year to deal with our tax, the last thing we like to think about is our death or that of a partner – and particularly what this may mean in practical terms for the survivors.

The fact is that it's very important that our financial affairs are in order before we die. Dealing with the death of a loved one is traumatic for those left behind, and financial worries should not be added to their burden. In addition, knowing that our finances are organised and our wishes are clear brings a certain peace of mind that allows us to get on with life and enjoy it while we have it.

So this section looks at the things you, and your partner if you have one, should think about as far as estate planning is concerned.

WHERE THERE'S A WILL...

Having a valid will ensures that your property is distributed according to your wishes, and helps minimise confusion and distress at a time when family members are least able to cope. A will can be made by anyone 18 years and over. If you are concerned about who will receive your assets or look after your children when you die, or you want to choose the executor of your estate, you should make a will.

Why a Will is so Important

Little more than a century ago, women were not entitled to own property in their own right, and even their earnings were deemed to belong to their husband. Unfortunately there are still some people whose attitude towards making a will reflects these values.

Don't let this be the case: even if you are married and your husband owns most of the assets, you still need to have a will. At the very least, if you die intestate (that is, without having made a will) the government will decide how your assets are to be distributed among your surviving relatives (each state has its own rules about the hierarchy of such beneficiaries, which may or may not include de-factos). And if you have neither family nor a partner, the government could, in theory at least, appropriate all your assets, though it does have discretion to distribute them to anyone you might reasonably have been expected to provide for.

You are particularly vulnerable if your partner hasn't made a will, as his assets may be distributed according to the formula laid down in your state. You may not be automatically entitled to all his assets, particularly if there are children or a previous spouse involved. Without a will, the distribution of assets is slower and the estate could cost more to distribute.

Do You Need a Solicitor?

A will doesn't have to be prepared by a solicitor for it to be valid. It must, however, be written, typed or printed, and every page must be signed by you and two witnesses who are not your beneficiaries or the spouses of beneficiaries.

It is not, on the other hand, expensive to use a solicitor, and this is probably the safest course in the long run. A 'home-made' will may not stand up in court if it is not clear or not properly drawn up. Also, if your estate is at all complex (for example, if you or your spouse have children from a previous relationship or own a business), legal advice may be helpful. You can expect to pay between $80 and $150 for a straightforward will, and $300 upwards for a more complicated one. It is worth getting quotes from a few solicitors.

If you do decide not to use a solicitor, you can get a printed will form

---

WHEN SHOULD YOU MAKE OR REVIEW A WILL?

A will can be reviewed at any time, but it is common sense to do so in the following circumstances:
- when you turn 18, if you have any assets
- when you marry, divorce or enter a de-facto relationship
- when you travel
- when you become a parent or grandparent
- when you buy property, investments or a business
- when you retire

You can make minor changes to your will by means of a codicil (a separate document witnessed by two people). If the changes are at all substantial, you should make a new will.

---

from a newsagency; kits for around $20 are also advertised widely. Alternatively, the Public Trustee can prepare a will for you, which is a free service on the condition that they administer the estate (for which they do charge a fee, and this can be fairly substantial – about $1600 on a $40 000 estate, $4000 for a $100 000 estate, and $9000 for a $300 000 estate).

Appointing an Executor

An executor is a person you appoint to carry out the instructions in your will. It is not compulsory to name an executor, but if you don't do so the Probate Court will have to be approached to appoint an administrator (usually the major beneficiary) to discharge your estate.

If you decide to name your own executor, choose someone that you trust – be this your partner, a friend, a relative or a solicitor. The advantage of appointing your partner your executor (and vice versa) is that it keeps control of your finances in the family. You should consider appointing more than one person – after all, if you choose only one, there is always the possibility that he or she could die before you do. Ask whomever you

A TAXING LEGACY

When their mother died, Alison and her sister Judy were the only beneficiaries. Alison was left the family home in Melbourne, and Judy the holiday home on the coast. While both properties were worth about the same, their mother had not realised that they would get quite different tax treatment when they were sold.

Alison decided to sell her mother's home. Because it was sold immediately, there was no capital-gains tax payable and Alison was able to keep the entire proceeds. Their mother had bought the holiday home in 1988, after capital-gains tax was introduced, which made it a different case: if Judy sold the property, she would have to pay tax on any increase in value it had undergone (taking inflation into account), as if she had purchased the investment herself. Its value had more than doubled over this period, so the capital-gains tax was significant. It was not her mother's intention to disadvantage Judy – she was simply unaware of the capital-gains tax laws when she wrote her will.

choose if they are prepared to take on the task, and explain their duties (which may include organising the funeral, filing for probate, and ensuring that any outstanding debts are paid and that the balance of the estate is distributed as you asked).

An executor may have to be paid for the work involved, if he or she is not a beneficiary: the fee may be a percentage of the estate or based on an hourly rate; ask your solicitor.

WILLS: THE TRICKY BITS

In many B-grade movies, the (rich) dead person's will is read out before a greedy and disgruntled cluster of relatives. Often containing surprises (such as the whole lot being left to the poodle), the will allows the plot to thicken ... In real life, there could be nothing worse.

Your will is there to express your wishes as clearly and unambiguously as possible, so there are a few things to bear in mind when making one. If, for example, you want your will to remain relevant for a decent period of time (so you don't have to update it constantly), don't be too specific when listing assets to be left to certain individuals. For example, cite 'my car' rather than 'my Peugeot 504' as you may one day replace it with a Toyota Corolla. Similarly, don't specify names when distributing your estate to children or grandchildren, as another child may be born or the situation change in some other way before you update your will. Instead, use terms like 'in equal shares amongst my surviving children' (or, in the event of their death, *their* surviving children).

A will is also the best place to name your child's or children's guardian, and the trustee of their assets and income. This can be a difficult choice, but it is an important thing to do in case both parents die at the same time. And because this is a large responsibility, you must ask the person you'd like to appoint if they are prepared to take it on. You may consider reviewing your choice as your child or children get older.

Capital-gains Tax

Be aware of capital-gains tax implications on your estate. If, for example, you've stated in your will that your assets are to be sold and the proceeds

POWER OF ATTORNEY

Power of attorney is the legal authority to act on someone's behalf should he or she be unable to manage their own affairs owing to illness or extended absence abroad. General power of attorney, which is often used for business purposes, ends if the person who granted it loses mental capacity; enduring or 'protected' power of attorney, which is usually recommended for individuals, continues after such an event. You can give power of attorney to one or more people (it's common to appoint your spouse and adult child jointly) or to a company – obviously, it should be someone you trust.

If you are over 55 and have any assets, it is definitely worth considering this step. You can get the appropriate form from a law stationer or newsagent, but it's advisable to discuss the matter with a solicitor before going ahead, as a person holding power of attorney has substantial authority. Alternatively, you can have the document prepared by a solicitor (this will cost about $150–$300) or by a trustee company (for a nominal fee). Many solicitors recommend that the document be lodged with the General Register of Deeds, which costs about $50, as this offers extra protection.

are to go to your family, any profit made on the sale could be subject to capital-gains tax. (The principal home is exempt from this tax if it is sold within twelve months of the owner's death.)

Death Duties

While no death duties are payable in Australia, this is not the case in many other countries. If you hold investments outside Australia, find out whether, on your death, they will be subject to death duties in the other country. If so, consider whether you can structure your investments to avoid this: you could, for example, invest via an Australian company or a unit trust, as technically the investments would thus continue after your death and therefore no death duties would be payable.

Other Things to Think About

You should also think about allowing in your will for funeral expenses (see page 245 for typical costs). As an alternative, you could set up a specific savings account to meet these costs and note in your will how you want the account to be used. Another option is to buy funeral bonds (an investment specifically designed to meet funeral expenses), up to $5000 of which is exempt from all means-testing; any earnings on them are tax-free, provided they are used only to pay funeral costs.

Once you've made a will, keep it in a safe place – in a filing cabinet or other fireproof container, or with your bank, solicitor or trustee. It is sensible to keep at least one copy and note on it where the original can be found. Give a copy to your executor or, if you want to keep the contents of the will confidential, give the executor instructions to be followed in the event of your death. Also keep with your will an up-to-date list of all your assets and liabilities, citing in whose name they are held.

Wills and Other Relatives

Under present law, your will may be challenged by your spouse/partner, children or step-children if they believe you have not made proper provision for them. It may also be challenged for other reasons, including if there is doubt whether the will presented for probate is the most recent one made or was altered after being signed. This is a complex area, so discuss it with your solicitor if you have any doubts.

Testamentary Trusts

You may wish to consider setting up a trust within your will. This is known as a testamentary trust and means that a trustee will manage your assets on your behalf after you die.

Trusts can be set up to benefit an organisation, a single family member or the whole surviving family. You may choose a private or professional trustee and it is up to you to decide the extent of discretion vested in that person, which could include the power to buy, sell or run a business. Consult a solicitor if you are considering such a move.

A trust is a waste of time if you have few assets, and similarly should be viewed with caution if it means your partner's assets are to be administered by the trustee and you have access only to the income. A rigid trust agreement could spell unintentional hardship and heartache for the recipients.

Conversely, a testamentary trust may be an excellent idea if you have substantial assets and under-age children. This type of trust allows you to protect your estate from claims by step-children, a second partner or other unintended beneficiaries, as the trustee has the ability to control where your income and assets go after your death. Also, and unlike an ordinary family trust (see page 212), not only can you control the amount that young children receive each year but any income distributed to children under 18 is taxed more favourably (for example, they benefit from the higher tax-free threshold of $5400).

IF YOUR PARTNER DIES

When your partner dies, your world can turn upside down and for a time you are likely to feel adrift. Whatever the impulse, don't make any major decisions for quite a while, as you will probably be in no state to take a balanced view. Knowing beforehand what steps you should take in such an event can help reduce at least some of the strain.

The Funeral

Arranging a funeral is invariably painful. This is a time when you may unintentionally spend more than you can really afford, so try to keep a sense of proportion. Contact a few funeral directors for quotes, and if you need to keep costs down consider organising things such as flowers and notices yourself. A rough guide to costs is as follows:

▲ church service	$1200
▲ civil service	$1000
▲ burial (including coffin/casket, grave and headstone)	$5000
▲ cremation and disposal of ashes	$3500

The Death Certificate

Usually the undertaker arranges registration of the death, although you can do this yourself: the form is available from the Registrar of Births, Deaths and Marriages in your state. You need copies of the death certificate in order to access any joint accounts which require two signatories, to claim life insurance, to access your partner's superannuation and to transfer assets into your name.

The certificate costs about $20 and takes about six to eight weeks; if you need it more urgently (if, for example, you need money quickly), it can be organised (through the funeral director) in five to ten days, at a cost of about $40.

Probate

Depending on the will, you may have to apply for probate (that is, to have the will declared valid). If the estate is small (less than $15 000) and uncomplicated, or if all assets are held as joint tenancies, probate may not be required.

If probate does need to be sought, this is done by the executor of the will or by your solicitor, through the state Supreme Court. You generally need the will, the death certificate, an affidavit from the executor, a copy of the funeral advertisement (which must be inserted in a newspaper fourteen days before the application for probate is made), and a list of assets and liabilities of the deceased.

A filing fee must be paid, the amount of which depends on the value of the estate. (It is normally free for estates under $50 000 and the maximum fee is $1000, for estates worth more than a million). If you use a solicitor, he or she will also charge a fee: average fees are $750 on an estate valued at $20 000, sliding up to $1700 on an estate of $200 000. Fees may vary slightly from solicitor to solicitor, so shop around. Obviously, if you feel comfortable obtaining probate yourself, you can save quite a bit of money.

The granting of probate, which can take from one week to a few months, authorises the executor to administer the estate. Some accounts, such as small investments, can be administered without probate: in such cases, most financial institutions require only a certified copy of the will, a copy of the death certificate, and an indemnity signed by the beneficiaries.

Q *My partner hasn't made a will. What would happen if he died?*

A If he died before making a will, you would need to apply to the court
for Letters of Administration. This allows the estate to be administered, and any assets to be distributed according to the laws in your
state. The procedure to obtain these is similar to that for probate.

Assessing Your Financial Situation

Once the will has been validated, you will be able to establish your financial position. If you intend to use a solicitor to obtain probate or administer
the estate, ask him or her to estimate as far as possible the expected costs
and have these drawn up in a contract.

If at this stage you find that your partner has left debts, it is important
that you understand how this places you and what your responsibilities
may be. Creditors may not be sympathetic and are unlikely to waste too
much time before requesting payment. If the debt was unsecured and in
your husband's name, you are not responsible but the estate may be.

If your partner carried life insurance, it may take several weeks before this
is paid out. If you have mortgage insurance, approach your bank to make a
claim. In the case of joint accounts or cards, you will need to change everything over to your name and amend the signatory procedure. If your
partner had any independent investments, contact his broker or financial
adviser and have these explained to you before transferring them into your
name. Also, contact his employer to find out what the procedure is for
accessing any superannuation.

Not too far down the track you should review your will, especially if your
partner was the beneficiary.

Going It Alone

After a period of time, and when you feel more able to deal with them,
there will be larger issues to think about. If you weren't working before the
death of your partner, you may want or need to consider doing so. If he had
a business, you may also find yourself having to think about taking it over
or selling it. If there were partners in the business, seek professional advice.

If you were both reliant on the pension, your situation will be reassessed.

To help people in such circumstances adjust to their reduced income, the Department of Social Security pays no less than the combined amount of both pensions for fourteen weeks after the death of one spouse. Special assistance for funeral and other expenses is also available as a lump-sum payment. Contact the Department of Social Security for more information.

If you receive a substantial amount of money, either directly from your partner or from a life-insurance payout, you will need to decide what to do with it. If this is the first time you have had money to invest, you may be daunted. Whatever the case, don't do anything in a hurry: the best course in the short term is to put your money somewhere safe – perhaps in a cash-management account or trust or a fixed-term deposit, which will earn you interest while you consider all the options carefully. (See Chapter 3, which sets out the different investments available and offers some practical advice on maximising your returns.) Whatever you do, never relinquish control, no matter how inexperienced you are financially.

Now for Some Time Out

So, this chapter has looked at some of the key points in your life. The next chapter focuses on another watershed – when you retire. Hopefully, this will be a time when you will have fewer obligations and responsibilities, and more time to do what you want to do, so in the following pages we look at some ways of making sure you have enough income to enjoy yourself.

6

GETTING YOUR REWARD: YOUR MONEY, YOUR FUTURE

'MONEY IS SOMETHING YOU'VE GOT TO MAKE IN CASE YOU DON'T DIE.'

— MAX ASNAS

It's hard to envisage wanting to rest for twenty or thirty years of your life. And today, more than ever before, our longer life expectancies (80 years for women and 74 for men) and better health care make it possible for us to lead very active lives when we retire and are no longer restricted by work commitments.

You may see retirement as a time to move to the mountains or the beach, to pursue your hobbies, to travel the world, to start a new business or just to take it easy. Whatever the case, your chances of having a good time are greatly improved if you have sound health and a sound bank balance. Don't forget that we are talking about a period which may well be longer than your total years of employment.

So this chapter looks at the realities of retirement at the end of the twentieth century. How much money will you really need? Where will it come from? And what other things might you need to think about? And if you're nowhere near even thinking about retiring, don't think that what follows doesn't concern you. It does – so please read on!

WHO'S GOING TO PAY?

Many of us, particularly those over 40, have tended to take it for granted that something or someone – the age pension, a partner – will support us to some extent in our later years. But times have changed.

By 2010, it is estimated that people aged 65 and over will outnumber those under 15, and governments' most pressing problem will be how to provide for them. Put plainly, there simply won't be enough of a working population to provide future oldies with the government support that is available now: the pension is likely to become only a safety net for the most needy, and the dollars available are likely to be less than adequate for all our needs.

Second, and this is why planning for retirement is particularly important for women, with one in three marriages ending in divorce, and most married women outliving their partners, the majority of us are going to be totally responsible for our financial situation at some stage in our lives. And, of course, there are many women who will be the main breadwinner or will remain single.

In other words, it's vital that you make independent plans, as soon as possible, to fund your own retirement.

SO, WHAT'S RETIREMENT ALL ABOUT?

Imagine having twenty or more years in which to do anything you like. If you look back over the last decade or so, you can probably think of innumerable ways in which your life and your career have developed. You may have married, had children, met lifelong friends. You may have done one or two courses, and changed jobs several times. Think of the holidays you've had and the places you've visited; the meals out and the theatre and movies you've enjoyed; the hobbies which have enhanced your life. Why would this stop?

The dramatic point of difference between the retirees of the past and those of the future is that retirement no longer represents the short space of time between giving up work and waiting for death. We're living much longer, we're retiring earlier, and we're expecting much more out of life. And there's no doubt that, used productively, those twenty or so years represent another lifetime – a lifetime that does, though, need to be provided for, and more and more the onus for this is on us.

THE THREE AGES OF RETIREMENT

If yesterday you went to work and tomorrow you retire, you're not suddenly going to turn into a little old lady sitting by the fire. Given the long period that retirement represents, to think that your interests and activities will be constant over several decades is, of course, a nonsense. In fact there are more likely to be three phases to your retirement, none of them distinct, none of them immutably tied to a chronological age, and each as individual as you are. Each of these stages will make different demands on your income and assets.

When you first retire, assuming that this is anywhere from the age of 55 onwards, you'll be merely middle-aged. (Remember that a generation or two ago, 40 was 'middle-aged' and 60 'old': today 60 is middle-aged and 80 is old.) Assuming you're in good health, you may not retire at all at this stage but continue to work, wind down to part-time, or start your own business. You may have your children off your hands, but you may have aged parents to care for, or a spouse who is not as hale and hearty as you. This is a time when you may want to travel and take up new hobbies, and/or you may choose to move to your favourite holiday spot for good. In other words, this early part of your retirement, which will probably last until at least your late sixties or so, is likely to be a very active period.

The second stage covers roughly the decade of your seventies. At this time you may look for smaller or more manageable accommodation. It may become a priority to have your family and friends close by, and you may be more concerned about access to community and health services.

The third stage is when you're 80 years plus, an age group in which women greatly outnumber men. At this time your physical capabilities are likely to diminish, and you may need increased assistance and medical care.

RETIREMENT – THE CHALLENGE

'YOUNG PEOPLE, NOWADAYS, IMAGINE THAT MONEY IS EVERYTHING AND WHEN THEY GROW OLDER, THEY KNOW IT.'

— OSCAR WILDE

Ideally, you started work at 18 and put some of your first pay packet towards your retirement plan, in the form of superannuation and/or other investments and savings. In truth, this didn't happen: but don't worry – you're not alone, and you're not necessarily destined for poverty. No matter how late you start planning, you'll be better off than if you didn't plan at all. What you can achieve, though, depends on your age and your disposable income.

If you're in your twenties, you're sitting pretty. You should be contributing to a superannuation fund, but not an exorbitant amount as these are early days and you may prefer to save for or pay off a home. At this age it also makes sense to spend some money on anything (such as training) which will increase your earning capacity in your thirties, forties and fifties.

If you're in your thirties, you should keep up your superannuation payments (and even increase them if you have any spare money, though again not to an excessive degree). At this stage it's important to pay as much as possible off your mortgage and, if you don't have children to support, to try to build up any savings you have to cover emergencies (see Chapter 2 about this). You may even wish to dip your toe in the waters of investments such as shares: although they can be risky in the short term, you have the time to ride out the ups and downs of the market and will learn a lot along the way.

If you're in your forties, you're likely to be at your peak earning capacity. You should continue reducing your mortgage and increase your super contributions and other investments. This is the time when many people buy an investment property or build up a share portfolio.

Your fifties and sixties are a time to really turn up the heat and top up your super to a large degree. With between five and fifteen years until you retire, you need to know how you'll be placed when it's time for the gold watch. You may well start revising your attitude towards investments: until now you probably chose investments which offered the best capital growth, but at this stage you should start looking for a balance between growth and income. Your final years of employment are also a time to concentrate on becoming debt-free. Credit cards will, of course, still be useful in retirement, but try to avoid borrowing for consumables and holidays.

THAT'S ALL VERY WELL, BUT...

These scenarios assume an orderly progression and acquisition of assets – and life isn't always like that. You may have had children late, and be struggling to pay for their education at an age when your parents were beginning to wind down to retirement. You may be almost 40 and still renting, you may be starting again after a divorce, or you may be facing a shrinking job market in your field. Equally, you may be 50 and have few assets, and be worried about being retrenched. So, what do you do then?

RETIREMENT: TIME FOR A RETHINK

- **Clear all debts**, including your mortgage (you could use some of your superannuation payout for this). Doing this will not only give you peace of mind, but will also leave you free to focus on investing the remainder of your money.

- **Redo your budget.** Think about the things you might want to do once you've retired – travel? take up new hobbies? – and how much they will cost you, then take this into account when you are doing your budget. Remember that some of your expenses will be reduced when you retire, so you may have some spare cash to put towards your new plans.

- **Get some financial advice.** A financial adviser can help you decide where the income you are going to need could come from, suggest what to do with your superannuation, and recommend tax-effective strategies. Estate planning (which is mainly about what you want to happen to your assets when you die) should also be a priority, and a financial adviser can help you with this.

- **Think about where you want to live.** Are you happy where you are, or is your house too big? Do you need to sell your home to free up some cash? If so, are there any alternatives? This may not be an immediate priority, but you should think about it sooner rather than later, so that you are not forced into any hasty decisions.

The answer is that you do the best you can with the resources available, and you make choices. Perhaps instead of saving for a house, you should contribute aggressively to your super or other investments; perhaps you could consider a second job for a while; perhaps you could consider retraining for a career you can carry on into retirement, or start your own business while you have the fall-back position of a paid job. These options are particularly pertinent if you are in your fifties.

WHEN IT'S TIME TO THINK ABOUT RETIRING

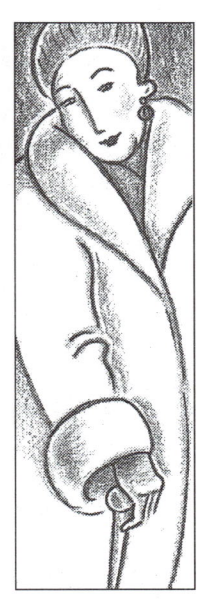

'FROM BIRTH TO EIGHTEEN A GIRL NEEDS GOOD PARENTS, FROM EIGHTEEN TO THIRTY-FIVE SHE NEEDS GOOD LOOKS, FROM THIRTY-FIVE SHE NEEDS A GOOD PERSONALITY, AND FROM FIFTY-FIVE ON SHE NEEDS GOOD CASH.'

— SOPHIE TUCKER

Your later working years are the ideal time to prepare yourself – mentally, physically and financially – for your retirement. The day you retire marks a transition in your way of life, and if your job has literally been your life you may find the change difficult. You may be concerned about the amount of free time you have and how you are going to organise yourself without the discipline that work provides. Your self-esteem may be tested each time someone asks you 'What do you do for a living?'

So don't wait until you retire to think about or develop interests outside work. Try out a range of hobbies and sports now, so that you get to know your talents, likes and dislikes. This may well have financial benefits if your talent or skill can be sold. Also consider your other needs when you're not working, such as keeping fit, expanding your social network through clubs or volunteer organisations, or perhaps taking time to study. The Council on the Ageing offers advice on just about every topic relevant to retirement.

Q *I really enjoy the mental stimulation and the company my job provides. What will happen when I retire?*

A Retiring from work doesn't mean you're retiring from life. There are lots of groups which provide meeting-places and a range of activities for like-minded women, from Rotary and Probus (Professional Business Retirees) to traditional women's clubs, which nowadays cater for a very wide range of interests. The Council for Adult Education and the University of the Third Age also give you the chance to meet new people as well as study.

THE NO-RETIREMENT OPTION

If you've had a challenging and rewarding career, and your health is good, why should you stop work at all? Or perhaps you need to work, because you've done the sums and you realise that you can't live comfortably enough on your savings.

Existing anti-discrimination legislation means that generally you can't be barred from continuing to work if you so wish. And as the baby boomers move through the age ranks their collective economic and political power will further influence our attitudes about older people and employment. Unfortunately, though, many older people still report problems in finding work, or feel pressure to accept being sidelined once they reach a certain age.

Of course, planning for a 'post-retirement' career should be undertaken well before the day arrives: you may need to do a course, build up contacts, or establish your credibility by undertaking projects in your chosen field.

Even if you're nowhere near retiring, take the time to consider whether you'll be physically or mentally up to your job further down the track: a career such as nursing or landscape gardening may be too demanding when you're 60 or 70.

Why should you stop work at all?

If you are approaching retirement age, you could perhaps consider moving from full-time to part-time work, which amongst other things will free you up to re-establish contacts and activities outside work. Or you could think about setting up some kind of arrangement with your current employer or within your profession, which allows you to organise work on your own terms. If you have been approached by other companies during your career but turned the jobs down, think about making contact with them now so that you can begin to build up clients.

A Whole New You?

Perhaps you will choose to change careers altogether. This is an attractive option for anyone who has always wanted to explore another side of their personality – to cash in on a creative talent, to teach, to counsel others, to write.

Given that you may well have twenty years to pursue your chosen path, you could find your second career every bit as rewarding – or even more so – than the first.

Going Out on Your Own

Or you may decide to start a business of your own – and, of course, being self-employed has the added benefit of allowing you to work for as long as you want to. If you're thinking about this option, see the section 'Going into Business' in Chapter 4, as many of the suggestions there apply equally to setting up a business once you've 'retired'. Be warned, though, that if your enterprise booms it may require more of your time than you envisaged. You may even find yourself working harder than ever before, at a time when you had planned to ease back.

Of course, do your homework first. Local councils and chambers of commerce and industry are good sources of information about local activities.

Most state libraries also have a business information service. Also consider whether the business you are considering is suitable as a part-time or home-based concern.

HOW MUCH MONEY WILL YOU NEED?

One of the most difficult things to get used to when you retire is the lack of a regular pay cheque. Obviously, you will have to rely on other sources of income, which might include interest from a bank or cash-management account or from fixed-interest investments such as debentures, rent from a property, dividends from shares, distributions from units in a managed fund, payments from a superannuation pension or annuity, or payments from a government pension.

Managing your money at this stage of your life is not just about watching how you spend – it's also about getting the most of what you have in hand. As you get older, your way of life will depend greatly on your health, income and access to transport. So how much money will you need for a comfortable and active retirement?

There are some simple sums you can do to work out what you'll need, but first up it's important to realise that your spending patterns are likely to be quite different once you've retired. If, for example, you own your own home outright, there'll be no more mortgage payments. You'll probably have all the household goods you need, and although these need replacing from time to time you're unlikely to be spending as much on them as you did in your twenties, thirties and forties.

If you're retiring from the workforce, your expenditure on clothes will undoubtedly diminish. Even if you're a clothes-aholic, casual clothes will probably best suit your new life and these tend to be less expensive than work gear. And you'll have more time to shop for bargains! On the other hand, when you work there are quite a few things you take for granted: for some, this might be the odd free pen, photocopying or lunch; for others, it might be a company car. These expenses will now be paid out of your own pocket – on the other hand, though, you'll no longer be paying daily for parking or transport. If you are lucky enough to have had a car through the company, you will of course have to consider buying one of your own: the expenses may be tax-deductible if you continue to work, though, and some insurance companies offer special deals for those over 55.

And, of course, your leisure expenditure is likely to increase. You may want to travel, to try new hobbies and sports, or to catch up on all the books, plays and movies your heart desires. Although you may be able to take advantage of Seniors Card discounts (see page 271), all such activities may eat into your available capital. And if you have plans to start a business of your own, you may need money to get it going.

Back to the Books

Some experts suggest that we should aim for an annual income in retirement of about 60 per cent of our final average salary: to achieve this you would need a savings pool of approximately 8.5 times your final salary at age 65 (more if you retired earlier than this age). To work out a realistic retirement income for *you*, it's worth taking the time to redo your budget (see Chapter 1), taking into account the changes in both your income and your expenses. If you're not yet close to retirement age, your sums will need to allow for the long-term effects of inflation and compound interest.

The budgeting exercise will give you a clear picture of where you are and what income you are likely to need. A financial adviser will be invaluable here. Once you've reassessed your budget and have a good idea of your financial position, the big question is: how long will your money last? This, of course, will depend on how much of your capital you spend each year, relative to how much your investments earn. You can work this out by using the table on page 260.

WHY STARTING TODAY IS JUST IN THE NICK OF TIME

So what do your figures look like? If the above exercise has given you a shock, what are your options?

Compulsory superannuation is the main solution put forward at present to provide income in retirement, but it has lulled some people into a false sense of security. If you think your employer's superannuation contribution is sufficient, you may be terribly wrong – remember that compulsory super has only been around for a relatively short time. But if

HOW LONG WILL YOUR MONEY LAST?

The following figures show that if you have investments earning 7 per cent a year, and each year you withdraw the equivalent of 8 per cent of your original sum, your money will last thirty years. If, on the other hand, you withdraw 12 per cent of the original sum each year, your money will last only twelve years.

ACCOUNT EARNINGS RATE	RATE AT WHICH ORIGINAL CAPITAL IS WITHDRAWN									
	6%	7%	8%	9%	10%	11%	12%	13%	14%	15%
12%								22	17	14
11%							23	17	14	12
10%						25	18	15	13	11
9%					26	20	16	14	12	11
8%				28	20	16	14	12	11	9
7%			30	22	17	14	12	11	10	9
6%		33	23	·18	15	13	11	10	9	8
5%	36	25	20	16	14	12	11	9	9	8

Source: *Kiplinger's Personal Finance Magazine*, June 1992

You can also use this chart to estimate the amount of savings you will need to fund your retirement. Assuming, for example, that you get 7 per cent return on your savings and that you need your savings to last thirty years, you would have to withdraw 8 per cent per year. So an annual income of $30 000 would require a savings pool of $375 000 (i.e. $30 000 x 8%), $20 000 would require $250 000, and so on.

you are young and expect to remain in the workforce full-time until you retire, it will probably provide you with more than enough to live on when you retire.

If, say, you are 20 and pay 10 per cent of your earnings into super until you are 65, your annual estimated income from super will be around 75 per cent of your salary throughout retirement. If, on the other hand, you begin contributing at 35, you would need to put in a staggering 22 per cent of your salary to achieve the same result.

But don't panic about these figures – they do assume that you will be relying totally on super. Hopefully you will have other savings or investments – and if you're young you've got plenty of time to reap the benefits of compound interest. (But even if you're 55 and have only just started to save, it's not too late: you'll still be better off than never having started at all.) And finally, of course, there's the traditional security blanket of owning your own home: although continuing low inflation may mean you're no longer guaranteed a big profit if and when you sell, well chosen real estate is still a good investment.

HANDLING YOUR MONEY
WHEN YOU RETIRE

'AN ANNUITY IS A VERY SERIOUS BUSINESS.'

— JANE AUSTEN

When you first retire it's an ideal time to visit (or revisit) a financial adviser. You could also consider contacting the National Information Centre on Retirement Investments (tel. 1800 020 110), which is government-funded but independent: it cannot offer financial advice, but can suggest what to think about when you are making financial decisions, including the pros and cons of different types of investments.

Now that you are no longer earning, you need to determine whether any investments you have are still appropriate to your income needs. Also, there may be new factors affecting your investment decisions, such as social-security provisions and any superannuation payout you may have received. A professional adviser can help you to get the best possible returns on your money and to take advantage of any tax concessions that might be available. Making uninformed decisions, on the other hand, may well see your capital and your income dwindle – and at this stage in life you may not be able to afford to make up those losses.

YOU'LL NEED MORE INCOME, BUT SOME GROWTH TOO

When you retire, you'll probably be more interested in a reliable income than you will in having investments that increase in value, but if you expect to live to a ripe old age you shouldn't overlook the danger of your money running out if you don't invest for capital growth as well.

It can't be said too often that the returns from 'safe' investments such as bank deposits are unlikely to counter the effects of inflation and taxation, and you could see your savings going backwards. If you want your money to last, you need to consider putting some of it into growth investments such as shares and property, which can provide increasing income to meet rising living costs. It's also important to spread the risk over a range of investments.

Don't overlook the danger of your money running out

Controlling the amount of income you get from your investments can be difficult, as the distributions are not always fixed, but there are ways to handle this. Fixed-interest investments such as term deposits, debentures and annuities do, of course, offer predictable returns. Some unit trusts (see the section 'Managed Funds' in Chapter 3) also allow you to nominate the amount of income you wish to

receive: this is paid to you out of distributions from the trust and, if necessary, from your capital. While this does make it easier for you to budget,
remember that the higher the income payment you request, the more likely
it is that you will have to draw on some of your capital as well. All in all, it's
a good idea to get professional advice on the best approach for your particular circumstances.

Q *I've invested in a unit trust, and my income cheque sometimes includes profits
from the sale of some of the trust's assets. These are hard to plan around, as they
alter the payments considerably. Is there anything I can do to make the
payments more even, so that I don't overspend in the months when I receive
larger amounts or, as happened recently, find money tight when the payments
are smaller?*

A One option might be to put all the irregular payments into an account
where you keep any additional at-call savings you have, and then
write a cheque from there into your transaction account for a set
amount each month.

DEEMED IF YOU DO, DAMNED IF YOU DON'T

For the purposes of determining people's eligibility for social-security benefits, the government assumes that any income pensioners receive from
savings or investments is earning a certain percentage each year. This is
known as *deeming*: the investment is deemed to have earned a certain return.

New legislation on deeming came into effect in 1996, which affects any
deposits with banks, building societies and credit unions, as well as listed
shares, investments in managed funds, and bonds issued by life-insurance
companies and friendly societies. Under these regulations, the first $30 000
($50 000 for couples) of your investments will be deemed to earn 5 per cent
a year, and anything over these amounts will be deemed to earn 7 per cent
– whether or not this is in fact the case. A couple with $60 000 worth of
shares, for example, will be deemed to earn an income of $3200,
as follows:

$2500 ($50 000 x 5 per cent) + $ 700 ($10 000 x 7 per cent) = $3200

GOLDEN RULES FOR GOLDEN OLDIES

- Your savings and investments will be your most secure source of income. So, if possible, lock into high interest rates if rates look like falling, as this will shelter you if they do drop, at least until your investment matures. A cash-management account or trust, or a fixed-term deposit, may offer higher rates.

- Unless you have a lot of money, you will inevitably have to draw on some of your capital in periods when investment returns are low. Don't be overly worried about this as long as you have a balanced portfolio offering some capital growth, which in the long term should replace some of the money you've drawn down.

- When you have retired it is a good opportunity to use 'income splitting' to reduce your tax, by putting any investments in the name of the partner with the lower income. But be aware that there may be capital-gains-tax implications if you rearrange your assets: your financial adviser can help you with this.

- Retirement is also an ideal time to think about estate planning and to review your will. You may want to consider arranging for an enduring or protected power of attorney, in case at some later date you become unable to look after your own affairs.

- Try to remain debt-free. But as, if you do need to borrow, it is unlikely that financial institutions will be knocking down your door to accommodate you, consider retaining at least one of your credit cards for emergencies.

- Always base your investment decisions on the merit of each product, *then* take into account its tax treatment and its impact on your social-security entitlements. A product chosen for its favourable social-security or tax treatment may not give you the best possible return. Make use of the Department of Social Security's Financial Information Service (tel. 13 23 00), which can help clarify the impact of investments on any pension entitlements.

At the time of writing you could, in effect, have up to $43 000 ($75 000 for couples) in financial assets without affecting your pension. If you have cash in a bank account which is earning less than 5 per cent, $2000 of this ($4000 for couples) will be deemed to earn either 5 per cent or the actual interest rate – whichever is lower: this is part of the $30 000 ($50 000) threshold.

Under this system you won't be penalised – in fact you'll be ahead – if the percentage return on your investments is greater than the deemed rate. But if your investments return you less than the deemed rate, you'll lose out. The new system does make things to some extent fairer for pensioners who own shares or other capital-growth investments purchased after September 1988. Whereas any capital gain was included as income for the purposes of deeming even if you hadn't cashed in your investment, since July 1996 this has no longer been the case. Any such profit is, though, counted for the purposes of the assets test.

What Do I Do With My Superannuation?

When you stop working, you will have to decide what to do with any superannuation you have accumulated. The complexities of the superannuation system are dealt with in more detail in Chapter 3, but there are quite a few things to think about (not least of these being the tax implications) before you decide where to put your super benefits when you retire. Do you, for example, need immediate income or not? What's the tax situation?

Depending on your age, you can 'roll over' your super payment within the superannuation system, cash it in, or do a mixture of both. If you roll it into any of the following, you will continue to benefit from tax concessions:
▲ a superannuation fund
▲ an approved deposit fund or a deferred annuity (up to age 65)
▲ an allocated pension or annuity
▲ an immediate annuity
The last two of these, and some super funds, will pay you an income.

If you don't need regular income from your superannuation, it's probably most sensible to invest it in a super fund, an approved deposit fund or a deferred annuity. These are available from major financial institutions such as banks, fund managers and insurance companies, and offer you a wide range of options, from cash to shares. This is particularly advantageous if you have a partner under 65 years of age, because men's super is exempt from social-security means-testing until they reach 65 and even if he has a substantial amount of superannuation it won't affect your entitlement to the age pension. Women's super, on the other hand, is means-tested as soon as we become eligible for the pension, which can be at 60.

'SUPER' INVESTMENTS THAT PROVIDE INCOME

If you need income or have reached the age of 65, it is worth looking at the income-producing investments available within the superannuation system. The two main types are *immediate annuities* and *allocated pensions and annuities*.

As well as looking at the tax implications of such investments (see the box on page 268), you should also consider their effect on your social-security entitlements. This is a complicated area, so it's advisable to seek advice from a financial adviser, the Department of Social Security or the Department of Veterans Affairs.

Immediate Annuities

These pay you an income for the rest of your life (lifetime annuity) or for a set period (term-certain annuity). The best time to buy a **lifetime annuity** is when interest rates are high, as these annuities are linked to the current interest rates. The gamble is, of course, that you may get run over by a bus the day after you buy the annuity and the insurance company keeps the money. On the other hand, you could live to be 100, in which case it would be a terrific investment. You can build in a minimum period for which payments are guaranteed, or you can have the payments continue to a spouse on your death, but these features come at a price and your payments will be reduced accordingly. By their very nature, lifetime annuities are not a good investment if you are suffering ill-health. Shop around for the best rates, and check the financial standing of the company offering the annuity, so you can be sure they will keep up the payments.

A **complying annuity** is a lifetime annuity which allows you to increase the amount of superannuation benefits you can receive at the concessional tax rate. It must comply with regulations set down by the Insurance and Superannuation Commission, which include the following: it must be payable for a lifetime; your payments must be increased annually either in line with inflation or by 5 per cent (whichever is lower); it cannot be used as security for borrowings; it cannot be com-muted (withdrawn) after six months; you cannot elect to have any residual amount paid out on your death, although you can nominate a spouse to receive future payments and a guaranteed period for which payments are made to your estate if you and your spouse die within ten years of purchasing the annuity.

With a **term-certain annuity**, the payments continue for an agreed length of time. If you die before the end of the term, payments will be made to your estate for the rest of the agreed period.

A Tale of Two Sisters

At the age of 60, Julie decided to opt for an annual minimum payment of $6000 from her allocated pension (this was about 6 per cent of her account balance). Her twin sister Maureen took the maximum permitted amount, which was 11 per cent of her account balance. As they each had $100 000 invested and the return was 10 per cent over the year, Julie increased her balance by $4000 while Maureen had to draw down some of her capital. So always do your sums carefully, and get advice if you are not sure of the implications of your decisions.

Allocated Pensions and Annuities

Allocated pensions and annuities allow you to choose the amount of income you get, subject to minimum and maximum levels set by the government. You can choose your own portfolio of investments, but of course you need to be aware that poor investment decisions will reduce your capital. Not only will your capital last longer if you draw down the minimum amount, but you will also benefit from deferred tax as any extra earnings from your investments (over and above what you receive as income) are not taxed. While your investments can increase in value, you face the risk that your money may run out before you die.

PENSIONS AND ANNUITIES: TAX ADVANTAGES

To encourage people to opt for income rather than a lump sum, the government offers a number of tax concessions if you roll your super into a pension or annuity.

- Tax on your superannuation lump sum is deferred until you make a withdrawal, and is eliminated completely if you receive income payments only and never make a withdrawal.
- You pay no tax on any earnings kept within the fund.
- Some of your payments (referred to as the undeducted purchase price or UPP) are returned to you tax-free.
- There is a 15 per cent tax rebate (which is generally available only if you are 55 or over) on the part of your pension or annuity payment which is included as assessable income – which greatly increases the amount of income you get tax-free. If, for example, you receive an assessable income of $18 000 a year from from a pension or annuity, you could get all of this tax-free because you are eligible for the normal tax-free threshold of $5400. The balance of $12 600 is taxed at the next personal tax rate (including the Medicare levy) of 21.5 per cent ($2709), but as the rebate (15 per cent of $18 000) equals $2700, you effectively get the $18 000 tax-free!

THE SOCIAL-SECURITY SAFETY NET

Today, nearly 80 per cent of 65-year-olds in Australia receive part or all of the age pension, which amounts to $335 per fortnight for a single pensioner and around $280 each per fortnight for a married couple. It's worth noting that more women than men in the 55+ age group expect this to be their main form of income when they retire. But as we said at the beginning of this chapter, in the not-too-distant future the pension is likely to support only the most needy.

A TESTING TIME: WHEN ARE YOU ELIGIBLE FOR THE PENSION?

Until recently, women were eligible for the age pension at 60, but this is now being raised to 65 (as is the case already for men). In order to take account of the differing expectations of different generations, this will be a staggered system: women born before 31 December 1936 will still be eligible at 60.5 years, but the qualifying age increases thereafter in six-month age brackets with the effect that those born after 1 January 1949 won't be eligible until they're 65.

Whether or not you are eligible for the pension also depends on both your assets and your income. The more you own or earn, the less you receive.

The Assets Test

At the moment, if you're single and own your own home, you're entitled to the full age pension if your assets (excluding your home) are not worth more than $118 000 ($167 500 for a couple). The cut-off point for a part pension is around $232 000 ($367 000 for couples). For non-home-owners the assets limit for a full pension increases to more than $200 000 for singles, and about $251 000 for couples. The pension reduces by $3 per fortnight for every $1000 worth of assets above these limits.

The Income Test

If you're single, you can earn up to $94 per fortnight and still be eligible for the full pension; a couple can earn a combined income of $164. For every dollar of income over this amount, the pension reduces by 50 cents in the dollar for a single pensioner, and 25 cents each in the dollar for a couple, until a cut-off point (currently around $776 per fortnight or $20 176 a year for a single person, and a combined income of around $1295 a fortnight or $33 670 a year for a couple) is reached.

TIPS ON IMPROVING YOUR POSITION

There are a few ways to improve your position as far as means-testing is concerned. As well as making the most of the new deeming rules (see page 263), these include the following:

- If you receive a pension, you can give away up to $10 000 every twelve months without this affecting your eligibility. If you give away more than this, you will be assessed on the extra amount as if you still had the money: if, say, you give $15 000 to a relative, the excess $5000 is treated as an asset as far as the assets test is concerned, and the current deeming rate is applied under the income test.

- Funeral bonds (a friendly-society bond specifically designed to meet funeral expenses) up to the value of $5000 are exempt from all means-testing and any earnings on them are tax-free, provided they are used only to cover funeral costs.

- Investment property, although included in the assets test, can work well for you as far as the income test is concerned, as you are assessed only on rent you actually receive.

- Any payment from a lifetime annuity (after expenses) which is considered to be a return of your capital is not assessed as income.

There are various other government payments available (such as support for the disabled, and ex-services pensions), which also depend on your circumstances. To find out if you're eligible, contact the Department of Social Security or the Department of Veterans Affairs.

THE SENIORS CARD – CHEAP AT HALF THE PRICE

Once you retire, you're likely to spend a much larger proportion of your income on enjoying yourself. The government's Seniors Card is a real plus here: it entitles you to discounts on a wide range of government and private services (including transport, entertainment, legal and other professional services and education) and consumer goods.

In most states the Seniors Card is not means-tested, but to be eligible you must be over 60 and work no more than twenty hours a week. To apply, contact the Seniors Card Office in your state. The benefits do vary from state to state though, and not all have reciprocal agreements, so investigate the situation if you're crossing the border.

THERE'S NO PLACE LIKE HOME

By the mid-1990s, 84 per cent of Australians aged over 60 owned their own home and research shows that most of them would prefer to remain there. Certainly there are big advantages in staying put: you're familiar with the local shops, transport and other services, and are likely to have friends nearby. And moving is also a large, costly and often stressful undertaking.

Yet you may at some stage have reasons to move. Later in the chapter we look at your choices if you decide to move because you want a change in lifestyle. If, on the other hand, you feel you *have to* move – perhaps because you've got too much capital tied up in your home and you need to free up cash, or because you need to modify your home and again cash is the problem – selling up may not be the only alternative. So let's look at your options.

STAYING PUT

If you want to stay put but think you can't afford to, there are many alternatives to selling your home. Local councils offer some indirect financial

---

LOAN AND SALE PLANS: YOUR MUST-DO LIST

- Contact the Department of Social Security to find out if any plan you're considering will interfere with your pension entitlements.
- Make sure you get an up-to-date valuation of your house before you commit yourself.
- Don't sell your home too cheaply just to free up some cash in the short term.
- As the contracts can be complex, make sure you understand everything in them before you sign. If there's anything you're not clear about, see a lawyer.

---

assistance for pensioners, such as deferring or giving rebates on rates. Alternatively, you could convert your home into cash through what is known as a home-equity conversion (HEC) scheme. The main types are loan plans and sale plans: you can get information about these from banks and real-estate agents.

Loan Plans

These arrangements allow you to borrow a percentage of the value of your home, either as a lump sum or in the form of regular payments. You pay interest on the loan, and the loan and interest are usually repaid when you stop living at home. The benefits are that you retain title to your home, which may make you feel more secure, and you are entitled to any capital gain on its full value. You will, though, have a compounding debt and will not know the final value of your holding (that is, its worth when you die or stop living there).

Sale Plans

Here you sell your home at an agreed value, but you and your partner can go on living there for the rest of your lives. The purchaser pays the agreed price up-front, or in instalments (in which case the remaining balance is payable upon your death or departure from the house). One plus is that you will know in advance the nominal value of your stake in the property. On the other hand, you will be a tenant rather than the owner and may have to pay rent; you will also forego all future capital gains.

Funding Modifications to Your Home

There is also an arrangement between the federal government and the Advance Bank to make loans of up to $7500 available for modifications to houses. For more information, contact the Advance Bank on 1800 051 234.

THE NEXT BEST THING

Many older people consider 'a granny flat' at their children's home the next best thing to staying in their own home, as it gives them independence as well as proximity to their family. A granny flat can also add to the value of a property.

If this is something you are considering, and while such arrangements are often informal, it really is wise (and you may feel more secure) to have a written agreement, especially if you contribute money for construction of the flat. An agreement may also protect both you and your direct offspring should the property become part of a divorce settlement.

Also bear in mind that if the 'flat' is worth more than $84 000, it will be considered a 'home' – and you will be considered a home-owner – for the purposes of the social-security assets test.

It is also worth noting that while such an arrangement can be financially beneficial to all concerned, it can be emotionally stressful.

If a granny flat is not an option and you want to stay at home, financial assistance from the Department of Social Security may be available to help with rent, or to provide a carer's pension.

WHEN YOU WANT TO MAKE A MOVE

Even when you're sure you're ready for a move, don't rush into anything. Stories abound of retirees heading off for good to their favourite holiday spot, only to find that while the weather was glorious in spring it became unbearable in summer. Spending some time in the area you are considering – by way

HOLIDAY-HOME HELL

Barbara and Ron had always holidayed at Peregian Beach in Queensland. It was peaceful, yet close to Noosa where they could enjoy good restaurants and shops. So when they retired, they sold up and bought a hilltop house there.

The first few months were great. But when Ron's eyesight suddenly began to deteriorate and he no longer felt happy driving, it was far more difficult to get around. Barbara hadn't driven for years and wasn't keen to start again; and public transport in the area was less frequent than they would have liked. Increasingly, they felt isolated from their friends and deprived of the activities they had so enjoyed in the city.

Eventually they sold up and moved back to town, though by the time they had paid two lots of relocation expenses they could only afford a small apartment. When their old friends Jill and Graham told them that they were considering moving for good to their favourite holiday spot, Barbara and Ron had some practical tips to give them.

of holidaying there at different times of the year, or by renting before you buy – will give you a feel for the climate and for the services available. If you are moving to a quieter spot, remember that the range of activities and services may be reduced.

On the other hand, there are some areas (notably the central coast of New South Wales and the Queensland Gold Coast) to which retirees have traditionally flocked and where the services are great. The only danger here is that real-estate developers are well aware of this fact and some build specifically for this market. Should you wish to (or have to) sell such a home at a later date, you could find this difficult if there is a glut of such properties or if you have paid an inflated price (relative to a standard local property). This doesn't, of course, mean that you shouldn't make such a move – it simply means you need to be sensible and apply the same criteria that you would if you were buying any property.

Of equal importance are relocation costs, which can be very high. So do your sums: if you're moving in order to free up some cash, make sure these costs don't have the opposite effect.

PURCHASE PRICE – PLUS!

In 1994 the Real Estate Institute estimated the cost of purchasing a $250 000 property in the Northern Beaches area of Sydney. It may come as no surprise to anyone who has ever bought a house that the basic costs (stamp duty, conveyancing, surveying and inspection fees, insurance, removal) added up to more than $12 600 – and this did not include expenses such as loan-establishment fees. And if, in order to move, you sell another property of similar value, legal fees for the transaction would be about $1250 and the agent's commissions a further $6000 or so. Thus the total cost of such a move would be almost $20 000, or 8 per cent of the purchase price. So do your figures carefully before you throw away the key to your present home. (The typical costs associated with buying and selling a house are outlined in the section 'Buying a Home' in Chapter 4.)

Moving On Up?

If you find a property you like but it is worth more than your current home, you could consider a shared equity arrangement. This is where someone else (a family member, say) lends you the difference between the two prices and you pay rent on the borrowed portion. This situation can be worthwhile if a beneficiary of your will wants to provide the additional funds, as it means both that you have a better place to live in and that your beneficiary potentially has a better investment in the long term.

RENTING

The pros and cons of renting versus owning your home are discussed in the section 'Buying a Home' in Chapter 4. If you have the means to do so, you may well decide to live in rented accommodation when you retire. But you will need fairly substantial means and should always do your sums carefully, as a large proportion of your income may go in rent and there is little protection against rent increases.

Hopefully you won't find yourself forced to rent because you have no other choice. Rental assistance for those on low incomes is available from the Department of Social Security, but the maximum amount is little more than $72 per fortnight for a single person and around $68 (combined) for a couple. This could well limit the choice of accommodation to public housing, which can only accommodate a small percentage of people aged over 65, and for which waiting lists are long.

What Do Retirement Villages Offer?

Retirement villages are increasingly popular with older retirees. By 1994 there were an estimated 60 000 people throughout Australia living in such centres, and this figure is expected to double by 2011.

Moving to a retirement village is largely a lifestyle choice: they provide safety, security and a social life, which appeals to many women who would otherwise be living alone. But they are not necessarily a good financial investment: under some tenancy agreements, you may outlay a significant amount up-front for your home but you may not be entitled to the full capital gain when you sell. This results from a deferred management fee, where the costs of managing the village, rather than being deducted initially and thus reducing the money available to residents, is deducted on the sale of the property. Such a fee is linked to the duration of your occupancy: it can be 2.5 per cent of the initial purchase price per annum (up to a given limit of years), or a percentage of any capital gain. As long as you understand the contract when you sign, this fee should not come as a shock when you want to sell.

Where Can You Find Out About Them?
The Council on the Ageing (which is a government-funded organisation) should be one of your first ports of call if you are considering a retirement village. Its useful publication, *Consumer's Guide to Resident Funded Retirement Villages*, provides information and comparisons on individual villages.

Word of mouth, particularly references from existing village residents,

RETIREMENT VILLAGES: THINGS TO CONSIDER

- There may be substantial entry costs (purchase price, stamp duty, legal fees), ongoing costs (maintenance, insurance, rates and services) and outgoing costs (deferred management fees).
- Your financial gain may be limited if the contract provides the operator with a share of the sale price, either through a deferred management fee or a portion of the capital gain, or both. You could also be liable for ongoing maintenance and service costs until your unit is sold, even if it is vacant.
- You may not have any control over the choice of contractors employed to maintain the property and facilities, and you are vulnerable to the cost of rising maintenance fees.
- If no nursing facilities are provided, you may have to sell your unit if a time comes when you need nursing care, which could put pressure on you to sell at a low price. In addition, there is no guarantee of a place in a nursing home even where one exists in the retirement village, and you could be faced with extra costs for this care if it is available.
- Your social-security entitlements may be reduced depending on what you sell your home for and the amount you pay for entry into the retirement village.

is also a good source of information – although, of course, everyone has different priorities. The Retirement Village Association, comprising the proprietors of most of the major retirement villages, will answer queries and supply a booklet called *Guidelines for People Contemplating Retirement Village Life*.

A 1995 amendment to the Retirement Villages Act introduced a new code of conduct. Many of the essential points deal with the calculation of fees and the resolution of disputes: the code is supervised by the Department of Consumer Affairs, which you should contact if you have a complaint.

Which Kind of Village is Right for You?

There are two main types of retirement village.

▲ DONOR-FUNDED VILLAGES are run by welfare and church organisations, and are the cheaper option. The main advantage is that your initial contribution is minimal and after this you are only required to pay maintenance costs. There are criteria for eligibility and there are usually long waiting lists, which reflect the affordability and relative popularity of this kind of accommodation. For more information, contact your local church or the Council on the Ageing.

▲ RESIDENT-FUNDED VILLAGES are privately operated and offer a range of tenancy arrangements, including leasehold, strata title, company share, and 'loan or licence' agreements. Some of these (like leasehold, and strata or company title) are similar to the agreements used for buying any property, while loan and licence is a special village-oriented arrangement. Resident-funded villages are, in the main, expensive, because you are usually paying for improved amenities and a range of recreational facilities – in other words, a particular lifestyle. As the contracts are complex, it's advisable to enlist the assistance of a solicitor before signing anything. This is particularly the case with loan and licence arrangements, as the agreement directly affects your security of tenure, your ability to borrow against your unit, and also your entitlement to any capital gain.

WHAT HAPPENS IF YOU NEED ONGOING CARE?

If you need a high level of daily care and the services provided by the state government's Home and Community Care Program are not sufficient, a nursing home or hostel may be the only solution. Nursing homes provide 24-hour nursing care, while hostels cater for people who do not require continuous care but need help with daily tasks such as dressing, feeding or bathing.

The financial arrangements vary, depending on your circumstances and the range of services provided. If you are receiving a full pension and rental assistance, 85 per cent of this will be used towards meeting the costs of your care in a nursing home; the government subsidises the rest. If you have sufficient financial means, a hostel may require an initial contribution, most of which is returned to you when you leave.

The institution should give you written information about the financial arrangements and services, and a contract which sets out your rights and responsibilities. If you don't understand the contract, seek legal advice. Standards in approved hostels and nursing homes (which may be privately run or government-funded) are monitored by the Commonwealth Department of Health and Family Services. The department has a charter covering things such as personal rights and money matters: copies of this and of reports on individual nursing homes and hostels are available from the department, public libraries, and most of the institutions themselves. If you sell your house to move into a hostel or nursing home, the change in your assets situation may affect your social-security entitlements.

HEALTH ISSUES

The Australian Bureau of Statistics projects that the fastest-growing age group through the next decade will be those older than 75. Economic forecasts also estimate that, by 2051, 52 per cent of health expenditure will be on the 65+ age group, compared to 33.5 per cent at the beginning of the 1990s.

At the same time, recent evidence has shown that the majority of older people remain in relatively good health until the last year or two of their lives. But with Medicare struggling to cope with spiralling demand, and increasing pressure on the hospital system, health insurance in our later years is something all of us need to think about.

We look at the general arguments for and against private health cover in Chapter 2, but there are some special considerations for those in the 60+ age group. A recent health survey by the Australian Bureau of Statistics found that hypertension, arthritis and heart disease were the three most common health problems of the aged. There are also, of course, 'lesser' afflictions that tend to increase hand-in-hand with the years – such as eyesight, hearing and mobility problems. Private health cover can help offset the costs of treatment for many of these problems. You may also be eligible for government assistance: if, for example, you receive at least $1 of a social-security pension, you are entitled to a range of benefits, including free or concessional dental care, eye care and pharmaceutical prescriptions. And even if you do not receive a pension, you may qualify for the Seniors Health Card, which entitles you to concessions on prescriptions, hearing aids and dental care. You can apply for this card via the Social Security Teleservice line on 13 24 68.

In the end, the decision to have (or not to have) private cover is not a purely financial one – it involves peace of mind, which is very hard to put a price on. If you do choose private cover, as usual it pays to shop around, because not only will premiums vary but the terms of the policy will too. In particular, get quotes from organisations which have developed health-care plans specifically for older people (some offer up to 20 per cent off the premium): contact the Council on the Ageing for information about such policies.

REAPING THE REWARDS

Retirement, then, is all about reaping your rewards, both personal and financial. If you have good health, you should be able to enjoy this time actively. And if you have enough income, you will also enjoy financial security.

A FEW FINAL WORDS

My main aim in writing this book has been to suggest some practical ways of managing your money and so help you along the road to financial independence. I also wanted to make it clear that you don't need to be a financial whiz to get ahead. We all have the ability to be successful investors. We just need to know where to access the necessary information and where to get good advice, and above all to have the right attitude.

So what are the keys to developing good money habits?

▲ Give financial decision-making the attention it deserves. Even if you are trying to juggle family and work responsibilities, it's vitally important to take the time to understand your options.

▲ Value whatever money you earn, and try to regularly save a portion of it.

▲ Have a positive attitude, which really will affect whether you succeed or fail – and this goes for most things in life, not just money.

▲ Set some goals. The real motivation for being a good money manager comes from having a reason to save.

▲ Don't spend beyond your means, tempting as it can be. Control your credit, rather than letting it control you.

▲ Don't be afraid to try. Put down any 'mistakes' to experience, and learn from them.

▲ It's never too early or too late to start planning – so do it now! You'll be better off than if you didn't plan at all.

I hope that this book has given you the confidence and belief that you can become a better money manager. But remember that while money will certainly give you more choices about how you live your life, it is in the end only a tool. So try to take a balanced view, and don't, in pursuit of your financial goals, neglect your personal needs and wants.

USEFUL CONTACTS

- As addresses and telephone numbers may change, it's advisable to check your current directory.
- FREECALL (prefix 1800) numbers are available only to people who live outside the metropolitan area.
- You can call numbers with the prefix 13 from anywhere in Australia for the cost of a local call (don't add an STD code).

BANKRUPTCY

The **Insolvency and Trustee Services of Australia** (ITSA) provides advice and information about credit problems, insolvency and bankruptcy.

ACT Level 2, 42 Macquarie St, Barton 2600; tel. (06) 250 6994

NSW Level 10, 255 Elizabeth St, Sydney 2000; tel (02) 9581 7822

NT 8th floor, National Mutual Building, 9-11 Cavenagh St, Darwin; tel. (08) 8943 1450

Qld 13th floor, 340 Adelaide St, Samuel Griffith Building, Brisbane 4000; tel. (07) 3360 5444; 1st floor NAB Building, 315 Ross River Rd, Aitkenvale 4814; tel. (077) 21 1177

SA 18th floor, 25 Grenfell St, Adelaide; tel. (08) 8205 4295

Tas. 22 Elizabeth St, Hobart 7000; tel. (03) 6221 7777

Vic. Level 9, Melbourne Central, 360 Elizabeth St, Melbourne 3000; tel. (03) 9272 4800

WA 2 The Esplanade, Perth 6000; tel. (09) 268 1222

- see also *financial counselling* and *law and legal services*

BANKS AND BANKING

Banking Ombudsman: tel. 1800 337 444 (all states); PO Box 14240, Melbourne City Mail Centre, Melbourne 8001
- see also *credit*

BUSINESS ADVICE

The following government organisations provide advice and assistance if you're starting up a business.

ACT (nearest office – Goulburn): Department of Fair Trading, 39 Goldsmith St, Goulburn 2580; tel. (048) 22 1277

NSW Office of Small Business, Grnd Floor, 140 Philip St, Sydney 2000; tel. 13 11 45

NT Small Business Advisory Service, Development House, 76 The Esplanade, Darwin 0800; tel. (08) 8999 7914; or 1800 193 111 (NT only)

Qld Queensland Small Business Corporation, Level 20, 111 George St, Brisbane 4000; tel. (07) 3834 6789 or 1800 177 324 (Qld only)

SA The Business Centre,145 South Tce, Adelaide 5000; tel. (08) 233 4600 or 1800 188 018 (SA only)

Tas. Tasmania Development & Resources, Small Business Service, ANZ Centre, 22 Elizabeth St, Hobart 7000; tel. (03) 6233 5712

Vic. Small Business Development Corporation, Level 5, 55 Collins St, Melbourne 3000; tel (03) 9655 3300 or 1800 136034 (Vic. only)

WA Small Business Development Corporation, 553 Hay St (cnr Pier St), Perth 6000; tel. (09) 220 0222 or 1800 073 340

CARS – BUYING AND SELLING

The **state Automobile Associations** offer a range of services , including mechanical inspections and other checks, and loan finance.

NSW and ACT
    NRMA, 151 Clarence St , Sydney 2000; tel. (02) 13 2132
NT AANT, MLC Building, 79-81 Smith St, Darwin 0800; tel. (08) 8981 3837
Qld RACQ, GPO Building, 261 Queen St, Brisbane 4000; tel. (07) 3361 2565
SA RAA, 41 Hindmarsh Square, Adelaide 5000; tel. (08) 8202 4600
Tas. RACT, Murray St (cnr Patrick St), Hobart 7000; tel. (03) 6232 6300
Vic. RACV, 360 Bourke St, Melbourne 3000; tel. (03) 9790 2211
WA RAC of WA, 228 Adelaide Tce, Perth 6000; tel. (09) 421 4000

Government Registers of Vehicles can tell you whether a car you're considering buying is stolen or has money owing on it.

NSW and NT
    Register of Encumbered Vehicles Service (REVS): tel. (02) 9600 0022
Qld Motor Vehicle Securities Register: tel. (07) 3246 1599
SA Vehicles Securities Register: tel. (08) 8232 0800
Tas. Vehicle Security Register: tel. (03) 6233 5201 (outside Tas. only)
Vic. Vehicle Securities Register: tel. (03) 9348 1222
WA Register of Encumbered Vehicles Service (REVS): tel. (09) 222 0711

CONSUMER AFFAIRS

These departments deal with consumer complaints on a wide range of matters.

ACT Consumer Affairs Bureau, 2nd Floor, GIO House, City Walk, Canberra City 2601; tel. (06) 207 0400
NSW Department of Fair Trading Service Centre, Stockland House, Level 6, 175 Castlereagh St, Sydney 2000; tel. (02) 9286 0006
NT Office of Consumer Affairs and Fair Trading, Law Department of NT, Tourism House, 43 Mitchell St , Darwin 0800; tel. (08) 8999 5184 or 1800 019 319 (NT only)
Qld Office of Consumer Affairs, 50 Ann St, Brisbane 4000; tel. (07) 3246 1500
SA Consumer Affairs Section, Office of Consumer and Business Affairs, 4th floor, 91 Grenfell St, Adelaide 5000; tel. (08) 8204 9777
Tas. Office of Consumer Affairs, 99 Bathurst St, Hobart 7000; tel. (03) 6233 4567
Vic. Office of Fair Trading and Business Affairs, Level 2, 452 Flinders St, Melbourne 3000; tel. (03) 9627 6000
WA Ministry of Fair Trading, 4th Floor, 251 Hay St, East Perth 6004; tel. (09) 222 0666 or 1800 199 117 (WA only)

CREDIT

Credit Reference Association: GPO Box 9991, Canberra 2601; tel. 1300 364 141
• see also *financial counselling*

DIVORCE AND FAMILY LAW

The **Family Court** offers counselling, mediation, and information about procedures in the event of marriage breakdown.

ACT cnr University Avenue & Childers St, Canberra 2600; tel. (06) 267 0511
NSW Lionel Bowen Building, 97-99 Goulburn St, Sydney 2000; tel. (02) 9217 7326
NT cnr Mitchell & Herbert Sts, Darwin 0800; tel. (08) 8981 1488
Qld GPO Box 9991 Brisbane 4001; tel. (07) 3248 2200
SA 25 Grenfell St, Adelaide 5000; tel. (08) 8205 2666

Tas.   39-41 Davey St, Hobart 7000;
       tel. (03) 6232 1725
Vic.   Level 18, Marland House,
       570 Bourke St, Melbourne 3000;
       tel. (03) 9604 2900
WA   150 Tce Rd, Perth 6000;
       tel. (09) 224 8222

Relationships Australia (formerly the Marriage Guidance Council) provides advice and assistance on financial and other matters for anyone experiencing difficulties in a relationship.

ACT   15 Napier Close, Deakin 2600;
      tel. (06) 281 3600
NSW   5 Sera St, Lane Cove 2066;
      tel. (02) 9418 8800
NT   75 Woods St, Darwin 0800;
      tel. (08) 8981 6676
Qld   159 St Pauls Tce, Spring Hill 4000;
      tel. (07) 3839 9262
SA   55 Hutt St, Adelaide 5000;
      tel. (08) 8223 4566
Tas. 306 Murray St, Hobart 7000;
      tel. (03) 6231 3141
Vic. 46 Princess St , Kew 3101;
      tel. (03) 9853 5354
WA   755 Albany Highway, East Victoria
      Park 6101; tel. (09) 470 5109

Child Support Agency: tel. 13 1272 or 13 1107
Child Support Review Office: tel.13 1141

EMPLOYMENT

The **Federal Department of Industrial Relations** provides information on awards and other employment matters.

ACT   Federal Award Inquiries:
      tel. (06) 247 0144; State Award
      Inquiries: tel. (02) 266 0688
NSW   Federal and State Award Inquiries:
      tel. (02) 9282 0888
NT   tel. (08) 8946 1666 or 1800 815 642
      (NT only)
Qld   Federal Award Inquiries:
      tel. (07) 3231 2533; State Award

      Inquiries: tel. (07) 3236 3733
SA   Federal Award Inquiries:
      tel. (08) 8237 6299; State Award
      Inquiries: tel. (08) 8207 1999
Tas. Federal Award Inquiries:
      tel. (03) 6235 1912; State Award
      Inquiries: tel. (03) 6233 7657
Vic. Federal Award Inquiries:
      tel. (03) 9240 1000; State Award
      Inquiries: tel. (03) 9655 1333
WA   Federal Award Inquiries:
      tel. (09) 321 7060; State Award
      Inquiries: tel. (09) 481 0647

FINANCIAL ADVICE AND PLANNING

The **Financial Planning Association of Australia** produces a booklet on how to select a good financial planner and also has a list of financial planners in your state.

ACT   29 Bentham St, Yaralumla 2600;
      tel. (06) 281 3351
NSW   Suite 404, 89 York St, Sydney 2000;
      tel. (02) 9299 8300
Qld   Level 23, Central Plaza 2, 66 Eagle St,
      Brisbane 4000; tel. (07) 3229 0455
SA   Level 1, 28 Greenhill Rd, Wayville
      5034; tel. (08) 8373 3936
Tas. 2nd floor, 25 Davey St, Hobart 7000;
      tel. (03) 6224 8855
Vic. 6/50 Queen St, Melbourne 3000;
      tel. (03) 9614 2289
WA   11 Angwin St, East Fremantle 6158;
      tel. (09) 319 1941

• see also *financial counselling* and *investing*

FINANCIAL COUNSELLING

NSW and ACT
      Credit Helpline: tel. (02) 995 15544
      or 1800 808 488
Qld   Financial Counselling Services (Qld)
      Inc: tel. (07) 3257 1957
SA   Department of Family and Community
      Services: tel. (08) 8226 7000

Tas.   Anglicare Financial Counselling
        Service: tel. (03) 6223 4595
Vic.   Credit Helpline (Vic.) Ltd:
        tel. (03) 9602 3800 or 1800 803 800
        (Vic. only)
WA   Family & Children's Services:
        tel. (09) 222 2555

HEALTH AND COMMUNITY SERVICES

• see *retirement and ageing*

HOMES – BUYING AND SELLING

Real Estate Institutes provide advice on
buying and selling homes.
Real Institute of Australia, PO Box 234,
Deaken West 2600; tel (06) 282 4277
NSW   30-32 Wentworth Avenue, Sydney
        2000; tel. (02) 9264 2343
NT   191 Stuart Highway; Parap 0820;
        tel. (08) 8981 8905
Qld   Turbo Dve, Coorparoo 4151;
        tel. (07) 3891 5711
SA   249 Greenhill Rd, Dulwich 5065;
        tel. (08) 8366 4300
Tas.   33 Melville St, Hobart 7000;
        tel. (03) 6223 4769
Vic.   335 Camberwell Rd, Camberwell
        3124; tel. (03) 9205 6677
WA   215 Hay St, Subiaco 61800;
        tel. (09) 380 8222
    The **Housing Industry Association** mainly
represents builders, but also provides services
such as building inspections for consumers.
ACT   25 Geils Court, Deakin 2600;
        tel. (06) 249 6366
NSW   10 Pitt St, Parramatta 2150;
        tel. (02) 663 4488
Qld   58 Hope St, South Brisbane 4104;
        tel. (07) 3846 1298
SA   Station Place (cnr Port Rd),
        Hindmarsh 5007; tel. (08) 346 5091
Tas.   163 Campbell St, Hobart 7000;
        tel. (03) 6234 8922

Vic.   70 Jolimont St, Jolimont 3002;
        tel. (03) 9280 8200
WA   28 Walters Dve, Osborne Park 6017;
        tel. (09) 244 3222

INSURANCE

The **Insurance and Superannuation
Commission** provides independent advice
and information on superannuation and
insurance schemes. The postal address for all
states is GPO Box 9836.
ACT   tel. 247 2299
Qld   tel. (07) 3221 2533
NSW   tel. (02) 9395 7222
SA   tel. (08) 8232 5130
Vic.   tel. (03) 9246 7500
WA   tel. (09) 481 8266
    The **Life Insurance Complaints Service**
handles consumer inquiries and complaints
about insurance claims: tel. 1800 335 405
(national); Melbourne: (03) 9629 7050

INTERNET

You can always surf the Internet. The list
of services is continually expanding: information supplied by governments and companies
includes such things as amenities in your
area, banking and investment services, and
price comparisons when shopping.

INVESTING

The **Australian Securities Commission**
provides a range of information and advice
about investment advisers, business and
company procedures, etc.
ASC Infoline tel. 1300 300 630
    **Investment Funds Association of
Australia** Ltd has a range of leaflets on the
basics of investing and managed funds: Level
4, 345 George St, Sydney 2000;
tel: (02) 9262 3599
    The **Australian Stock Exchange** has an
Investor Centre in each capital city
(except Canberra and Darwin) which

provides information, free lunchtime seminars, courses and other educational programs for new investors. Each centre also has a bookshop and research library.

NSW Level B1, Exchange Centre, 20 Bond St, Sydney 2000; tel. (02) 9227 0660

Qld Shop 3, Retail Plaza, Riverside Centre, Brisbane 4000; tel. (07) 3835 4014

SA 91 King William St, Adelaide 5000; tel. (08) 8216 5028

Tas. Level 12, 86 Collins St, Hobart 7000; tel. (03) 6234 7333

Vic. 530 Collins St, Melbourne 3000; tel. (03) 9617 8611

WA Exchange Plaza, 2 The Esplanade, Perth 6000; tel. (09) 224 0044 or (09) 227 0660

LAW AND LEGAL SERVICES

Most local councils have a **citizens advice bureau** which provides free legal advice and assistance. Government-funded **community legal centres** provide free legal advice and referrals; the National Association of Community Legal Centres can provide details: Suite 602, 383 Pitt St, Sydney 2000; tel. (02) 9264 9595

State **law societies** give legal advice and referrals:

ACT 1 Farrell Place, Canberra City 2601; tel. (06) 247 5700

NSW 170 Phillip St , Sydney 2000; tel. (02) 9373 7300

NT 1st floor, 18 Knuckey St, Darwin 0800; tel. (08) 8981 5104

Qld. 179 Ann St, Brisbane 4000; tel. (07) 3233 5888

SA 124 Waymouth St, Adelaide 5000; tel. (08) 8231 9972

Tas. 28 Murray St, Hobart 7000; tel. (03) 6234 4133

Vic. Law Institute of Victoria, 470 Bourke St, Melbourne 3000; tel. (03) 9607 9311

WA 33 Barrack St, Perth 6000; tel. (09) 221 3222

Legal Aid services provide legal advice, information and assistance. This is free for people on low incomes (based on means-testing).

ACT Legal Aid Commision, Civic Offices, North Building, London Circuit, Canberra City 2601; tel. (06) 243 3411

NT 9-11 Cavanagh St, Darwin 0800; tel (08) 8999 3000 or 1800 809 616 (NT only)

NSW Legal Aid Commission, 323 Castlereagh St, Sydney 2000; tel. (02) 9219 5000

Qld Legal Aid Office, 44 Herschel St, Brisbane 4000: tel. (07) 3238 3444

SA Legal Services Commission, 82 Wakefield St, Adelaide 5000; tel. (08) 8205 0155 or 1800 188 126 (SA only)

Tas. Legal Aid Commission, 123 Collins St, Hobart 7000; tel. (03) 6230 0900

Vic. Legal Aid Commission, 179 Queen St, Melbourne 3000; tel. (03) 9607 0234

WA Legal Aid Western Australia, 55 St Georges Tce, Perth 6000; tel. (09) 261 6200 or 1800 809 616 (WA only)

The **Law Consumers Association of NSW** has kits about family law, wills, probate and conveyancing: 3rd floor, Porter House, 203 Castlereagh St, Sydney 2000; tel. (02) 9267 6154

• see also *divorce* and *family law*

PENSIONS

For inquiries and information, including advice on the deeming rules, contact the Department of Social Security: tel. 13 23 00.

PUBLIC TRUSTEES

State government trustees provides a range of advice and services in areas such as personal financial planning, tax, trusts, and estate matters.

ACT Level 4, 4 Mort St, Canberra 2601;
tel. (06) 257 1222
NSW 19 O'Connell St, Sydney 1000;
tel. (02) 9252 0523
NT 47 Nuckey St, Darwin 0800;
tel. (08) 8999 7271
Qld 444 Queen St, Brisbane, 4000;
(07) 3213 9313
SA 25 Franklin St, Adelaide 5000;
(08) 8226 9200
Vic. 168 Exhibition St ,Melbourne 3000;
tel. (03) 9667 6444 or 1800 133 095.
WA 565 Hay St, Perth 6000;
tel (09) 222 6777

RENTING – TENANTS
AND LANDLORDS

For help with solving disputes, in all states
except NSW and Tas.contact the Consumer
Affairs (CA) office.
ACT CA Information and Assistance;
tel. (06) 207 0400
NSW Tenancy Service, Office of Real Estate
Services, tel. (02) 9377 9100 or
1800 451 301.
NT CA office; tel. (08) 8999 5184 or
1800 019 319 (NT only)
Qld CA Inquiries; tel. (07) 3246 1500
SA Tenants' Landlords Rights Office, CA;
tel. (08) 8204 9544
Tas. Tenants Landlord Disputes
Community Mediation Service, 11
Liverpool St, North Hobart 7000;
tel. (03) 6231 1301
Vic. Residential Tenancies Office, CA;
tel. (03) 9627 6000
WA CA office; tel. (09) 222 0666 or 1800
199 117 (WA only)

RETIREMENT AND AGEING

The **Commonwealth Department of Health
& Family Services** provides information and
advice about aged-care issues such as domiciliary care, and nursing-home and hostel
standards.

Central Office: 1800 020 103
ACT tel. (06) 274 5111 or 1800 020 102
NSW tel. (02) 9225 3555 or 1800 048 998
NT tel. (08) 8946 3444 or 1800 019 122
(NT only)
Qld Brisbane tel. (07) 3360 2555 or 1800
177 099; north Qld tel (077) 27 2225
or 1800 019 030 (Qld only)
SA (08) 8 237 6111 or 1800 188 098
Tas. tel. (03) 6221 1423 or 1800 005 119
(Tas.only)
Vic. tel. (03) 9285 8888 or 1800 133 374
(Vic. only)
WA (09) 346 5111 or 1800 016 023 (WA
only)
Department of Veterans Affairs:
ACT Ground Floor, Drake Centre,10
Moore St , Canberra City 2601;
tel. (06) 267 1411 or 1800 046 088
NSW 280 Elizabeth St, Surry Hills 2010;
tel. (02) 9213 7777 or 1800 257 251
NT Suite 8, Cascom Centre,
15 Scaturchio St ,Casuarina 0810;
tel. (08) 8927 0044
Qld 10 Eagle St, Brisbane 4000;
tel. (07) 3223 8333 or 1800 113304
(Qld only)
SA Blackburn House, 199 Grenfell St,
Adelaide 5000; tel. (08) 8213 2611
or 1800 113 304 (SA only)
Tas. 21 Kirksway Place, Battery Point
7004; tel. (03) 6221 6666 or
1800 113 304 (Tas. only)
Vic. 300 Latrobe St, Melbourne 3000;
tel. (03) 9284 6000 or 1800 113 304
(Vic. only)
WA Level 12, AMP Building, St Georges
Tce, Perth 6000; tel. (09) 366 8222 or
1800 113 304 (WA only)
The **Home and Community Care Program**
handles home help and carer services.
ACT tel. (06) 207 1122
NSW tel. (02) 9230 1583 or 1800 226161
(State Library switchboard)
NT tel. (08) 8999 2400
Qld tel. (07) 3234 0818
SA tel. (08) 8237 6111

Tas.   tel. 1800 806 656 (Tas. only)
Vic.   tel. (03) 9616 7777
WA   tel. (09) 346 5111

The **Australian Pensioners' and Superannuants' Federation** provides research and information on a wide range of issues affecting older people. Th central office is at Suite 62, Level 6, 8-24 Kippax St, Surry Hills 2010; tel. (02) 9281 4566.

The **Council on the Ageing** provides information and assistance about a wide range of matters affecting the over-55s:

ACT   Hughes Centre, Wisdom St, Hughes
        2605; tel. (06) 282 3777
NSW Level 6, 93 York St , Sydney 2000;
        tel. (02) 9299 4100 or 1800 449102
NT   18 Bauhinia St, Nightcliff 0810;
        tel. (08)8948 1511
Qld: 82 Buckland Rd, Nundah 4012;
        tel. (07) 3256 6766
SA   45 Flinders St, Adelaide 5000;
        tel. (08) 8232 0422
Tas.   2 St Johns Avenue, New Town 71800;
        tel. (03) 6228 1897
Vic.   Mezzanine Level, 290 Collins St,
        Melbourne; tel. (03) 9416 0822 or
        1800 136381 (Vic. only)
WA   99 William St, Perth 6000;
        tel. (09) 321 2133

The **Retirement Village Association** represents most of the major retirement villages.

NSW and ACT
        Unit 3, 17 Burwood Rd, Burwood
        2134; tel. (02) 9747 4732
Qld   41 Silvester St, Wilston 4051;
        tel. (07) 3857 1438
SA   198 Greenhill Rd, Eastwood 5063;
        tel. (08) 8373 2116
Vic.   4/335 Flinders Lane, Melbourne 3000;
        tel. (03) 9629 4520
WA: 55 St Georges Tce, Perth 6000;
        tel. (09) 221 2217
(*No offices in Tas. or the NT*)

Seniors Card Information Line
ACT tel. (06) 205 0518
NSW tel. (02) 9502 3754

Qld   tel. (07) 3224 2788
SA   tel. (08) 8226 7200
Tas. tel. (03) 6233 4532
Vic. tel. (03) 9616 8241
WA   tel. (09) 222 18001/2/3
• see also *pensions* and *social security*

SOCIAL SECURITY

The Department of Social Security handles pensions, family and child-care payments, and other government benefits.
Inquiries and information: tel. 13 2468
Family Hotline: tel. 13 13 05
Childcare Cash Rebate: tel.13 21 24
Pensions: tel. 13 23 00
For information in languages other than English: tel. 13 12 02
• see also *divorce and family law* and *retirement and ageing*

SUPERANNUATION

Commonwealth Superannuation Administration: tel. (06) 252 7911
Superannuation Hotline: tel. 13 1020
The **Insurance and Superannuation Commission**: tel. 13 1060
Superannuation Complaints Tribunal: tel. 13 1434

TAX MATTERS

The **Australian Taxation Office** has a number of inquiry lines.
Deeming Hotline: tel. 13 2300
fringe-benefits tax: tel.13 3328
income tax: tel. 13 2861
PAYE: tel. 13 2866
Superannuation Helpline: tel. 13 1020
Tax Agents Board: tel. 374 8800

WILLS AND PROBATE
• see *Public Trustees*

Index